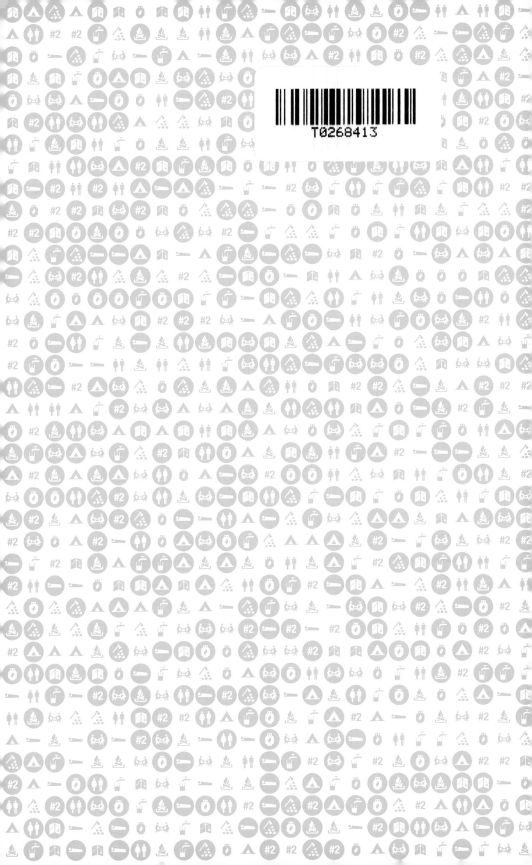

T0268413

MAKING CAMP

A Visual History of Camping's Most Essential Items & Activities

MARTIN HOGUE

PA PRESS

PRINCETON ARCHITECTURAL PRESS
NEW YORK

CONTENTS

INTRODUCTION

Lamentable is the fact, that during the six days given over to creation, picnic tables and outdoor fireplaces, footbridges and many other of man's requirements, even in natural surroundings, were negligently and entirely overlooked.[1]
—ALBERT H. GOOD

There is a deeply satisfying immediacy about the prospect of establishing and occupying an encampment for the night—clearing the site, erecting the tent, chopping wood, building a fire, and cooking over the live flame. It undoubtedly suggests a meaningful connection to landscape, place, and the rugged life of backwoods adventurers. Every summer forty million Americans take to the open road in search of this powerful experience of nature.[2] They travel to state parks, national parks, and other federally managed lands. They summer at commercial campgrounds like KOA (Kampgrounds of America) or at private, luxury glamping sites advertised on Airbnb and Tentrr. Less discriminating campers even overnight their RVs in Walmart parking lots. Despite the hundreds of campsites available at popular facilities, demand has

◐ ◑ **c. 1930**
Automobile camp in Elysian Park, Los Angeles. Photographer unknown. During the 1920s, large campgrounds nationwide introduced an important management innovation: the individually numbered plot. Note the marker for campsite 2 visible between the woman and man at the center of the scene.

➋ **c. 1900**
Wallace Emerson and Reuben Carey camping at Brandreth Preserve in upstate New York. Photographer unknown.

➌ **1925**
Camping at the Foot of a Giant Redwood, Motor Camper & Tourist, May 1925. Photographer unknown.

become so great that reservations must be booked months in advance of arrival, with the result that the near-mythical sense of spontaneity and adventure associated with camping (*this* is the spot!) is greatly diminished.

Recreational camping emerged in the United States after the American Civil War as a form of escape from the hustle of city life. Spurred by the 1869 publication of *Adventures in the Wilderness; or, Camp-Life in the Adirondacks* by Reverend William Henry Harrison (aka Adirondack) Murray (1840–1904), visitors flocked to the region in search of spiritual and physical renewal, marking what the historical geographer Terence Young characterized as the birth of the practice as we know it today.

From the outset, camping presented destructive impacts: as early as 1896, Col. Samuel Baldwin Marks Young, the army commander in charge of Yosemite, observed that

> the spectacle of empty tins that had contained preserved fruits, soups, vegetables, sardines, etc., together with offal from the cook fire, and other more objectionable [wastes], is detestable anywhere, but is abominable in the superlative degree when included in the view of a beautiful mountain stream skirted with meadows, luxurious grasses and gardens of wildflowers.[3]

Seventy years later, the American photographer Rondal Partridge's (1917–2015) 1965 photograph of a congested parking lot in view of Half Dome in Yosemite is similarly arresting. More recently, the camping enthusiast and author Dan White wrote with rare vividness about the hundreds of WAG (Waste Alleviation and Gelling) bags he encountered and tried to collect while hiking to the summit of Mount Whitney in California.[4] The dispersal of these bright blue bags here and there only seems to have intensified the presence of human waste (however

⬆ c. 1965
Rondal Partridge, *Pave It and Paint It Green, Yosemite National Park, Circa 1965.*

➡ 1915
Overflow Crowd of Campers in Stoneman Meadow, Yosemite National Park. Photographer unknown. With its breathtaking view of Half Dome, the point of view in this scene is similar to the one Rondal Partridge would capture fifty years later.

deodorized) along the venerated trail. After all, these never made it to a proper trash can.

As a new type of spatial landscape during the 1920s and '30s, automobile campgrounds helped mitigate some of these destructive impacts; they did not close the door on the increasing masses of visitors, but instead concentrated campers and their motor vehicles in designated enclaves, sparing more delicate and ecologically sensitive natural areas. The motor campground offered visitors an environment that perpetuated the myth of roughing it in nature, albeit within a dense and highly structured spatial setting. Numbered signs around the campground pointed to dedicated, cleared sites where the car could be parked and the tent erected; there, a stone firepit singled out the location of the campfire, while an empty picnic table provided an ideal spot to prepare a meal, relax, read. The architectural character of larger structures like restrooms was rusticized with local stones and wood that were painted deep brown so as to blend into the natural environs.

I set out to write this book to help recapture some of the shock and wonder I experienced when I first laid down a friend's tent at a KOA campground at the edge of the Badlands in June 2000; I expected to be let loose on the property to find my own shady spot. What I found instead was a highly structured spatial setting, rows of parked, humming RVs, lawn chairs, and the like. How can I square the mythical image of camping that many of us hold in our minds with the reality I later experienced? Are they even connected? To be clear, I'm not so much interested in recapturing the original mythical image of the old-time camper; those who do might read *Camping in the Old Style* (2009) by the author David Wescott, one of the leading authorities on the subject. Readers interested in a comprehensive history of camping in the United States should consult Warren James Belasco's *Americans on the Road: From Autocamp to Motel, 1910–1945* (1979); Charlie Hailey's *Campsite: Architectures of*

➲ 1959

A Typical Campsite, in National Park Service, *Campground Study: A Report of the Committee to Study Camping Policy and Standards—Region Four*. With callouts such as "Tent," "Fireplace," and "Table," this illustration of a typical campsite features many of the thematic elements discussed in this book.

A TYPICAL CAMPSITE

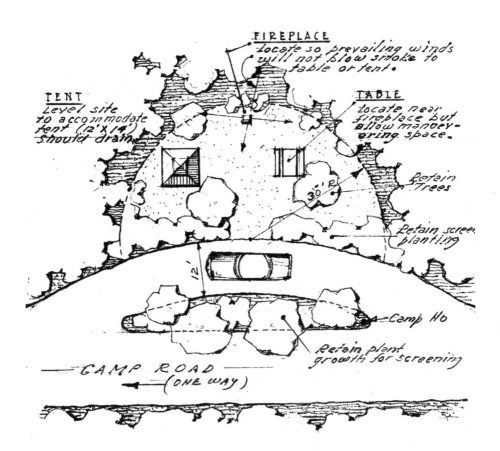

FIREPLACE locate so prevailing winds will not blow smoke to table or tent.

TENT Level site to accommodate tent (12'x14') should drain.

TABLE locate near fireplace but allow maneuvering space.

Retain Trees

30' R

Retain screen planting

12'

Camp No

Retain plant growth for screening

CAMP ROAD (ONE WAY)

IN THE DEVELOPMENT OF A CAMPSITE THE NATURAL CHARACTER OF THE AREA SHOULD BE RETAINED AS MUCH AS POSSIBLE. IN WOODLAND AREAS THE SHRUBBY GROWTH SHOULD BE REMOVED IN AN IRREGULAR MANNER IN DEVELOPING A SITE. CLEAR CUTTING SHOULD BE AVOIDED.

MAXIMUM DISTANCE TO WATER 100 FT.
MAXIMUM DISTANCE TO GARBAGE DISPOSAL 100 FT.
20 TO 35 SITES PER COMFORT STATION.

Duration and Space (2008); Terence Young's *Heading Out—A History of American Camping* (2017); or Phoebe Young's *Camping Grounds: Public Nature in American Life from the Civil War to the Occupy Movement* (2021), all excellent books on the subject. What interests me specifically is the profound disconnect that exists between the image of those late nineteenth-century recreational campers and the contemporary reality of the modern campground.

The title of this book, *Making Camp*, refers to what campers "make" when they camp, a set of constructions (a tent, a fire, a meal) resulting from actions that provide the practitioner with a tangible stake in their temporary settlement. Each task requires a different degree of investment: when the camper makes a tent, for example, she is not constructing the structure from scratch, cutting nylon shapes along a precise pattern and sewing the parts together; nonetheless the process of erecting the tent, of assembling its structural poles and threading them through the nylon envelope to provide the shelter with volume, comprises a set of actions that occur every single time the camper arrives at a new site. The sequence of events is reversed when the camper departs: the fully sewn tent is properly rolled up in its stuff sack and stowed in the trunk of the car, lying in wait of its next deployment at another site—next day, next week, or next year. The title of the book also refers to elements of the camp that are already fully "made." The numbered campsite that greets the camper upon arrival, for example, is cleared of trees, marked by a distinct parking spot, a firepit, and a picnic table. In this regard, these various forms of *making* camp connect what we now know as camping with a more physically demanding and unadulterated vision of the craft: What is the lineage of the Coleman gas stove to the wood fire, for example? How can sitting at a picnic table be traced back to sitting on a blanket or a log? How is it that we can find picnic tables virtually everywhere in the American landscape, not just

⊕⊕ 1924

Illustration from *Motor Camping & Tourist*, December 1924. The caption reads, "There is a lot of hard work, wholesome, physical labor, associated with motorcamping, and everyone should be willing to do his or her part, so that many hands may make the tasks light."

⊕ c. 1970

Promotional image from the Coleman Company depicting a family enjoying a meal at their campsite. Photographer unknown.

at campgrounds? Why does a two-person duckbill tent from the turn of the century weigh ten times as much as its nylon analog?[5] How does potable water get into a cup now, and how did it get into a cup then? And when did campgrounds become so complex that a visitor might need maps to navigate their confines?

Making Camp traces the individual histories of eight important architectural campground components. I approach the term *architecture* broadly to include a range of elements—some brought in by the camper, some made from scratch, others already in place when the camper arrives. Ingeniously, it is the subtle interplay between these various components that helps ensure the illusion that the camper retains some agency in *making* their own *camp*.

1. Water: Late nineteenth-century recreational campers often mistakenly placed their trust in quaint, scenic roadside tableaus; little did they know that the sparkling water from a cold, clear stream might be polluted by a nearby town or even by other campers upstream. Nowadays, there is little to distinguish the potable water inside large public campgrounds from that which can be found in any municipality: it issues freely from water taps, is available hot or cold in showers and washing basins, and services flush toilets connected to modern sewer systems. For the off-grid, backpacking enthusiast, a discussion of water will also include a range of equipment like bottles and hydration reservoirs, filters, purifiers, and portable showers.

2. Campfire: Long considered the social and functional heart of the camp as well as an important test of skill, the wood fire has been supplanted by modern gear like the lightweight gas stove, on which a full cooking flame can be attained within seconds.

3. Campsite: In the early days of late nineteenth-century recreational camping, wilderness enthusiasts simply hiked into the woods and settled on a spot they deemed promising, based on its scenic value, its proximity to a stream or lake, and other key

↑ ↑ 1900
Elias F. Everitt, photograph of a family camping and fishing by a stream in the San Bernardino Mountains in California.

↑ 1976
Maurice Zardus, *Buildings and Utilities, Water Foundation at Potwisha Campground*, Sequoia National Park

factors. Today, the campsite functions as the standard unit of management of any campground. Campers settle in and out of predetermined spots, with new visitors arriving only hours after the very same site has been vacated by its previous occupants.

4. Map: Early campgrounds were no more than large open fields inside which campers, along with their tents and motor vehicles, were confined. The emergence of campground maps during the 1930s suggests that this spatial territory quickly became far more complex and needed to be carefully managed. The map plays a dual role, acting as a geospatial reference for its occupants, while simultaneously perpetuating a unique spatial code of one-way driving loops, automobile parking spurs, and RV pull-throughs that underpins the generic layouts of over 20,000 campgrounds nationwide.

5. Picnic Table: Sitting in camp was often improvised using local materials—a simple log might present a serviceable bench, for example, while experienced campers traveled with foldable tables and chairs or simply crafted their own furniture by lashing together sticks and branches. A place to congregate, to prepare and eat food, the picnic table has become a deep part of the American vernacular not only in campgrounds but nationwide, to the extent that we cease to recognize the origins of this highly singular form.

6. Tent: Tents predate recreational camping by several millennia; however, the structure remains the single most iconic element of camping gear. When driving tent stakes into the ground, the camper establishes a tangible, if temporary, connection with place. The technological innovations following the invention of nylon by the DuPont Company in 1938 have propelled the tent as a center of research and innovation with respect to weight, compactness, permeability, durability, and structural stability.

7. Sleeping Bag: A point blanket? A bed roll? A sleeping robe? Even the name could not be agreed on.

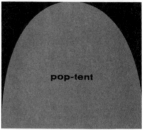

⊕ 1957

What the Hell is a Pop-Tent, promotional brochure issued by the Sports Manufacturing Company of Ann Arbor, Michigan, highlighting different uses for the iconic tent designed by Bill Moss.

An artifact of modern manufacturing, the sleeping bag is a relatively recent invention dating back to the 1870s, when commercial entrepreneurs like the Welshman Sir Pryce Pryce-Jones (1834–1920) contracted with the Russian Army to deliver 60,000 units of his Euklisia Rug, a patented, sewn blanket featuring a built-in, airtight pillow. Other technologies such as the zipper (1913), nylon, and other synthetic fibers combined to affect the sleeping bag's compactness, weight, and insulating value. A history of the sleeping bag would not be complete without a discussion of mattresses, cots, and bedding, all of which affect comfort and experience.

8. Trash: The histories of sewage, water, and trash management systems have always been closely linked in campgrounds. While bear-proof trash bins, RV dumping stations, incinerators, and landfills run counter to romantic notions of wilderness and are best kept out of view (and out of mind), this "landscape we do not see" is one of the most critical parts of the camping experience.[6]

In preparing this book, I imagined finding a copy of *Making Camp* years from now at an REI store like the one in Salt Lake City, where I first purchased some of my own equipment, or on the shelves of the Grant Village gift shop in Yellowstone National Park, where I camped a few years later. I thought of *Making Camp* as another piece of equipment, something to be packed at home and later brought out, along with the rest of the gear and provisions, at the campsite. Each of these eight narratives is a self-contained story that can be read on its own, under the light of the evening campfire, in about an hour's time—enough material, in other words, to last for an entire week of camping. And though it won't help the uninitiated with tips on erecting their tent or building a proper fire (there are plenty of manuals around for that), the book does provide both new and experienced campers with a broader historical perspective on the evolution of the campground as a spatial setting, as well as key

⊙⊙ c. 1888
Pryce Jones Patent Euklisia Rugs, in Pryce Jones, *Royal Welsh Warehouse, North Wales, Newtown* mail-order catalog. The Euklisia Rug is widely recognized as the first commercially manufactured sleeping bag in the world.

⊙ 1920
Walter Crane, frontispiece illustration from Robert Louis Stevenson, *Travels with a Donkey in the Cévennes*, depicting the author in his sleeping bag, his fateful donkey, Modestine, grazing nearby.

elements of camping gear. Ironically, the reader may discover that camping has always constituted what author Dan White characterizes as a "standoff between domesticity and the wild," and that even late nineteenth-century campers were not so prepared to completely abandon modern comforts themselves.[7] Have we traveled so far between then and now?

References

Spanning 150 years, the respective arcs of these eight histories pass through shared reference points. When I first came across the camping scenes captured by the American photographer Bruce Davidson (b. 1933) in Yosemite National Park between 1965 and 1966, I felt that he had seen, and been intrigued with, something similar to what I had experienced myself when I first set out camping twenty years ago. Encountering Davidson's work for the first time validated my own intuitions and gave voice to the profound sense of irony that I often still experience today when checking in at a busy campground. Davidson built his early reputation on an interest in outsider communities, and his beautiful black-and-white photographs bring dignity to the people he worked with: a dwarf clown in *Circus* (1958), the tattooed, leather-clad, pompadoured young men of *Brooklyn Gang* (1959), the struggles of the civil rights movement in *Time of Change* (1961–65), and the vibrant community living in a single block of Harlem of *East 100th Street* (1966–68). Though the published body of work from Yosemite is relatively small, it's easy to imagine why Davidson chose to spend some time there. Campers are outsiders themselves, and many of the people he met in Yosemite are captured glaring defiantly at the camera, as if to ask what the photographer might be doing there in the first place. Davidson helped me see that it's human action, not wilderness or nature, that defines camping. If it weren't for the title of the series, alternately known as *Yosemite Campers* (1965)

↑ 1965
Bruce Davidson, *Woman with Rollers in Her Hair*, from *Yosemite Campers* series.

↗ 1965
Bruce Davidson, *Three Women Fixing Their Hair*, from *Yosemite Campers* series.

↘ 1966
Bruce Davidson, *Camp Ground No. 4, Yosemite National Park*, from *The Trip West* series.

and *The Trip West* (1966), or *Ugly Americans*, there would be no way to tell that these pictures were taken in one of the most iconic national parks in the United States. This may have been part of the artist's plan. Davidson's photographs are characterized by a refusal to aestheticize the campsite or romanticize its beauty. If anything, the reverse may be true: the campers that populate these images are never active in the way that one might imagine them to be—cutting wood, hunting, cooking over a live flame, etc. Instead they are seated, in lawn chairs and at picnic tables, staring into the distance, looking bored. Each campsite is a field of inanimate debris, populated by cars, trailers, cardboard boxes, suitcases, cosmetic cases, chairs, coolers, stoves, laundry drying on clothing lines strung between trees, an occasional tent, even a television. Packed like sardines, it's hard to tell where one campsite begins and another ends. Some campers resorted to putting up bedsheets between trees to create some privacy. Though thirty-five years and hundreds of miles separate Davidson's experience in Yosemite and my own initial forays into camping, these places felt in many regards much the same. Sanctioning my own perspective and direction, Davidson made it possible to talk about camping for what it actually was— unvarnished, dry, and, from my perspective, bitingly funny—not what we imagine it might or should be like. Rather than looking away, the photographer simply chose to double down.

Bruce Davidson's photographs appear several times throughout this book. This deliberate, repetitive pattern is matched only in frequency and quality by the technical drawings produced by the architect Albert H. Good (1892–1945), the second key protagonist in this story. Hired by the National Park Service at the height of the Great Depression, Good produced a compendium of drawings and specifications titled *Park Structures and Facilities* (1935) to be implemented by the Civilian Conservation Corps (CCC) in national and state parks and forests across the country. To be

❷ 1938
Picnic Unit, Caddo Lake State Park, Texas, Albert H. Good, ed., *Park and Recreation Structures,* vol. 2, *Recreational and Cultural Facilities.*

Picnic Unit

Caddo Lake State Park   –   –   –   Texas

Free from accusation of fragility, yet capable of being relocated if occasion demands, this unit and the variations shown on the plate opposite rate well for primitiveness and practicability. Wood construction of this husky character is only truly appropriate if the surrounding standing timber is in scale with the log members of the table and benches.

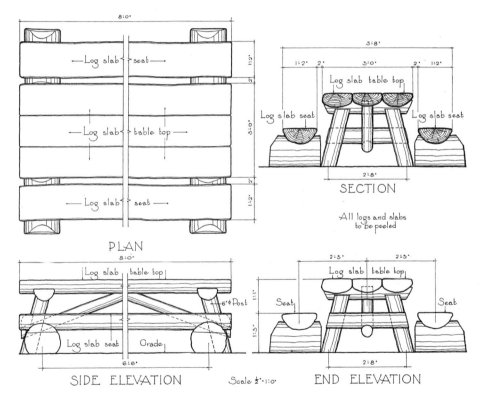

PLAN

SECTION

All logs and slabs to be peeled

SIDE ELEVATION   Scale ½"·1:0"   END ELEVATION

sure, there were several books and reports on the topic authored during this period, including Charles Parker Halligan's *Tourist Camps* (1925), the US Forest Service's *Public Camp Manual* (1935), the National Park Service's *Campground Study* (1959), and the United States Department of Agriculture's *Forest Recreation for Profit* (1962). Of these, Good's is easily the most comprehensive. Featuring chapters such as "Signs and Markers"; "Seats and Tables"; "Outdoor Fireplaces and Camp Stoves"; "Campfire Circles and Amphitheaters"; and "Comfort Stations and Privies," the book provides a glimpse of the expansive infrastructure required to meet the public need. Each chapter features a range of examples documented at facilities the architect had visited around the country. Meant as a survey of current specifications, Good's work could prove generative and inspire new design approaches as well, based on the availability of materials, site constraints, and the like. The architect later revised his research in an expanded 1938 edition titled *Park and Recreation Structures*, which features information on motor campgrounds, including new chapters on "Tent and Trailer Campsites"; Camp Lay-Out"; "Campstoves"; and Picnic Tables." These new sections suggest the growing importance of this type of infrastructure in the area of outdoor recreation. This later edition was reprinted in a beautiful 1999 volume published by Princeton Architectural Press, and it only seems fitting that they agreed to publish my own book on the subject.

I was particularly taken by the detail and craft of Good's drawings. In an age when the distance between digital representation and reality is growing narrower still, his spectacular, delicately hand-lettered illustrations are a reminder of another time. For architects, drawing constitutes the primary vehicle through which ideas are studied and expressed. Drawing is a language, a way to represent, to view, to understand, and to transform the world. Like Good, I am an architect, and my attention is

⊘ 1938

Amphitheater, Yellowstone National Park, Albert H. Good, ed., *Park and Recreation Structures*, vol. 2, *Recreational and Cultural Facilities.*

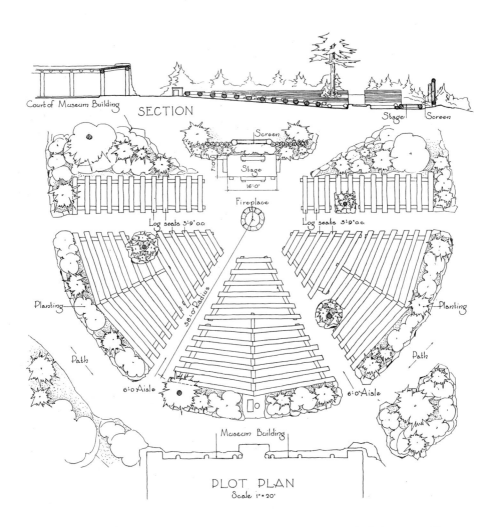

Court of Museum Building   SECTION   Stage   Screen

Screen

Stage
16'0"

Fireplace

Log seats 3'9' o.c.   Log seats 3'9' o.c.

Planting   Planting

58'0' Radius

Path   Path

6'0' Aisle   6'0' Aisle

Museum Building

PLOT PLAN
Scale 1"=20'

Amphitheater   Yellowstone National Park

In this large national park are two outdoor theaters of nearly identical arrangement. On the facing page both are pictured. The plan shown above is of the Old Faithful amphitheater, which differs from the one at Fishing Bridge, mainly in the greater elaboration of its platform and background. Both platforms are quite shallow front to back.

The campfire pit is axial in both instances. The seating of large, barked logs, resting on log stringers, is boldly scaled to the out-of-doors. The perching of the housing for the projector on log 'piles' is of interest. The rocks which outline the paths of one example are so unfortunately placed as to force their eventual removal, unless Nature hastens to supply some ground cover to obliterate them in considerable degree.

always piqued in the presence of such skilled illustrations. Highlighting Good's rigorous, analytical mindset, the patience and care with which he approached the design of even the most commonplace campground element like the firepit or the picnic table suggested that these were in fact worthy of study. I am impressed by the way Good decided to isolate these elements in individual chapters, and the rich character he uncovered for each element. The table of contents of the 1938 edition offers a strong point of departure for my own efforts, which I knew could be expanded to include additional chapters like the campground map, the tent, and the sleeping bag. I also admire the way in which Good mixed drawings with written observations and field photographs, resulting in a book that is equal parts visual and verbal—a model that has paved the way for my own research. To be sure, *Making Camp* is a single book, but one that is formed by putting two records side by side, one written, one graphic. Each written page is matched by illustrated counterparts selected from a range of representations, including master plans, maps, technical drawings, patents, diagrams, sketches, paintings, and photographs. The book gains its subtitle by combining both in equal measure and, at its essence, presents a history of graphic specifications similar to the one Good authored nearly ninety years ago. Under the light of the campfire, the written narrative can be read on its own; alternatively, the book can be read by connecting image to text or by consulting the images and their related captions in the order in which they appear in each chapter. And because each history is a discrete narrative, the adventurous reader may begin with any chapter deemed of greatest interest; simply find one of the eight full-spread illustrations in the book and read on…

❷ **1934**
*Bubbler, Letchworth State Park,
New York*, Albert H. Good, ed.,
Park Structures and Facilities.

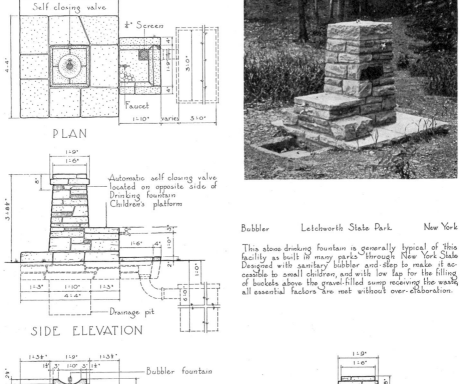

PLAN

4:4"

Self closing valve

¼" Screen

Faucet

4:4"

3'-0"

1:10"   varies   3:0"

SIDE ELEVATION

Automatic self closing valve
located on opposite side of
Drinking fountain
Children's platform

1:9"
1:6"
8'
3:8½"

1:6"   4"

1:3"   1:10"   1:3"
4:4"

Drainage pit

Bubbler   Letchworth State Park   New York

This stone drinking fountain is generally typical of this
facility as built in many parks through New York State.
Designed with sanitary bubbler and step to make it accessible to small children, and with low tap for the filling
of buckets above the gravel-filled sump receiving the waste,
all essential factors are met without over-elaboration.

SECTION

1:3½"   1:9"   1:3½"
1½" 3" 1:10" 3" 1½"
3'·2¼"
2:10"
2:5¾"
1:3"
9"·3"
9"·3"
1:6"
G.I.Pipe   Drainage Pit   4" Vit.Tile
1:10"

Bubbler fountain

Cement

Self closing valve
Self closing lever
Handle valve

Screen
Stone·slab

Dry·Well

3:0"

FRONT ELEVATION

1:9"
1:6"
8'
1:3"
1:0"
5'   9"
1:3"   1:10"   1:3"

Scale ⅜" = 1:0"

UNITED STATES DEPARTMENT OF THE INTERIOR · NATIONAL PARK SERVICE

WATER

*Dreamily, deliriously, I waded into the waist-deep water
and fell on my face. Like a sponge I soaked up moisture
through every pore, letting the current bear me along
beneath a canopy of overhanging willow trees. I had no
fear of drowning in the water—I intended to drink it all.*[1]
—EDWARD ABBEY

Postcard-ready images of a lone tent at the lake's edge
form an integral part of camping iconography, and
with good reason: access to water for drinking, cooking, and bathing; for boating, fishing, and swimming;
or the mere enjoyment of scenery is connected to a
broad range of daily camping activities. For noted
camping experts like the Reverend William Henry
Harrison (aka Adirondack) Murray, whose 1869 book
helped extoll the virtues of camping to the American
public, or Daniel Carter Beard (1850–1941), founder
of the Sons of Daniel Boone (later to become the Boy
Scouts of America), siting the rustic encampment in
direct proximity of a lake, river, or stream, and within
reach of an ample supply of firewood, represents a

◐ ◑ 1883
Krebs Lithographing Company,
Cincinnati, Ohio, *Camping Out.*

◓ **1938**
*A Medium-Sized Organized
Camp on a Lake-Front Site,*
Albert H. Good, ed., *Park and
Recreation Structures,* vol. 3,
*Overnight and Organized Camp
Facilities.* This typical layout for
a campground at the edge of
a lake illustrates the continuing
power of camping near a body
of water. Of roughly 20,000
facilities nationally, more than
3,500 campgrounds feature
the terms *Lake* or *River* in their
names. Emphasis on water by
the author.

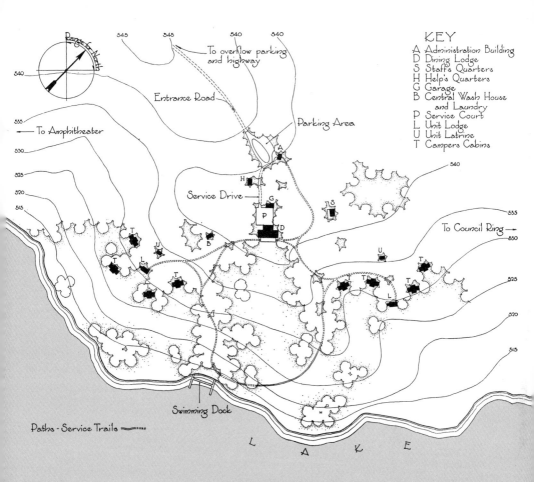

KEY
A Administration Building
D Dining Lodge
S Staff's Quarters
H Help's Quarters
G Garage
B Central Wash House
  and Laundry
P Service Court
L Unit Lodge
U Unit Latrine
T Campers Cabins

Range for North

To overflow parking
and highway

Entrance Road

Parking Area

To Amphitheater

Service Drive

To Council Ring

Swimming Dock

Paths - Service Trails

L   A   K   E

strategic decision of great consequence, a near-implicit guarantee of success.

And yet the proliferation of iodine tablets, filtering systems, biodegradable soaps, kettles, hydration reservoirs, bladders, water bottles, insulated jars, cups, mugs, gravity-fed solar showers, portable pressure washing systems, and other assorted camping gear signals that our attitude to water *in situ* has become far more nuanced. Traveling around Yosemite National Park in 1918, writer Mary Roberts Rinehart (1876–1958) observed that she liked "water in a tub or drinking-glass or under a bridge. I am very keen about it. But I like still water—quiet, well-behaved, stay-at-home water."[2] As seductive as Murray's poetic exhortation to "quench your thirst at the coolest, sweetest spring of pure water from which you ever drank," many modern campers, both on and off the grid, would probably side with Rinehart: when faced with a choice, they too prefer their own water domesticated rather than from the source—drinkable, on-demand, and in whatever state (hot, cold, misted, pressurized) suits their specific daily needs.[3]

Reputable Sources

We flee from cities, but we bring the best of cities with us.[4]
—RALPH WALDO EMERSON

By the time Rinehart arrived in Yosemite, traffic had increased steadily since the artists Thomas Ayres (1816–1858) and Albert Bierstadt (1830–1902) had first visited the area, in 1855 and 1863 respectively—from a few dozen visitors annually to more than thirty-five thousand a year. Bierstadt's dramatically lit scenes had the same effect on the valley that Murray's prose had for the Adirondacks: for hordes of intoxicated tourists, wild nature was often met with enthusiasm, but not always with high regard. Careless campers used streams as latrines and wash basins;

❯ 1903–1904
William Adams Vale, photograph of Fern Cliff Camp, located along the Arrowhead Reservoir Toll Road in California's San Bernardino Mountains. For the camping author Arthur H. DesGrey, "A camp may possess all the apparent requisites for a good location and still be a menace to its inhabitants."

even the most respectful were not immune, since they might inadvertently consume water polluted by towns, factories, or even campsites upstream. In an ironic twist, the very places Murray and Bierstadt had touted for their thrilling scenery and regenerative properties were turning into breeding grounds for diseases like typhoid and cholera long eradicated from large urban agglomerations nationwide.[5]

The autocamping expert Elon Jessup (1885–1958) may have been pining for the comforts of home when he complained in 1923 that "the trusted city water system is exchanged for one which you may know nothing whatever about."[6] Indeed, a visual inspection of the loveliest sparkling stream simply did not suffice, since dangerous bacteria could only be detected under a microscope or by proper testing—not part of the camper's regular arsenal. Instead, experts recommended boiling water with charcoal or dissolving it with a light chlorine solution before it could be safely consumed. On a 1907 inspection trip to Yosemite, Marshall O. Leighton (1874–1958), the US Geological Survey's chief hydrographer, became so concerned by the impacts that tourism had placed on water quality along the Merced River that he recommended channeling drinking water from a remote, uncontaminated source two miles upstream of major hotels, campgrounds, and other concessioners.[7]

Replacing the spring at the foot of Glacier Point that had once supplied the valley, the proposed thirty-inch gravity-fed pipe and low dam at the new intake near Happy Isles was designed to supply one million gallons of drinking water daily.[8] Inaugurated by the time Rinehart arrived in the valley, the improved delivery system took a cue from New York City's Croton Aqueduct (1842), a forty-one-mile southbound infrastructural span that linked Manhattan to the Croton River. What else was Yosemite Valley quickly becoming than a small municipality? As the stream made way for the pipe,

↑ 1923
Campgrounds along the Merced River in Yosemite National Park, in Elon Jessup, *Roughing It Smoothly: How to Avoid Vacation Pitfalls*. Photographer unknown. In order to avoid significant sewer discharges, most campgrounds in the park were located upriver from major hotels and concessions.

➜ c. 1965
Rondal Partridge, *Campground by the River, Yosemite* (detail). Writing in *Camp Planning and Reconstruction* (1935), the plant pathologist Emilio Pepe (E. P.) Meinecke observed, "The public's tendency to crowd down to running water is undesirable from the point of view of sanitation."

the latter also represented a form of trust, a guarantee of purity: rather than being viewed with suspicion when encountered at the source, safe drinking water could be secured over great distances until it issued directly from a faucet or hydrant at the desired spot. To be sure, Yosemite's new service was worth the investment, since it was intended for thousands of visitors. However, wealthy off-grid campers such as the philanthropist and suffragist Phoebe Apperson Hearst (1842–1919) spared no expense to safeguard their own water supply; Hearst ran three thousand feet of iron pipe from a spring of pure water to her personal summer encampment in Sonoma County, California, in 1891.[9] With the traditional narrative linking topography, gravity, water, and place properly upended, the landscape architect Frank A. Waugh (1869–1943) was undeterred by the lack of water for a new campground at the South Rim of the Grand Canyon in 1918; he simply proposed that the entire allotment of drinking water be supplied with water hauled in by railroad over a distance of 120 miles.[10]

Out of Sight, Out of Mind

A hydrant yielded water faster than a stream.[11]
—WARREN JAMES BELASCO

In response to the growing popularity of camping during the early decades of the twentieth century, the noted expert Frank E. Brimmer (1890–1977) boasts in the *Coleman Motor Campers Manual* (1926) that "drinking water, one of the greatest problems for the old-time camper, is one of the easiest today, because the universal need for water on the part of millions of motor campers has compelled all camps to pipe or drive wells that would always ensure a pure supply."[12] By the 1960s, the National Park Service had embarked on an ambitious modernization program of its infrastructure, completing 535 new water systems

↑ 1932
Arthur Holmes, water station at Summit Lake Campground in Lassen Volcanic National Park, in California.

➲ 1919
United States Geological Survey topographic map of Yosemite National Park showing the original water intake at the base of Glacier Point (bottom left) and the new pipe on the Merced River at Happy Isles (bottom right).

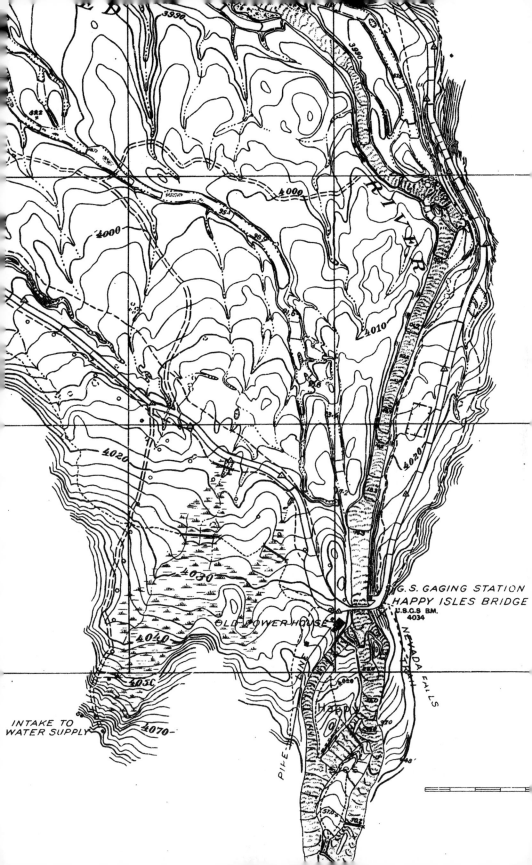

supplying campgrounds, visitor centers, and other high-traffic facilities throughout the United States.[13]

But with the availability of drinking water emerged new considerations. As it now safely issued from a tap, how could the thrill of dipping straight from a "lake of crystal water" described by Adirondack Murray be recaptured?[14] The historians Linda Flint McClelland and Ethan Carr both discuss strategies employed by the National Park Service for rusticating campground infrastructure like drinking fountains, toilets, pavilions, and related facilities by using local materials like rough-hewn stone and by staining wood beams, posts, and sheathing in dark-brown tones that helped match these structures to the local setting. The result was an uncanny sense that these buildings had always been part of the scene they were designed to service.[15] Citing a recent installation at Lake Guernsey State Park in Wyoming, for example, Albert H. Good, whose previously mentioned *Park Structures and Facilities* (1935) and *Park and Recreation Structures* (1938) helped codify design standards for a major expansion of the national campground network by the Civilian Conservation Corps during the Great Depression, observed, "Here certainly is the peak accomplishment in naturalistic masking of a provision for bubbler and tap. It is a temptation hardly resistible to state that the rock was smitten with a rod and that the water gushed forth in the best biblical tradition."[16] But in a wonderful twist of irony, Good seemed to hedge on his own praise, so worried was he about the effects of doing such a terrific job that campers couldn't actually find the tap, "so elaborately draped as to fail to declare itself."[17] In a compromise of sorts, he recommended pointing out rusticated water stations with signage—a practice that remains in use to this day. Other manuals from this period similarly dictated that water infrastructure clearly appear on campground maps and that no individual campsite be located further than 150 feet from a water faucet.[18]

❍ **1934**

Drinking Fountain, Lake Guernsey State Park, Wyoming, Albert H. Good, ed., Park Structures and Facilities.

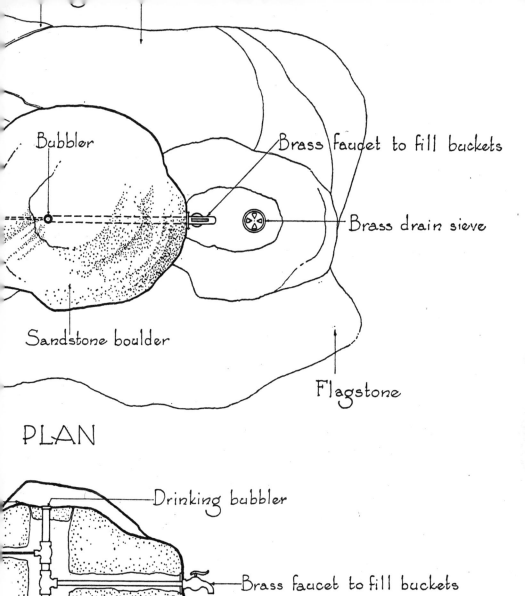

Bubbler

Brass faucet to fill buckets

Brass drain sieve

Sandstone boulder

Flagstone

PLAN

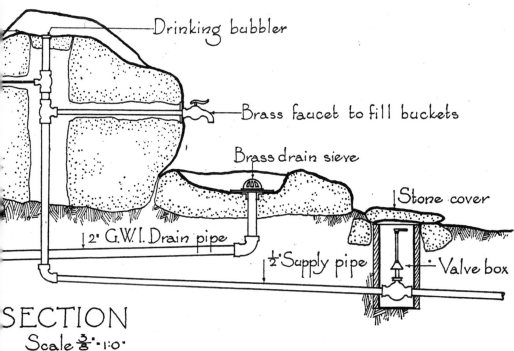

Drinking bubbler

Brass faucet to fill buckets

Brass drain sieve

Stone cover

$2''$ G.W.I. Drain pipe

$\frac{1}{2}''$ Supply pipe

Valve box

SECTION

Scale $\frac{3}{8}'' \cdot 1\cdot 0''$

Freed from rivers, lakes, and streams, the campground slowly transformed into an autonomous,
internally oriented territory whose coherence could
only be glimpsed from a paper map: multiple campsites serviced by drinking taps, flush toilets, a plenti-
ful wood supply, and the like. The Department of
Agriculture plant pathologist Emilio Pepe (E. P.)
Meinecke (1869–1957) described the overall concept
as bringing the city into the woods, noting its "float-
ing population."[19] But the reverse could be true as
well: as the twentieth century became increasingly
defined by movement and speed—a period during
which the term *flow* applied equally to running water
as it did to fast-moving motor vehicles—the campground was also free to "plug in" to water mains as
it did to major roads at the edges of towns and cities,
resulting in a kind of exurb that could meet the
demands of the blazing, cross-country motor campers during the 1920s. Over two thousand municipal
campgrounds sprang up during this period, among
them Overland Park, whose eight hundred campsites
were directly serviced by Denver's municipal water
system.

Nothing exemplified the new idea of "plugging
in" more than the early recreational vehicle (RV).
Meinecke described it as "truly a modern dwelling
on wheels, a moving bungalow provided with beds,
cooking stoves, sanitary equipment, running water,
ice boxes and electric lights."[20] For the historian
Warren James Belasco, the RV was like "an instant
hotel to which one only had to add water."[21] While
water taps were, initially, shared campground amenities to which campers brought buckets or other large
vessels for resupplying their own campsites, the
RV required its own personal hose fastened directly
under the vehicle. Other service amenities such as
electricity and sewage hookups were soon to follow,
with the effect that the rustic campsite looked more
and more like the comfortable domicile the visitor
had left behind. In the search for modern amenities,

➲ **1935**
Standard water station signage
from US Forest Service Region
5 (Pacific Southwest), *Public
Camp Manual.*

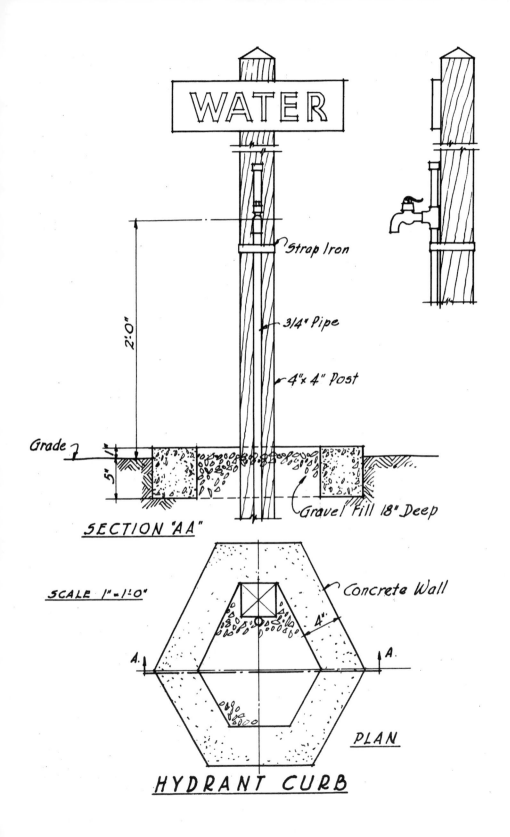

WATER

Strap Iron

3/4" Pipe

4"x 4" Post

2'.0"

Grade

5"

Gravel Fill 18" Deep

SECTION "AA"

SCALE 1" = 1'.0"

Concrete Wall

4"

A.

A.

PLAN

HYDRANT CURB

even the simple but no less meaningful labor of refilling a bucket at the nearby tap was no longer necessary.

Following World War II, camping continued to grow in popularity. Beginning in the early 1960s, large commercial chains like KOA (Kampgrounds of America) prioritized ease of access and comfort at the expense of the kind of woodcraft and local expertise that had once dominated the field. As writer John Steinbeck (1902–1968) traveled the country aboard his trusted *Rocinante*, a camper shell attached to the bed of a 1960 GMC truck that he named after Don Quixote's horse, all that was needed was to steer the RV or trailer to the designated spot, plug a few hoses in—and voilà! For the Nobel prize novelist, "A deep-dish sit-down in a tub with scalding water is a pure joy."[22]

On the Grid, Off the Grid

CONTINUUM WALK

WATER TAKEN FROM THE MOUTH OF THE RIVER DART

CARRIED ON A CONTINUOUS WALK OF THIRTEEN HOURS

AND POURED INTO THE HEADWATERS OF THE RIVER AT ITS SOURCE

DEVON ENGLAND 1998 [23]

—RICHARD LONG

As postwar Americans took to the new interstate highway system in record droves, Ethan Carr noted the emergence of a new environmental consciousness: in short order, the US Congress passed the Federal Water Pollution Control Act (1948), the Clean Air Act (1970), the National Environmental Policy Act (1970), and the Endangered Species Act (1973).[24] At the very same time, the Leave No Trace movement that emerged and grew during the 1960s dictated a new and more respectful ethos toward nature, conservation, and the traditional and ancestral

⦿ 1935
Site plan from US Forest Service Region 5 (Pacific Southwest), *Public Camp Manual*, showing the location of water faucets and underground pipes for Deer Creek camp in the Pacific National Forest of California.

U. S. DEPARTMENT OF AGRICULTURE
FOREST SERVICE
PACIFIC NATIONAL FOREST
DEER CREEK RECREATION AREA
DEER CREEK PUBLIC CAMP
S.W. ¼ Sec. 36 T. 5 N. R. 15 W. M. D. M.
CALIFORNIA

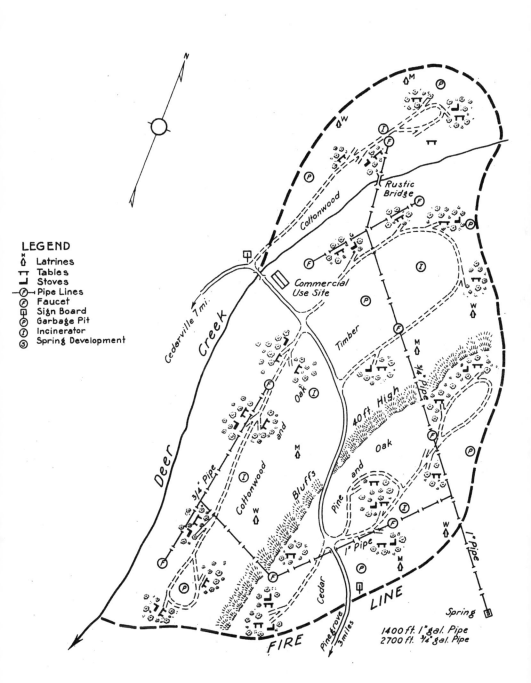

LEGEND
- Latrines
- Tables
- Stoves
- Pipe Lines
- Faucet
- Sign Board
- Garbage Pit
- Incinerator
- Spring Development

Rustic Bridge

Commercial Use Site

Cedarville 7 mi.

Deer Creek

Cottonwood

Timber

40 ft. High

Oak and Cottonwood

Bluffs

Pine and Oak

Cedar

Pinegrove 3 miles

FIRE LINE

¾ Pipe

1" Pipe

Spring

1400 ft. 1" gal. Pipe
2700 ft. ¾ gal. Pipe

homelands of Indigenous People and First Nations who were the original stewards of its resources. And though many continued to plug in, others were inspired by the counterculture of the 1960s to do just the opposite: tread lightly upon the land, pack out everything that had been packed in—and plug *out*.

Of the most current off-grid technological improvements, the Geyser portable shower system, which features a sponge connected to a pressurized tank of water, is one of the most interesting— though there may be no more ubiquitous symbol of the desire for independence than the Nalgene water bottle, long cherished by the camping and hiking communities. And to think that this match made in heaven occurred almost by coincidence. In 1949, the chemist Emanuel Goldberg (1911–1999), based in Rochester, New York, developed a large pipette jar for laboratory use made from medical-grade plastic. Taking inspiration from his wife's initials—Natalie Levey Goldberg—he founded the Nalge Company to manufacture and distribute its products, which rapidly increased in demand during the 1960s. Scientists found them an inexpensive alternative to glass labware, and hikers and campers liked them because they were sturdy, leak-proof, lightweight, and, most importantly, reusable. The company began advertising directly to the outdoor market in the 1970s, promising to reduce the impact plastics were already having on our planet. Because they could be refilled, Nalgene products guaranteed that fewer disposable plastic bottles would find their way to the landfill.[25] Unfortunately, over time, this guarantee did not prove entirely successful. In 2008, after it was demonstrated that Bisphenol A (BPA) plastics were detrimental to human health, Nalgene, in response, redesigned its line of bottles with Tritan, a BPA-free recyclable product, which remains in use to this day.

Instantly recognizable in the classroom, at the campsite, or on the trail, the Nalgene bottle signals broader lifestyle choices: water over soda and other

Fig. 14.—Bark Drinking-Cup

● **1908**
 An Improvised Bark Drinking-Cup, Edward Breck, *The Way of the Woods: A Manual for Sportsmen in Northeastern United States and Canada.*

● **1960**
"Nalgene serves You right!," Nalgene ad from *Science* magazine, June 1960.

Always dependable
NALGENE

NALGENE serves You right!

"Serves you right" the way it handles easily—no needless
weight, no slipping even when wet . . . no breakage
problems. You can ask a great deal of NALGENE Lab ware
and *get* it. Beakers, Carboys, Flasks, Funnels, Graduates,
Bottles, Pipets, Centrifuge and Test Tubes—all surprisingly
low in cost. NALGENE is the practical, efficient lab ware
that keeps its word . . . *always dependable!*

*Nalgene Lab ware is proving
its dependability in "Operation
Deep Freeze," McMurdo
Sound—Antarctica*

For our Catalog
H-459—write Dept. 156

 THE NALGE CO. INC. ROCHESTER 2, NEW YORK

bottled drinks. And despite their distinctive design, it may in fact be hard to find two bottles that are exactly alike: the company offers hundreds of models in different colors and sizes, spouts and caps, logos and messages ("Grizzly Crush," "Out There Together," "Bong Water"). For Nalgene, the opportunities for customization are virtually endless: there are even models celebrating the seminal British new wave band Joy Division ($35) as well as a wide-mouth, glow-in-the-dark model ($12), among many others.[26] For the true outdoor enthusiast who may be turned off by this shameless turn toward commercialization, the bottle can be adorned with stickers from national and state parks where the bottle was in service. In this practice, the camper is no different from the RV or trailer owner in broadcasting their outdoor adventures to the general public.

⊙ 2022
Geyser portable shower system. According to the company, "A small 0.8-gallon tank heats the water to a comfortable 95 degrees, while a pump supplies a stream of water to the sponge at the end of the hose—all powered by a 12V connection plugged into your still-running vehicle."

⊘ 1982
"The Anatomy of a Nalgene® Bottle," Nalgene ad from *Science* magazine, May 1982.

The Anatomy of a Nalgene® Bottle

Plastic bottles are not all alike.

Take a good look at the details that put Nalgene bottles in a class by themselves.

Our bottles have been designed and manufactured for tough applications. **We start with a bottle that's engineered to form a system with its closure; then we add the features described below to produce the best plastic bottle you can buy.**

Leakproof Bottle and Closure System

Closure

The durable, one-piece closure is molded of polypropylene.*

Shrink Seal Ring

Nalgene bottles, from 30mL to 1L in capacity, have a shrink seal ring at the neck, which can also be used for attaching an identification tag for security or shipping purposes.

Bottom

Even the bottom of a Nalgene bottle is special. The inner corners are curved for easy cleaning. The base is flat for a wide stance and greater flexibility. Molded into the bottom are letters identifying the plastic used, the capacity in ounces and milliliters, and—most important for your protection—the Nalgene name.

Seal Ring

The seal ring is molded inside the closure and fits tightly against the beveled inner edge (chamfer) of the bottle neck as the closure is tightened. **This makes the Nalgene bottle totally leakproof, with no need for a closure liner that can wear, leak or cause contamination.** Hand tightening is all that's needed for a positive seal. (Only with 100-mm and larger closures do we recommend an optional closure liner to guarantee leakproof service.)

Threads

Threads on Nalgene bottles and closures are continuous and deeper than you'll find on typical plastic or glass bottles. This greater contact area permits twice as much tightening force against the seal ring. And it's virtually impossible to snap Nalgene threads by over-torque because they're not round, but straight-shouldered "semi-buttress" threads —another mark of good design.

Heavy-Duty, Uniform Walls

Weight is an indication of strength and reliability in plastic bottles. Hold a Nalgene bottle in one hand and any other plastic bottle in the other. You can feel and see the difference. **The rugged walls of Nalgene bottles are exceptionally resistant to splitting or puncturing.** Nalge's advanced molding technology gives you walls with a uniform quality not found in other bottles

Specify Nalgene bottles when you need precision-molded bottles for lab applications. We put a lot of extra value into our bottles. Don't settle for anything less.

Order Nalgene labware from your lab supply dealer.

* or Tefzel ETFE
on Teflon FEP bottles

CAMPFIRE

The camp-fire is the living, life-giving, palpitating heart of the camp; without it all is dead and lifeless.[1]
—DANIEL CARTER BEARD

More than the tent, the sleeping bag, or any other single component described in this book, the camp-fire functions as the place around which all other activities revolve. David Wescott calls it the "prince of entertainers, the king of hosts," and no image or memory of camping is quite complete or suggestive without it.[2] Anyone who has ever camped overnight and built a campfire from scratch knows that even the most severely charred hot dog or a can of plain reheated beans tastes far better than the most carefully prepared home-cooked meal. Some longtime campers might say that the dark and smoky patina that envelops camp food is the secret ingredient that no supermarket is able to supply.

As one of the central technologies that has undergirded human civilization, the control of fire has been understood for nearly two million years—an interval

1880
Winslow Homer, *Camp Fire.*

1889
Seneca Ray Stoddard, *Game in the Adirondacks.*

of time well outside recorded history, not to mention the period under study in this book.[3] The celebrated American landscape painter Albert Bierstadt sought to evoke the primordial nature of fire when he and his companions reached Yosemite Valley in California in 1863, a scene he later completed in his New York City studio and titled *Cho-looke, The Yosemite Fall* (1864). Bracketed by a massive granite formation in the background and a modest campsite at the lower right of the canvas, *Cho-looke* tells a temporal story of times both far and near. Could the artist have imagined the role that this and other paintings would play in popularizing the region, and just how many individual campfires now burn at hundreds of campsites in Yosemite Valley on a chilly summer evening? The enthusiast building a wood fire at Upper Pines or Tuolumne Meadows may find little to distinguish the character of its live flame, its light, scent, and sounds, from the one Bierstadt and his companions enjoyed at their own campsite 150 years ago, or those built by the Ahwahnechee hundreds or even thousands of years earlier in the same area. Keeping in mind the general aim of this book and "the invisible delight in the campfire that escapes analysis," just when, and how, should such a history begin?[4]

It may be useful to consider this thorny question by quoting early twentieth-century outdoorsman Horace Kephart (1862–1931), who wrote that the cardinal rule of camping is to "never leave a fire, or even a spark, behind you. Put it out."[5] As a recreational camping enthusiast and one of its most important early advocates, "Kep" wrote eloquently about every aspect of rudimentary camping. At nearly nine hundred pages, *Camping and Woodcraft* (1917), his best-known book, grew out of an earlier, shorter volume titled *The Book of Camping and Woodcraft: A Guidebook for Those Who Travel in the Wilderness* (1906), which was later expanded to cover a broad range of topics, including outfitting, clothing, provisions, cooking, tents, bivouacs, wayfinding,

⊙ 1864

Albert Bierstadt, *Cho-Looke, The Yosemite Fall*. Bierstadt sought to capture the sublime and timeless character of the valley by organizing the scene around the four classical elements of nature: earth, water, air, and fire.

axemanship, even cave exploration. Kephart had a lot to say about campfires in particular—what they are used for, and how they are built and maintained over time. The decisiveness with which the author approached the end of the campfire's life, however, illustrates an interesting paradox: poorly tended, a campfire may die, but poorly tended the very same fire may also survive or, worse, thrive dangerously far beyond its intended use.[6] For Frank E. Brimmer, "A match may be the millionth part of the other wood where it is carelessly thrown; but it may burn a billion feet of valuable growing lumber."[7] In the highly regulated environment of the modern camp-ground, camping parties may occupy the same site and meet at the same picnic table, but the lifespan of each campfire is finite, and often associated with morning or evening meals. To be sure, common sense and courtesy dictate that no campfire should endure past the moment when a camper departs their campsite for good.

To write a history of the campfire, then, is to perhaps follow a series of parallel tracks: first, the recognition of the singularity of each fire as a display of practiced woodsmanship that is initiated and maintained over a certain period of time; second is the story that occurs once the blaze is put out and the infrastructure left behind—like the firepit and cook-ing grill—helps mark the spot where future campers will initiate their own campfire; finally, a history of the campfire would not be complete without a review of recent technologies that have emerged and sup-planted its effects (light, heat, etc.) and altogether reorganized the camp, its space and atmosphere.

⊘ **1916**
John Singer Sargent, *Tents at Lake O'Hara.*

A Display of Woodsmanship

A camper is known by his fire.[8]
—HORACE KEPHART

Naturalist, explorer, and author A. Hyatt Verrill (1871–1954) observed that "it may seem like a very simple matter to build a fire, and you may think that a description of how to do it is superfluous."[9] Issued at the height of the first recreational camping craze that gripped the United States during the late nineteenth and early twentieth centuries, Verrill's statement certainly rings true a hundred years later.
To be sure, fire is such a familiar feature in human life that we now seem to possess the quasi-magical ability to summon it on command, under any circumstances, and therefore give scant thought to how it came to be in the first place:. Safely packaged and easily available in the form of matches, disposable lighters, fuel-dipped coals, and piezoelectric gas stoves, it permits even those least experienced to succeed at safely resolving the age-old equation *[wood]+[spark]=fire.*

Offering a mélange of techniques and firsthand experience, Verrill, like Kephart, authored some of the first instructional books on camping at a time when the practice still held many of its rustic charms. Modern camping is often associated with specialized pieces of gear, but because campfires could not (yet) be purchased like a tent or a sleeping bag, both authors agreed that building a campfire constituted an important (perhaps *the* single most important) test of woodsmanship and resourcefulness. For them, campfire building was a rite of passage, the cost of membership in the burgeoning fraternity of campers; only after solving the equation *[wood]+[spark]=fire* could the camper call herself fully initiated. That this equation has lost much of its mystery, or that we should even conceive of the flame as more than a basic product (think of the Bic Lighter, for example),

⊘ **1920**
Fire Wood Sticks and Kindling, Daniel Carter Beard, *The American Boys' Handybook of Camp-Lore and Woodcraft.*

⊘ **1912**
Council Fire, Ernest Thompson Seton, *The Book of Woodcraft.* For Seton, "The high pyramid or bonfire, (a) goes off like a flash, roasts every one, then goes dead. The shapeless pile (b), is hard to light and never bright."

Bad   Bad   Good

The bonfire is always bad. It wastes good wood; is dangerous to the forest and the camp; is absolutely unsociable. A bonfire will spoil the best camp-circle ever got together. It should be forbidden everywhere.

shows just how far we have come over the last 150 years since the birth of recreational camping.

It is nowadays both instructional and amusing to read through the weathered pages of those books. One common trope of the period was to pit the wiser and more experienced camper against the novice. If their purpose was to instruct, Verrill and his contemporaries couldn't quite resist poking fun at those wannabe campers whose dollars and attention they sought but whose lack of skill they also mocked, characterizing them with epithets like "shirk," "quitter," "side-stepper," "arrant [sic], thoughtless, selfish Cheechako," "tenderfeet," and "blooming idiot."[10] Under the scold of their pen, the campsite, and the campfire in particular, became the locus of comical situations so laughable and hyperbolic that they felt made up on the spot. Conservation activist and writer for *Recreation* magazine George Oliver (G. O.) Shields (1846–1925) observed, for example, that "the great majority of men, when they undertake to make a camp-fire…proceed as if trying to put it out instead of to replenish it."[11] Picking up the thread, Daniel Carter Beard, observed that "there is not one in a hundred who can [build a campfire] successfully without a Sunday edition of the newspaper, a can of kerosene and an armful of kindling wood."[12] Pointing out that *[more wood]+[spark]=better probability of fire*, Kep expressed concern for the abundance of resources some may have deployed for such a modest task, describing a "higgledy-piggledy heap of smoking chunks…that will warp iron and melt everything else." Were these authors trying to stir up enthusiasm for the field or push new campers away?

While the contemporary reader cannot help but marvel at the ways in which campfire building has morphed from an artful and highly technical undertaking to a mere commodity, one particular aspect of these descriptions still rings true today: the sense of being observed—even judged—by others is played out not in the pages of an old book but on the very

⊘ 1917
Illustrations from A. Hyatt Verrill, *The Book of Camping*, depicting methods for starting a campfire without the use of matches. These include using flint and steel (fig. 2) as well as a bow and drill (fig. 8).

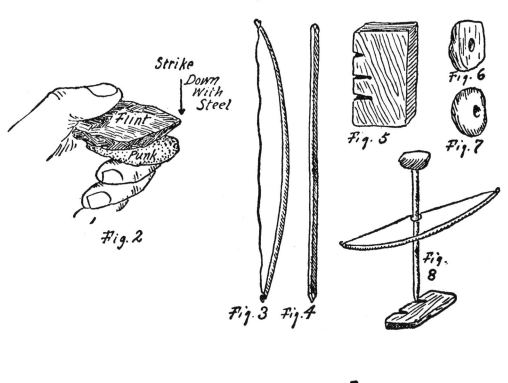

Strike

Down
With
Steel

Flint

Punk

Fig. 2

Fig. 3   Fig. 4

Fig. 5

Fig. 6

Fig. 7

Fig.
8

Fig. 9

public stage of the modern campground, where rows of densely arranged campsites only serve to magnify technical difficulties into real and lasting shame. Standing thirty or forty feet away at an adjacent site, nearby campers may be too far away to benefit from the glow and heat of the campfire; however, these bystanders can witness and critique the performance of building it.

The absurd situations described by Kephart, Verrill, Shields, and Beard served several purposes: first, they helped separate the initiated from the uninitiated, while simultaneously elevating, often quite blatantly, their own standing—not to mention their book sales—as recognized experts in the field. Frank E. Brimmer, for example, noted that he had "personally read and answered 10,000 letters from motor campers" over a period of two years.[13] More importantly perhaps was that their words of advice helped place responsibility squarely into human hands. Pouring rain? Wet wood? Howling wind? The writer and founder of the Bear Lake Trail School, Frank H. Cheley (1889–1941), offered, "If your fire won't burn, nine times out of ten it is you rather than the fuel or the weather."[14] For his part, Daniel Carter Beard suggested that "a man who can build one in the forest without the aid of matches and when everything is sodden and water-soaked, is entitled to wear fringe on his leggings and wamus, for he has earned for himself the title of the 'real thing', the true Buckskin Man."[15] For Beard, the equation $[wood]+[spark]=fire$ might be rewritten to take into account site and circumstance, leading to a far more complex proposition such as $[green\ wood]+[wet\ wood]-[ax]+[wind]+[rain]+[darkness]-[matches]=fire$ (and buckskin).

Even for the most skilled, there was a lot to think about. Not all lumber burned in the same manner, for example, and Verrill stated that "every wood has peculiarities of its own, and the wood which will give the best results for one purpose may be very

➲ **1906**
Pitch-Pine to Start a Fire and *A Camp Kitchen Range*, Daniel Carter Beard, *The Field and Forest Handy Book*.

PITCHPINE TO START A FIRE

Fig. 246.

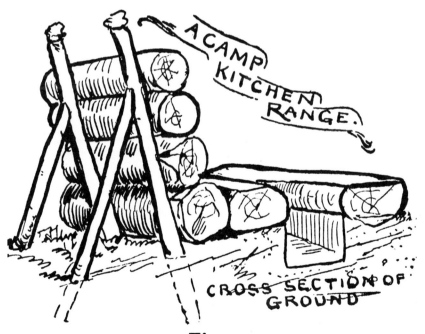

A CAMP KITCHEN RANGE.

CROSS SECTION OF GROUND

Fig. 247.

unsuitable for another."[16] Like the expert craftsman selecting the proper grade of timber for a table, Horace Kephart's observations about firewood, seen from the point of view of the fire builder, his knowledge and insight into the properties of various tree species, are a true wonder to behold. Under his gaze, lumber is no longer just wood, and even before it has been cut, dried, or lit, it takes on magical, alchemical properties informed by a lifetime's worth of experience. Kephart reserved his greatest praise for hardwoods like beech, white oak, and sugar maple, which he called the "favorite fuel of our old-time hunters and surveyors, because it ignites easily, burns with a clear, steady flame, and leaves good coals."[17] Best of all, in Kephart's opinion, was hickory, "a distinctly… American tree," and which, green or dry, "makes a hot fire, but lasts a long time, burning down to a bed of hard coals that keep up an even, generous heat for hours."[18] Speaking no doubt from experience, he cautioned that hickory "must be watched for a time after the fire is started, because the embers that they shoot out are long-lived, and hence more dangerous than those of softwoods."[19]

Once felled, the desired wood then had to be transported to camp on foot and dried for long periods before it could be fed into the fire. Toward this end, Frank Cheley described the sacredness of the ax above all other tools on the trail, an instrument so crucial that it should never be shared with others.[20] Under its sharp blade, wood could be managed into pieces of various sizes—from logs to kindling—to facilitate different stages in the process. A prodigious and skilled illustrator, Daniel Carter Beard drew careful sketches of various forms of fires and the ways in which wood should be stacked to meet desired expectations.

But even such a fundamental part of the camping experience as selecting and chopping wood could in time be eliminated, and even monetized. The now-familiar sight of small packets of precut and dried

⊘ 2011
A case of wood from Yellowstone Firewood, Inc., at campsite #153, Loop D of Madison Campground in Yellowstone National Park, June 22, 2011.

firewood at roadside stands or the local grocery store parallels the increasing parcelization of the campground. Throughout the 1920s, campfires were often built as large public displays for the benefit of an entire campground; however, by the 1930s the campfire had become a private, more intimate event to be experienced at individual campsites. The packet constitutes a guarantee of sorts that its contents would burn well; even the cardboard box holding the wood could provide easy ignition fuel. Indeed, buying wood meant that the tree-identification and fire-building skills prized by Kephart and his compatriots were no longer essential, and therefore would no longer need to be passed down from one generation of campers to the next. To be sure, the sale of firewood predated recreational camping, a fact that may have helped curtail many risky activities, such as the careless removal of trees around the campground or the use of dangerous tools in dense public settings. In the manual *Public Campground Planning* (1934), T. G. Taylor and W. L. Hansen state that "it is not good practice to let the gathering of wood to the user, who ordinarily is not particular as to the manner of acquisition or the adverse results that may occur by reason of his efforts which may be highly deleterious where a scarcity of dry wood exists." The authors conclude that "a handy supply of firewood is not only a desirable accommodation for public campground occupants but is of prime importance from the standpoint of protection of the vegetation" and that "permanent location of several places where wood may be piled and later removed to the various campgrounds [is] needed."[21]

Because they resulted from locally fallen trees, these wood piles may have also inadvertently helped limit the movement of threatening parasites from one campground to another. Despite its bulk, wood had acquired a certain mobility with the emergence of automobile camping during the 1920s. Campers set out on the road not only with their gear and food in tow but often with firewood as part of their supplies,

⬆ **2016**
California Firewood Task Force, *Buy It Where You Burn It* campaign poster.

➡ **2019**
Beaverkill Campground— Untreated Firewood Source, issued by the New York State Department of Environmental Conservation to every campground under its supervision. This type of map illustrates the area from which campground firewood can be procured.

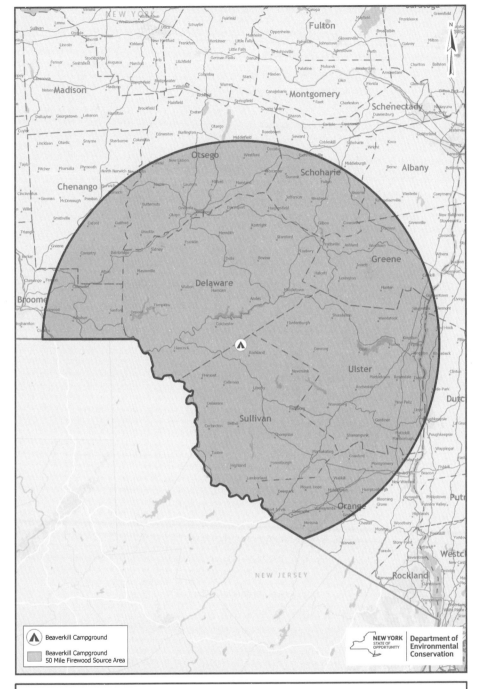

Beaverkill Campground - Untreated Firewood Source

New York State Firewood Regulations
☐ It is **illegal** to transport untreated firewood more than 50 mile from its source or origin.
☐ It is **illegal** to bring untreated firewood into New York State
☐ When transporting untreated firewood within 50 miles of its source or origin, you **must** carry proof of source or origin, such as a receipt.

For more information visit **www.dec.ny.gov** and search "firewood", or call toll free **1-800-640-0652**.

0	12.5	25	50
Miles

a factor that no doubt contributed to the spread of deadly pests whose infestations, such as Dutch elm disease, could be devastating. Unlike other sources of fuel, wood possesses an intimate geography that is tied directly to the place where trees grew and were later felled. Following regulations issued by the Department of Environmental Conservation, for example, New York State campgrounds now require campers to certify that any firewood inside their vehicles was acquired less than fifty miles from the campground they seek to enter.

Persistent Traces

Burn everything that will burn—bury the rest.[22]
—FRANK H. CHELEY

Early recreational campers never intended to move firewood from one campsite to another as they would the rest of their gear. This decision to link tree-cutting operations to the campsite was therefore both practical—*less distance=less effort*—and symbolic. Set in the middle of the forest, wasn't wood the most abundant renewable resource available in a typical camp?

Faced with the choice of what to do with a recently felled tree, the camper could use the wood for heat or to erect semipermanent structures, such as shelters, beds, tables, benches, chairs, and firepits. The architectural historian Reyner Banham (1922–1988) theorized this fundamental choice as a contrast between what he termed as "structural" and "power-operated solutions."[23] To the extent that it referred to any semipermanent structure erected around the camp, Banham's structural paradigm evoked the French abbot Marc-Antoine Laugier's Primitive Hut and the origins of the discipline of architecture.[24] Published in 1755 but referring to an Edenic time, this iconic image of rusticity and rootedness features a combination of felled lumber fastened to living trees, resulting in a shelter

⊕ 1755
Charles Eisen, engraving of the Vitruvian primitive hut, in Marc-Antoine Laugier, *Essai sur l'architecture,* 2nd ed.

⊘ 1933
Side View of Shelter and Fire, Frank H. Cheley, *Camping Out.* At the rudimentary turn-of-the-century campsite, shelters, tables, chairs, and campfire were often made from the same woody materials.

SIDE VIEW OF SHELTER AND FIRE

that would not have been out of place in a late nine-teenth-century rustic camp.

Each in their own way, Banham and Kephart were concerned with articulating the unique potentials embedded within the wood supply. Banham's insight was that the camp is made from both static (shelter, table, chairs) and dynamic (campfire) components, the latter requiring constant replenishment. Given the campfire's strong, entropic force, it would be easy to imagine that the entire architectural system of the camp could be disassembled and fed to the flames on the morning of departure—an interesting way to subvert Banham's original distinction. On the other hand, Kephart's strict focus on the burning potential of wood prefigured the ascent of high-tech gear famil-iar to modern campers. Unlike the tables and seats fashioned from branches lashed together, lightweight tents and mattresses purchased from suppliers like REI can be moved at will. As for the campfire, it too possesses unique qualities related to both mobility and immobility: on the one hand, its flame is depen-dent on trees that have been felled, split, dried, and set flat on the ground—in short, literally uprooted from where they first stood. Once ignited, however, the wood fire becomes the least mobile point in camp, a geographic reference around which the tent, table, and other features are positioned to maximize its impacts. Like Banham, who argued that "societies who do not build substantial structures tend to group their activities around some central focus," the archi-tect and author Charlie Hailey noted that "the camp-fire is an originary and centralizing feature from which the camping practice proceeds…and from which the practice's operational modes radiate."[25] Describing its effects, Banham observed that "the output of heat and light from a campfire is effectively zoned in concentric rings, brightest and hottest close to the fire, coolest and darkest away from it."[26] The concept of concentric rings described in his diagram is familiar to the camper. As the smallest and most

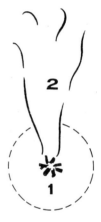

➊ 1969
Environmental Conditions around a Camp Fire, Reyner Banham, *The Architecture of the Well-Tempered Environment.* Banham describes a "1. Zone of radiant heat and light and a 2. Downwind trail of warmed air and smoke."

➋ 1935
Campfire Circle, Manzanita Camp Ground, Lassen Volcanic National Park, Albert H. Good, ed., *Park Structures and Facilities.*

Manzanita Campfire Circle

Lassen Volcanic National Park

A campfire circle with budding ambition to become a kind of outdoor theatre. The seating for three-quarters of its circumference is of full round logs, cut out to provide both seats and backs. The rest of the seating is without backs, anticipating the lecture platform, picture screen, and additional front row seats at some future time.

Proposed screen

Lecture platform

Grade

Campfire

2' Drain

Log seats

SECTION

3rd Row
2nd "
1st "   Round edge
1'-2" 1'-4" 1'-6"

LOG DETAIL

Proposed log seats

2' Fine gravel around seats

Log seats

2'-6"

2'-0"

1'-6"

Native stone

20'-0"

Campfire

2' Drain

Removable iron
fire shield

2'-6"

3'-0"

3'-6"

Gravel path

Proposed Screen

Lecture platform

Location of projector

18" Ø Log

2'-6"
2'-0"
1'-6"
1'-4" 1'-2"

Proposed log seats

PLOT PLAN
Scale 3/32" = 1'-0"

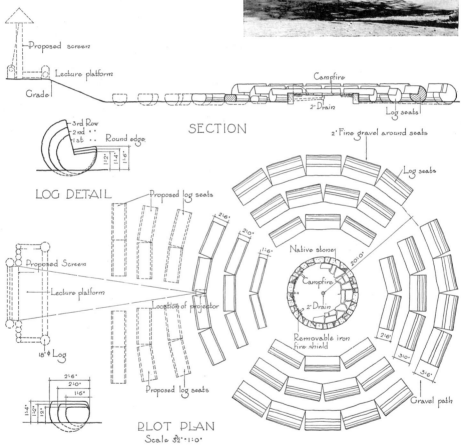

intensive of these rings, the firepit helps contain the spread of the wood fire. A permanent installation made from nonflammable materials like green logs or large stones, often partially embedded below the ground, the firepit also helps designate the location where the next fire should be initiated.

Writing in *Public Campground Planning* (1934) that "unless provision is made for stoves and bonfire places, the campground will be spotted with burned areas," T. G. Taylor, a professor of forestry at Utah State University, and W. L. Hansen, of the US Forest Service, expressed equal concern for the aesthetic impacts of such persistent traces as they did with the inadvertent spread of fire.[27] Writing in *Park Structures and Facilities* (1935), Albert H. Good thought so much of the issue that he dedicated two full chapters of his book to the subject. In a chapter titled "Campfire Circles and Amphitheaters," Good offered an architectural expression of Banham's diagram on a large scale, with heavy log benches arranged in concentric rings around a large bonfire. As places for campers to meet and socialize, these bonfires were not explicitly meant for cooking but instead fulfilled a broader, symbolic mission. It is easy to imagine how such a large-scale bonfire would prove hard to ignore for most campground visitors. As Reverend R. H. Waggoner of Cincinnati, Ohio, observed in the 1910 edition of the Wylie Permanent Camping Company's *Guide to Yellowstone*, the evening campfire was a major social event, a place for arriving visitors to meet and mingle with established veterans of the camp.[28] With an keen eye for the spectacular himself, James McCauley (1841–1911), an early pioneer of Yosemite Valley who ran a small hotel with his wife, Barbara, first conceived of the dramatic Firefall in 1872, a nightly summer event that emulated a waterfall by dropping burning embers down 3,200 feet from the top of Glacier Point. The Firefall proved so successful that it ran for nearly a century. Seeking safer grounds, perhaps, the National Park Service sought to preserve

⬆ **2009**
Long-exposure photograph of the Firefall at Glacier Point taken from the Ahwahnee Meadow in Yosemite National Park.

➡ **c. 1934–1950**
Ralph H. Anderson, photograph of an evening campfire talk led by park rangers, Yosemite National Park.

the social and visual functions of these nighttime rituals with campfire talks, evening public presentations led by a local ranger that served as a form of regional storytelling on a large scale. Good was careful to distinguish between such large public displays and the utilitarian firepits and stoves meant for individual campsites, which played more purpose-driven roles. Reading between the lines, we can sense the author's ambivalence about the impact of codifying firepits as he had other components of the campground. The author hailed "the pioneers, the plainsmen, who frequently cooked out of doors on the most primitive of contrivances."[29] Good included a number of field photographs of firepits from different campgrounds as illustrative examples of potential approaches but offered no technical drawings as he had for campfire circles or other installations in camp. Many of the field examples Good documented were so inconspicuous, they looked as if they resulted from little or no human agency. Instead, he proposed a simple level platform made of masonry or cement, featuring protective walls upon which a sturdy steel cooking grill could be raised at specified heights above the flame "to prevent...any but the most emaciated hot dog from dropping through."[30] This was certainly by design: the author may have had in mind the design of the Klamath stove that first appeared in a contemporaneous publication, the US Forest Service's *Public Camp Manual* (1935), when he observed that "our park vistas [have] become more and more encumbered with chimneyed eruptions that assume the monumental proportions, and even the appearance, of a dismal mortuary art."[31] Seeking a hybrid form, "part stove, part fireplace," Good argued for the "subordination of the fireplace to its surroundings," even "at some sacrifice of convenience in use."[32] An example of this idea can be found in firepit specifications published in the 1915 edition of the US Forest Service's *Handbook for Campers in the National Forests in California*. There we find a pit lined with

⬆ **1925**
Scene in Big Pine Recreation Camp, Los Angeles County. Photographer unknown. Each picnic table is equipped with a stone fireplace for preparing hot meals.

➡ **1934**
Two illustrations from Albert H. Good, ed., *Park and Recreation Structures*, vol. 2—*Recreation and Cultural Facilities*, depicting "picnic fireplaces" at Parvin State Park in New Jersey (top) and throughout national parks (bottom).

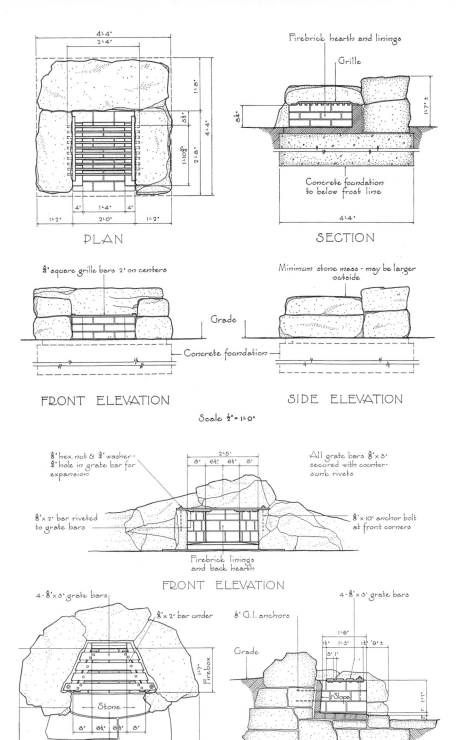

PLAN

SECTION

Firebrick hearth and linings

Grille

Concrete foundation
to below frost line

4'-4"

¾" square grille bars 2' on centers

Grade

Concrete foundation

FRONT ELEVATION

Minimum stone mass - may be larger
outside

Grade

SIDE ELEVATION

Scale ½" = 1'-0"

⅜" hex. nut & ¾" washer -
½" hole in grate bar for
expansion

All grate bars ⅜" x 3"
secured with counter-
sunk rivets

⅜" x 2" bar riveted
to grate bars

⅜" x 10" anchor bolt
at front corners

Firebrick linings
and back hearth

FRONT ELEVATION

4 - ⅜" x 3" grate bars

⅜" x 2" bar under

Firebox

Stone

Stone hearth

PLAN

4 - ⅜" x 3" grate bars

⅜" G.I. anchors

Grade

Slope

Foundation of rock
broken stone or cinders

SECTION

Scale ½" = 1'-0"

stones and sunken below the ground line to protect from surrounding winds, as well as a broad perimeter scraped free of flammable materials. The resulting "Camp Fire-Place" evokes the centrality and fixity of the installation inside the camp, and the care with which its construction should be approached.

Disappearance/Displacement

The open fire is more picturesque. Granted. But so is the tallow dip more picturesque than the incandescent bulb.... but we might as well face the fact that this is the age of electricity and motor cars.[33]

—FRANK E. BRIMMER

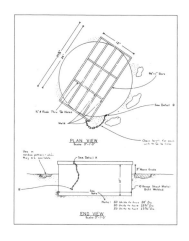

Good's hunches proved true—at least for the most part. By and large, the stone firepits and "soaring piles of masonry" that he deplored have become a thing of the past.[34] Among a new generation of structures that would replace stoves and earthen firepits was an ingenious, open-ended steel drum topped by a sturdy steel grill that Good referred to as a "cheese box." At once heavy but not too heavy, the design could be fabricated en masse in a metal shop and later moved to (and even around) the campsite where, like the picnic table, the tent, the sleeping bag, and many other preassembled components, it could take its rightful place.

By the time these drums were introduced, the campfire had completed a long historical arc. No longer a display of skill and experience, the flame and its many benefits had been turned into pieces of gear that could be compacted and made highly portable in the form of lightweight cooking stoves and lamps; generated with safe, high-yield sources of fuel such as propane gas, denatured alcohol, and kerosene; and summoned in an instant as a source of light or cooking flame with the push of a button. Like "a master magician who touches dull wood or coal with his wand, releasing the bright spirits of light and heat

➊ 1975
Back Country Fire Grates, Rocky Mountain National Park (detail). This firepit features a cooking grill connected to a steel drum by a large chain.

➋ 1938
Picnic Fireplace, Cook County Forest Preserve, Illinois, Albert H. Good, ed., *Park and Recreation Structures,* vol. 2—*Recreation and Cultural Facilities.* This is the earliest example of the now-familiar circular steel drum firepit.

Picnic Fireplace

Cook County Forest Preserve – – Illinois

A forthright answer to the need for picnic fireplaces in vast numbers in the heavily picnicked parks of the Chicago Metropolitan area. Surely here an endless duplication of "sculptured" rock fireplaces so fitting, for example, in the mountain parks surrounding Denver, would seem reasonable only to those who would limit current traffic on Michigan Avenue to the pioneer's covered wagon and the Indian's travois. Among the advantages of this "cheese box" type are low cost, suitability for quantity production, simplicity of installation, and range of orientation in adaption to prevailing winds. Possibly further development will make possible the unit revolving on its anchorage, which will give it more fixed location without sacrifice of orientation range and further provide it with a smooth hearth.

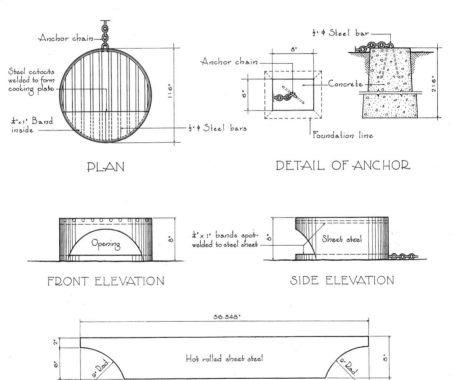

PLAN   DETAIL OF ANCHOR

FRONT ELEVATION   SIDE ELEVATION

DEVELOPED ELEVATION
Scale 1" = 1'-0"

that are imprisoned within them," the equation *[wood]+[spark]=fire,* in any of its forms, had by this time been elegantly rewritten: *fire=now, fire=any-where,* whether in the depths of an earthen firepit or on top of a picnic table.[35]

Daniel Carter Beard traced the origins of the "gearing" of the campfire to a single point in history. Though the invention of the sulfur match dated back centuries earlier, the British apothecarist John Walker (1781–1859) is largely credited with the commercialization of the friction match in 1826.[36] Walker developed pinewood sticks dipped in a phosphorous solution that could be ignited when struck against a hard surface. Wildly popular, his matches replaced laborious techniques for starting a fire, which included the use of a flint and steel. By the time that A. Hyatt Verrill published *The Book of Camping* (1917) nearly a century later, safety friction matches—and a pouch to keep them dry—had become de rigueur in any serious camper's equipment.[37] Appearing a century later in Elon Jessup's *The Motor Camping Book* (1921) is a table-grill hybrid perched on four folding legs set above the live flame, forming a flat surface over which cooking implements were stationed.[38] Having displaced the pot holder and other cooking implements that Beard had improvised from green branches, the clever design paved the way for— indeed seemed to *demand*—still more gear: What would the grill be used for, if not to set down kettles, pots, and skillets? And why not eat the camp meal on plates, in cups, and with silverware? How could all these items be made lighter and more compact en route to the campsite? Gone indeed were the days when the camper simply lopped off a chunk of meat from the roasting spit with a pocketknife and consumed the entire meal with his bare fingers. For many, the campfire had become safe enough that even children could gather and play at its perimeter.

In *Forever Wild: Environmental Aesthetics and the Adirondack Preserve* (1985), the author Philip G. Terrie

⬆ ⬆ **1933**
Method of Supporting Utensils, Frank H. Cheley, *Camping Out.* The author describes a range of techniques for placing pots and pans over the campfire, including the use of two long green poles, known as firedogs.

⬆ **1921**
A Grate Designed to Accommodate a Broiler in Addition to Pots and Pans, Elon Jessup, *The Motor Camping Book.*

⊘ **2020**
Plate from Jennifer K. Mann, *The Camping Trip,* depicting Ernestine (left) and her cousin Samantha preparing s'mores over the campfire.

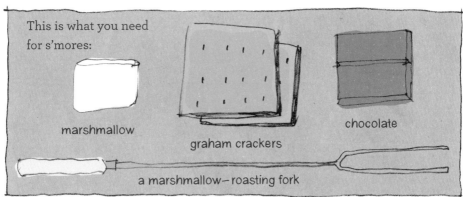

This is what you need for s'mores:

marshmallow

graham crackers

chocolate

a marshmallow–roasting fork

First you roast your marshmallow over a campfire.

argued that the nineteenth-century "sportsman never really felt at home in the wilderness, he depended on an insulating barrier of technology, civilized comforts, and psychological buffers to keep himself from being overwhelmed by the vastness of nature and by an environment in which he perceived himself to be somehow out of place."[39] As illustrated in *Camping in the Woods—"A Good Time Coming"* (1863) by the British-American artist Arthur Fitzwilliam Tait (1819–1905), this "insulating barrier of technology" included not only household imple-ments like cups, skillets, and plates but also the ser-vices of experienced local guides who hunted and prepared food, such that the recreational camper's own labor in camp was kept to a minimum. Later, camping writers like Kephart, Beard, and Verrill sought to change the narrative by placing the empha-sis on firsthand expertise; for them, a rustic approach was the only standard by which real camping should be pursued. Resourcefulness was key. Wet match? Beard instructs that it "may be dried by running it through one's hair."[40] No matches? Verrill offers instructions on the use of a bow and drill that were so mind-boggling and complex as to detract any but the most determined.[41] For his part, Frank Cheley sug-gests that "a fire may be kindled by focusing the sun's rays through the crystal of your watch (or even your eye glasses) onto a pile of fine lint, scrapings from a cotton garment, or fine bits of inner bark. If a live coal is secured, wrap the feeble spark in a bit of lint and fine litter placed in your handkerchief and gently blow until it breaks into flame."[42] For the truly des-perate, he even suggests firing a gun into the rag.[43] As camping became increasingly popular during the 1920s, the campfire and its attendant uses (i.e., cook-ing, heating, lighting) became perhaps the single most active area of experimentation with respect to the development of camping gear. The selling point was no longer skill, experience, or resourcefulness as measures of whether the camper belonged in the

⊘ 1906

Blowing on the Folded Rag to Make Fire, Daniel Carter Beard, *The Field and Forest Handy Book*.

Fig. 244.—Blowing on the folded rag to make fire.

woods or not, but the ease with which anyone, even the luckless "Cheechako," could summon the campfire's magical powers.

There may be no single implement more emblematic of this change in status than the Coleman portable cooking stove. Indeed, there may be no American purveyor of gear better known than Coleman, a company whose name has become synonymous with camping. Including tents, bug-proof shelters, chairs, air mattresses, sleeping bags, coolers, plates, cups, stoves, pots, kettles, and lights, Coleman's equipment has become so ubiquitous over the past century that any camper would confess to owning at least one piece of the brand's gear. Bruce Davidson's iconic photograph of Yosemite campers features an unlit Coleman stove and a tin gas can among the detritus of the campsite. For the author and editor Warren H. Miller (1876–1960), "the really practical dope is a tent stove."[44]

William Coffin Coleman (1870–1957) founded the Hydro-Carbon Light Company in 1900 with the initial purpose of selling hanging gasoline pressure lamps. By 1907, he had set about developing a portable model that could withstand domestic incidents such as falling off a table or leaking if turned upside down.[45] Following a long period of testing during which many early prototypes failed, Coleman shipped its first portable lamp in 1910.[46] From there, the historical geographer Terence Young suggests that it was a small step to adapt the technology for outdoor usage.[47] In 1922, Coleman shipped over ninety thousand units of its new Quick-Lite model, which William Coffin Coleman claimed to be "twenty times brighter, as well as rain proof and fool proof."[48] Following this important commercial success, Coleman began developing a line of gasoline-pressured portable ranges, which he introduced a year later to compete with the highly successful Swedish import Primus (1892) and American Gas Machine Company's (1912) camping stove models.

◯ 1966
Bruce Davidson, *Camp Ground No. 4, Yosemite National Park*, from *The Trip West* series. In this close-up detail, a Coleman stove can be seen on the picnic table at the middle right.

Later identified with its namesake, The Coleman Company hired Frank E. Brimmer to write a guidebook promoting its products. Brimmer, like Kephart and Verrill, was an established writer in the field of camping. Riding an early wave of enthusiasm when motor camping first swept the country during the 1920s, Brimmer transitioned specifically to the topic with books like *Autocamping* (1923) and *Motor Campcraft* (1923). Modest in size, *The Coleman Motor Campers Manual* (1926) is a sixty-four-page pamphlet that offered a twist on a time-honored formula of the age. Like many books of the period, it featured equipment lists, rations, recipes, and practical tips and suggestions. Unlike other similar titles, however, it also came richly illustrated with camping scenes, inside which Coleman products had been carefully arranged. Populated with men, women, and happy children busying themselves around their equipment, these photographs suggested that camping could be easy, fun, safe, and accessible to all. Coleman coined the slogan "The smooth way to rough it," a statement that foregrounded inherent contradictions inside the field that continue to define camping to this day: enthusiasts often fashion a rustic image of themselves in the woods, braving the elements, and the like.[49] At the same time, many of them like to be surrounded by modern domestic comforts—so campers embrace (and often find justification for) the many gadgets that will get them there. In this regard, camping gear seems to embody the perfect marriage between a problem and its resolution—even if one has to invent a fictional need wholesale. The Coleman stove is a good example of this idea: Brimmer knew that unlike other camping activities such as erecting a tent or chopping wood, cooking posed a gender bias that might prove a tricky sell to his male-oriented audience of the time. But he also knew that no piece of equipment was immune to the mysterious type of gear-envy that seems to possess most campers. Sensing an opportunity, he embraced fuzzy rhetoric

⬆ 1925
Cover illustration from *Motor Camper & Tourist*, April 1925, perpetuating stereotypical gendered divisions of roles at the campsite.

➡ 1926
List of Tools and Extras for the Car, Frank E. Brimmer, *Coleman Motor Campers Manual*. Part instruction manual, part promotional advertisement, Brimmer's book features camping photographs in which a range of Coleman products are given prime billing.

List of Tools and Extras for the Car

Naturally, for average trips the autocamper will seldom get beyond the grasp of the roadside garageman; just the same it is advisable to take extra tools for the car as well as other things that may come in handy at a critical moment. This is especially true when one is going on long transcontinental trips.

Tools to Take for the Car

Tire chains
Rim wrench
Pipe wrench
Monkey wrench
Socket wrench set
Pressure gauge
Tire pump in good condition
Valve tools
Vulcanizer outfit
Sandpaper, fine grade
Two pairs of pliers
Two jacks
Two blocks of wood or boards on which to stand jacks in mud or sand

Assortment of screws, bolts and cotter keys
Assortment of files—flat, round and triangular
Two hammers
Oil can with long reach
Plenty of wire
Tire irons
Iron bar
Small vise
Tow cable or rope
Grease gun
Trouble lamp

Extras for the Automobile

Two good spare tires
Two extra tubes
Extra bulbs
High- and low-tension insulated wire
Set of fuses
Assortment of gaskets
Fan belt

Rim lugs, if detachable
Box of tire valve stems
Auxiliary gas, oil and water tank
Set of spark plugs
Length of radiator hose
Insulating tape

On a canoeing and fishing trip, a Coleman Stove has a necessary place. Short stops for lunch, mountain trout to fry a crisp brown, coffee to make in a hurry.

when he suggested that "many husbands would surprise their wives with their adeptness in cookery. Give them a few staples to work with, a rabbit for a stew, and a Coleman, and they can concoct dishes which would cause a French chef to turn green with envy."[50]

It is no accident that motor vehicles appeared in the background of most of the scenes in Brimmer's pamphlet, for they constituted by far the most important technological innovation at the campsite—a place to store gear, sleep inside of, and, perhaps, cook from as well. Using similar sources of fuel, the Coleman No.2 stove had in a sense more to do with the car than it did with the traditional wood fire. For one thing, both embraced mobility and speed as central selling features. The Coleman stove was not only light and portable, it also short-circuited the traditional timeline for gathering, cutting, and drying wood and for building, igniting, and maintaining the campfire, until such time when the flame was primed for cooking. The camper in possession of a Coleman stove could "banish all old time cooking troubles [and] satisfy his cravings whenever Old Man Appetite says: 'Let's eat now.'"[51]

To be sure, much of the uncertainty in delivering and maintaining a steady fire had now completely vanished. With the later introduction of disposable, prepackaged gas cans that were screwed directly into the stove assembly, even fuel would soon become a complete abstraction.[52] And what about matches? A piezoelectric ignition system delivered an electric spark into a stream of pressurized gas, lighting the flame with the push of a button. Indeed, even the boxy design of the original Coleman stove, with its wind baffles—eventually branded as Wind Blocks— could be further simplified: for the backpacking enthusiast seeking economy of weight, portable stoves are no more than a gas can (doubling as the assembly's base), topped by a burner and a regulator. However elegant and reductive, the formula *fire=now*,

↑ 1924

Exhaust Heater, from *Motor Camper & Tourist*, July 1924. A woman is preparing a meal over the heat generated by the automobile engine.

➔ 1958

Portable Gasoline Heatmaster and Tank, in the Coleman Company, Inc., *Catalog Outing Products, Parts Catalog 32B*. This diagram illustrates the range of spare parts for the Coleman 460G Heatmaster stove.

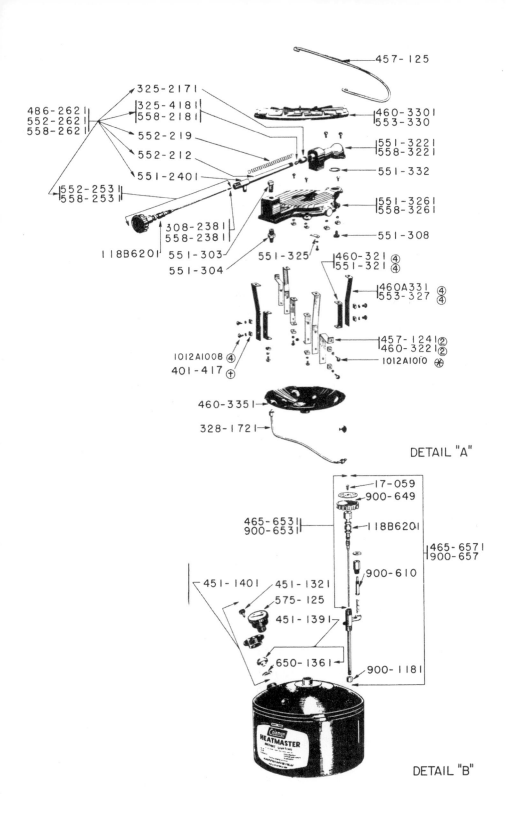

457-125

325-2171

486-2621
552-2621
558-2621

325-4181
558-2181

460-3301
553-330

552-219

551-3221
558-3221

552-212

551-332

551-2401

551-3261
558-3261

552-2531
558-2531

551-308

308-2381
558-2381

460-321 ④
551-321 ④

118B6201   551-303

551-325

460A331 ④
553-327 ④

551-304

457-1241 ②
460-3221 ②

1012A1008 ④

1012A1010 ✱

401-417 ⊕

460-3351

328-1721

DETAIL "A"

17-059

900-649

465-6531
900-6531

118B6201

465-6571
900-657

900-610

451-1401

451-1321

575-125

451-1391

650-1361

900-1181

DETAIL "B"

fire=anywhere could take on a complexity of
its own. Specifications for a midcentury model
Coleman stove illustrated the underlying complexity
of the system: the single line delivering and regulat-
ing the stream of pressurized fuel between the tank
and the burners was made of sixteen different parts,
many of which were incompatible from one model
to the next.

In the twenty-first-century digital age, marked by
instant gratification, the camping stove is experienc-
ing a (very) quiet, if somewhat counterintuitive,
revolution of its own. In *The Revenge of Analog* (2016),
the Canadian author and journalist David Sax celebrates the return of analog tools enjoyed by those
resisting the digital world—notebooks, vinyl records,
film, and board games. And if they're not quite ready
to abandon their iPhones and iPads at the campsite,
many campers are embracing a similar worldview,
sacrificing the immediacy of gas burners and piezoelectric ignition for a certain degree of environmental
consciousness. Does this mean a return to the traditional virtues of the wood fire? Not quite: a single-
burner stove, the Sierra Zip, employs a battery-
operated fan to aerate a small chamber in which
twigs, pine cones, and bark are fed. Residual matter
that only a few decades ago would have been used
to start a campfire now constitutes its main source
of combustible fuel.

Even more minimalist is the line of GoSun portable solar ovens, introduced in a 2013 Kickstarter
campaign. Solar cooking dates back to the late eighteenth century, but the company, having found a way
to make the appliance lightweight and highly portable, has brought about renewed interest in the technology, with an eye toward the camping market and
other off-grid situations such as disaster relief efforts.
When packed, two parabolic reflectors form a protective clamshell around a slim tube of insulated glass
that serves as an oven. When deployed, light is
focused by the reflectors onto the glass chamber,

➋ ➌ 2019
Publicity stills for GoSun solar
ovens. Top: GoSun Sport.
Bottom: GoSun Fusion, a hybrid
model featuring a rechargeable,
lithium-ion battery that allows
some off-grid use during
evenings or rain.

resulting in temperature buildups of up to 550°F and deliciously cooked meals.[53]

Conclusions

Cold food may yield sustenance and allow [the outdoor enthusiast] to continue a little longer, but to really restore his vigor he needs external heat, hot food cooked over the camp-fire, warm heat-rays to penetrate his body and relax the tired muscles, drive out the cold and rheumatic aches, and put him in a state of comfort that enables mind and body to recuperate.[54]
—WARREN H. MILLER

For David Wescott, the campfire constitutes "the means and emblem of light, warmth, protection, friendly gathering, council."[55] There is growing evidence that the traditional wood campfire is slowly being displaced as the primary source of these effects. The historian Warren James Belasco noted the introduction of electrical lighting in public campgrounds during the 1920s, an innovation which, in effect, stretched the day, allowing campers to stay on the road longer without the worry of setting up camp under the darkness of night.[56] During the 1990s, KOA (Kampgrounds of America) tested new ground with the introduction of a new model of outdoor kitchen, the Kamper Kitchen. A shared facility equipped with domestic electric stoves and sinks and constructed in the style of a log cabin, the Kamper Kitchen suggests that cooking may no longer be an activity that takes place at (or defines) the campsite but one that could be relegated to outside of the designated campsite.

On a 2017 camping trip to Acadia National Park, I noticed campers eating fast food at their campsite; it is now completely reasonable to think that food consumed at the picnic table may be prepared well outside campground limits, and by different hands. In 2018, Domino's announced 150,000 public Domino's

⊘ 2022
KOA Kamper Kitchen, Colorado Springs, Colorado. Photographer unknown. Featured at KOAs nationwide, this type of outdoor kitchen is a throwback to the 1920s, when many campgrounds featured public kitchens outfitted with cooking ranges.

Hotspots that don't have traditional street addresses, including parks and campgrounds, where their products could be delivered and picked up.[57]

Bruce Davidson's wonderfully ironic 1966 photograph (page 17) of campers at Yosemite National Park, with its lone box of Ritz Crackers as the only source of food, illustrates the extent of a radical physical transformation of many campsite components, including the campfire, far beyond what even advocates like Albert H. Good may have envisioned: the entire site has been reduced to a glorified pantry, where imported goods are not prepared, but consumed. Even Davidson himself, however, could not have envisioned how quaint his own vision would become only a few decades later. After picking up the evening meal at a local Domino's Hotspot, the camper can get their evening campfire experience by taking in a local ranger's PowerPoint presentation at the campfire circle talk—with no live flame in sight. In the era of climate change, some campgrounds formally forbid campfires, instead requiring campers to use roving flashlights to satisfy this important evening tradition.[58] For the architect Charlie Hailey, for whom "the backyard and living room campouts occur in the domesticated wilderness of the suburban lawn and garden or within the protected zones of the family's house," these modern experiences of the campfire as a mere "televisual flicker" come as further evidence that the distance separating campsite and the domicile is growing shorter still.[59]

➋ **1974**
C. E. Westveer, photograph of an evening amphitheater program at Crabtree Falls Campground on the Blue Ridge Parkway in Micaville, North Carolina.

CAMPSITE

*To be free, unbeholden, irresponsible for the nonce! Free to
go or come at one's sweet will, to tarry where he lists, to do
this, or to do that, or do nothing, as the humor veers; and for
the hours, "It shall be what o'clock I say it is!"*[1]
—HORACE KEPHART

Situated somewhere between what historians John
A. Jakle and Keith A. Sculle have described as the
"challenging new circumstances and the safe reassur-
ances of familiarity," the camp is a substitute for the
home—a place to dwell, to sleep, to interact socially,
to prepare and eat food.[2] Stripped of any but the most
essential conveniences and often merely shielded by
a single layer of paper-thin, 40-denier ripstop nylon,
the modern shelter, and the patch of ground upon
which it is located, is literally and figuratively *open*
to the external stimuli of its natural surroundings.

As the parcel of land upon which millions of
enthusiasts elect each summer to drive their car, set
up their tent, or park their trailer or RV, this patch of
ground upon which they lay down temporary roots is

◐◑ 1863
A. F. Tait, *Camping in the
Woods—"A Good Time Coming."*

◔ c. 1890
Open camp in the Adirondacks.
Photographer unknown. Three
men with rifles and a banjo
unwind in front of their lean-
to, near Lake Pleasant, New
York. A rudimentary table and
benches stand at right.

less an imagined ideal than the basic unit of management of the modern campground. There are over nine hundred thousand such campsites dispersed across twenty thousand campgrounds nationally.[3] Among these, KOA (Kampgrounds of America) alone reported a total usage of over 5.8 million campsite-nights annually in 2021, as well as 23 million unique visitors on its website.[4]

Modern campsites embody a peculiar contradiction: as Dan White correctly observes, they are defined and serviced by an increasingly sophisticated range of utilities and conveniences, and yet marketed to perpetuate the cherished American ideal of the backwoods camp.[5] The land art pioneer Robert Smithson (1938–1973)—whose deeply tuned sensibilities to site and site-making were in part informed by the childhood family camping trips he helped organize—might suggest that the campsite is merely a place upon which to reenact the making of a place.[6] Campgrounds indeed commodify the locus of this singular experience into multiple sites—often hundreds at the same facility. Record sales reported by sporting utility stores like REI and EMS are due in major part to their ability to successfully associate their equipment with the out-of-doors and the prospect of healthy living.[7] For many urbanites, high-performance gear—hiking boots, mountaineering vests, etc.—have now become staples of everyday casual chic.

Modern campgrounds are abundant with delightful irony: as an internalized setting of modern utilities, each lone campsite functions in part as a stage for cultural fantasies to be performed in full view of an audience of nearby campers that is itself interested in much the same "wilderness" experience. Who in the camping community has not experienced a certain degree of gear envy, among the equipment deployed at a neighboring site, of a brand-new Primus OmniLite Ti multifuel stove (with silencer), a Sierra Designs tent, or a Marmot sleeping bag? KOA even

⊘ **1965**
Bruce Davidson, *Photograph of a Couple at their Campsite*, from *Yosemite Campers* series.

goes as far as to lease permanently parked Airstream trailers on some of its sites to attract campers who want to spend the night inside a cultural icon. This experiment suggests that prospective campers can show up without *any* equipment of their own: as with a stay at a hotel or roadside motel, a simple change of clothes and a toothbrush will do. No wonder that the daily repetition of chores once associated with survival has now been recast as a series of disembodied rituals that attempt to reconnect the camper with something that is largely lost. By now most of the old necessities—hiking to and clearing the site, hunting for game, collecting water and firewood—have given way to less arduous activities, such as parking the car, pitching cable-free pop tents, buying cold cuts at the campground store, hooking up electrical and sewerage conduits, and setting up patio chairs. Serviced by pervasive networks of infrastructure and populated with trailers and $300,000 RVs, campgrounds celebrate a unique form of American ingenuity in which intersecting narratives and desires (e.g., wilderness, individuality, access, speed, comfort, nostalgia, profit) become strangely and powerfully hybridized.

To tell the history of the campsite is not to tell the story of any one specific site or even one specific campground, but rather to examine how this rugged cultural ideal came to be commodified into generic and largely replicated spatial patterns. It is to talk not only about campers but also about the crucial role that motor vehicles have played in shaping this narrative—one that begins rather innocuously with early twentieth-century roadside bivouacs and culminates with the tightly organized loops of dedicated plots that define the modern campground. The following four key concepts provide a way to understand the radical physical and cultural transformations undergone in the very short span of 150 years.

➲ 2013
Speculative montage by the author depicting four nineteenth-century campers spending the night at a KOA with gear purchased at Campmor, a popular outfitter located in Paramus, New Jersey.

Revivex Water and Stain Repellent
Item 36211-N
Page 139
price: $7.99

GSI Outdoors Hand Anodized Dutch Oven
Item 82500-N
Page 78
price: $139.95

Sierra Designs Lightning XT 3 Tent
Item 27667-N
Page 8
price: $269.97

Trekker External Frame Pack
295-N 3900
price: $19.99

Mac Sports Big Boy Comfort Chair
Item 41021-N
Page 47
price: $27.99

Camper Top Tent
Item 20745-N
Page 9
price: $211.99

Camp Stove Toaster
Item 23102-N
Page 78
price: $3.99

Sleep Screen
Item 41168-N
Page 45
price: $29.99

Eton Solarliink FR360 Radio
Item 88890-N
Page 89
price: $50.00

PIC Mosquito Coils
Item 81316-N
Page 99
price: $3.99

Heavy Duty Grid
Item 80288-N
Page 71
price: $17.99

Pocket Chain Saw
Item 27001-N
Page 92
price: $29.99

Telescoping Fork
Item 88097-N
Page 72
price: $4.99

Travel Pet Bed
Item 22750-N
Page 63
price: $34.99

Sea To summitt Sinks
Item 83204-N 20
Page 79
price: $24.99

Bison Fold A Bowl
Item 59700-N
Page 63
price: $12.99

Spatial Enclosure, Spatial Alienation

*If there is any message…that I would sear with words
deeply grooved into the plastic record of the brain so that
it could never be forgotten, it would be this: Autocamp
upon others as you would have others autocamp upon you.
This ought to be the Golden Rule—or the Gasoline Rule—
of motor camping.*[8]
—FRANK E. BRIMMER

It is easy to overlook the fact that organized camp-grounds originated just as much in the perceived need to protect unsuspecting or uneducated campers from nature's darker forces as in the wish to spare nature from human destruction. The very word *campground*, a noun, seems paradoxical in nature, with *camp*, a verb, describing an informal and often temporary shelter that is built over a formally dedi-cated territory, or *ground*. The term *campground* sug-gests dueling agencies, private and collective, freeing and restrictive, initiating and protective all at once. By tolerating a certain level of ecological degradation and concentrating campers within a defined territory, campgrounds prevent visitors from occupying just about *any* place they might otherwise gain access to. The subtlety of the spatial enclosure they occupy might help maintain the illusion of freedom—camp-ers think they are in nature, but are simultaneously protected from it, and, to take it one step further, it could be argued that they are actually captive within this artificial environment.

As a 1927 scene in Yosemite's Stoneman Meadow makes clear, the first public campgrounds in the United States were initially nothing more than large, dedicated clearings, free of trees, within which to concentrate large groups of tourists. The researcher and author Susan Snyder noted, "It was against the rules of the park to camp anyplace except in the prescribed grounds."[9] Later practices, including time restrictions, pillow counts, admission fees,

◈ 1927
Campers in Stoneman Meadow,
Yosemite National Park.
Photographer unknown.

physical barriers, and even deep moats surrounding campgrounds, would impose further controls on campers. The row of logs erected around Summit Lake Camp in Lassen Volcanic National Park in the early 1930s is a good example of a simple perimeter enclosure; more than restricting people, its purpose was to discourage the circulation of motor vehicles beyond the created boundaries. And as if it weren't clear enough, facility managers affixed a sign reminding the occupants of the "campground limits." In effect, spatial enclosures became not only a means to confine tourists but also to keep undesirables out.

The spatial enclosure both protects campers and isolates them *from* nature and, in some cases, from one another. Frank E. Brimmer liked to say that "the camaraderie of the motor camp is one of the best 'melting pots' of American Democracy—the one place where folks meet human beings in an informal and wholesome manner."[10] Tragically, in the decades before the Civil Rights Act (1964), the campground's open-ended joviality was not exempt from racial prejudice—even in national parks. From 1939 to 1950, the National Park Service operated a segregated campground at Lewis Mountain in Shenandoah National Park. In his book *The Negro Motorist Green Book*—in circulation from 1936 to 1966 and later known as *The Negro Travelers' Green Book*—travel writer Victor H. Green (1892–1960) euphemistically noted the facility on Skyline Drive in Luray, Virginia, as "Tourist Homes."[11] In his extraordinary undertaking, Green hoped to steer Black travelers toward facilities—restaurants, gas stations, nightclubs, hotels, motels, and, increasingly, campgrounds—that would welcome them as they moved across the country.[12] But this, of course, also meant that these travelers could not put down stakes at any of the other three much larger facilities inside the park. With respect to Brimmer's melting pot of American democracy, separate is never equal.

⊙ 1949
Cover illustration from Victor H. Green, *The Negro Motorist Green Book: An International Travel Guide.*

⊘ 1932
Art Holmes, *Summit Lake Camp Boundary*, Lassen Volcanic National Park in California.

⊙ c. 1939–1950
When Lewis Mountain Was Segregated, Shenandoah National Park. Photographer unknown. The sample description that appears at the top of the image was excerpted from Victor H. Green's 1949 *The Negro Motorist Green Book: An International Travel Guide* and superimposed by the author. During this period, the National Park Service operated four campgrounds in the park, including the segregated facility at Lewis Mountain.

LURAY
TOURIST HOMES
Camp Lewis Mountain—Skyline Drive

LEWIS MOUNTAIN
NEGRO AREA
COFFEE SHOP & COTTAGES
CAMPGROUND PICNICGROUND
⟶ ENTRANCE ⟶

With the introduction of basic utilities, such as electricity, drinking water, and toilets, campgrounds became internally oriented and campers were no longer expected to venture beyond these safe confines. Why should they fend for themselves, gather wood, hunt for game, or collect drinking water, when all this could be accomplished within the campground itself with a quick run to the bathroom, the nearby water tap, or the camp store?

This subtle form of alienation has led to an important cultural shift: the idealization of nature as peaceful and nonthreatening. Before the introduction of such modern amenities, early twentieth-century campers would often mistakenly place their trust in quaint, scenic roadside tableaus, unsuspecting that, say, the sparkling water from the cold nearby stream might be potentially harmful. And for many modern campers features such as water taps (with filtered water often piped in from distant sources) further reinforce the perception of nature as an abstraction. Nature is expected to remain comfortable, visually and emotionally inspiring, its atmospheric effects negligible. Campground operators themselves help reinforce this perception, typically closing facilities before seasonal temperatures reach the freezing point. As a result, most campers never confront the potentially brutal rigors of weather, to the point where an evening frost, a few persistent bugs, or a light rain might now count as major hardships during the course of a weekend trip, and that might create memories worthy of being recounted in family conversations for years to come.

The dramatic events of June 11 and 12, 2010, at the campground in the Albert Pike Recreation Area in the Ouachita Mountains National Forest in southwest Arkansas challenged this tenuous fantasy—practically a pact—that recreational campers had long entertained about nature. During the night a storm developed; heavy rains quickly saturated the ground and later caused a flash flood, bringing the levels of

⊘ 2010

Mike Stone, damaged RV off the bank of the Little Missouri River in the Albert Pike Recreation Area, following the June 11–12, 2010, storm during which twenty people perished, including six children.

the nearby Caddo and Little Missouri rivers twenty feet above their respective banks in the span of a few hours. While many alarmed campers managed to flee their campsites during the middle of the night, others were caught off guard, twenty of whom drowned. Among the dead were six children under the age of seven, whose youthful innocence was not much different than that of any other camper entering the woods. While a litany of geographical (e.g., isolation, rugged local terrain, poor phone reception) and design (i.e., lack of proper registration procedures and evacuation protocols) factors can be in part faulted for this tragic loss of life, the disaster also underscores crucial historical shifts within the culture of camping itself: an increasing lack of awareness of potential danger, as well as an implicit trust in the protective confines of the spatial enclosure of the campground and the resources at hand.

The Cleared Site and the Presumption of Rusticity

Usually old camp sites are undesirable, for health and sanitary reasons. Choose new ones whenever possible, even if it does take a bit more elbow grease to put them into livable shape.[13]
—FRANK H. CHELEY

Albert H. Good expressed mock surprise when he claimed that the wilderness was not initially outfitted with amenities like picnic tables and fireplaces. For an architect like Good, nature was an Eden meant to be consumed, and properly concealed infrastructural components were not obstacles to, but rather a necessary condition of, the full enjoyment of nature. These elements mark a specific potential for use: picnic tables suggested the possibility of sitting and eating, firepits and grills for cooking food, wooden steps for negotiating difficult grades, and the like. His *Park Structures*

⊘ 1938
Illustration from Albert H. Good, ed., *Park and Recreation Structures*, vol. 3—*Overnight and Organized Camp Facilities*, depicting a typical automobile campsite and a vehicle parked at what E. P. Meinecke referred to as its "garage spur."

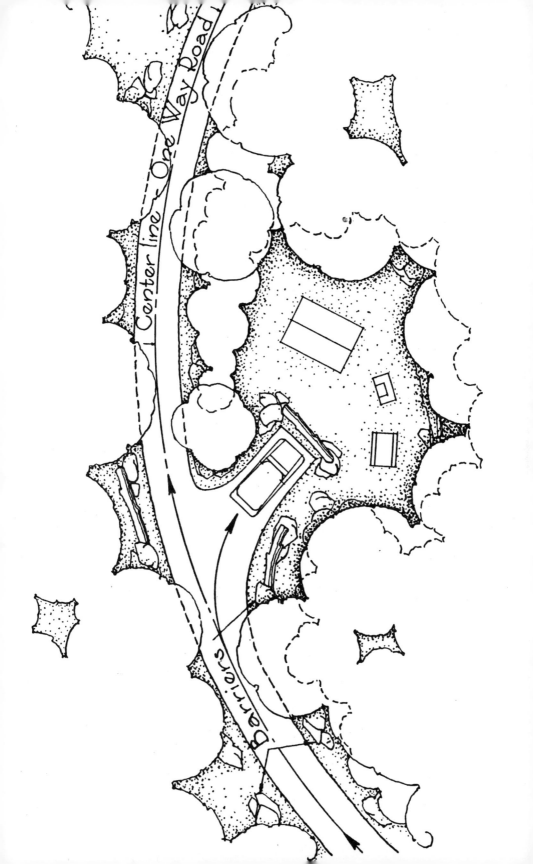

and Facilities (1935) and *Parks and Recreational Structures* (1938) were largely disseminated throughout the United States during the Works Progress Administration (WPA) and Civilian Conservation Corps era that oversaw a major expansion of recreational facilities in national and state parks. Good's architectural specifications, involving entranceways, signs and markers, fireplaces and camp stoves, seats and tables, drinking fountains, and more would form much of the backbone of contemporary campground design.

Good's observations set up a key dialectic between fixed infrastructural components located at the campsite, on the one hand, and those pieces of equipment that must be imported by the camper, on the other. Before the incremental and systematic implementation of modern utilities (e.g., water, bathrooms, electricity, firepits, food lockers), recreational campers had to transport a full array of domestic apparatus (e.g., water basins, tables, chairs, stoves, tents) from one campground to another. To accommodate these comforts, touring automobiles were outfitted with sideboard lockers, trailers, and even built-in components like tents and tables that sprang directly from the sides. The motor vehicle quickly became an integral part of the camping apparatus, not only for what it could transport, but literally as a spatial extension of the campsite. In the 1920s—an era that predated the arrival of campers and RVs—trade advertisements trumpeted curious inventions such as hammocks strung inside automobiles and specially outfitted engine surfaces that could serve as hot plates for preparing meals (page 80). And just as the improvised campsite and the automobile respectively exemplified wilderness rusticity and technological sophistication, these short-lived inventions suggest an unwillingness to abandon, even briefly, the modern comforts of home. Indeed, the presence of the automobile on the site seems, then as now, a reassuring presence in the face of an almost overwhelming change of environment.

RED HEAD BRAND
AUTO BED

Sleep in your car The RED HEAD BRAND Auto Bed is dandy to sleep in! Up or down in three minutes. Fits any sedan or touring car Weighs 30 lbs. Folds to package size of a golf bag

Many other useful articles in our "Auto Campers' Guide." Be sure to write for a copy.

ALWARD-ANDERSON-SOUTHARD CO.
Incorporated 1915
921 West Chicago Ave., Chicago, U. S. A.

⬆ 1925
Alward-Anderson-Southard Company, *Red Head Brand Auto Bed*, in Donald Wood, *RVs & Campers: 1900–2000.*

➔ 1921
Photograph captioned: "A home devised sheet metal, running-board food box....The camper is filling his gasoline stove," Elon Jessup, *The Motor Camping Book*. Photographer unknown.

To preserve anew the carefully staged illusion of discovery and dwelling in the wilderness, the modern campsite must function as a perpetually unfinished site, designed to be provisionally completed each time a new visitor checks in.[14] By physically clearing the campsite of trees and shrubs and limiting the number of fixed infrastructural components present on the site (e.g., firepit, table, water spigot), Good and other campground planners of the period ingeniously maintained the delicate yet persuasive illusion of rusticity experienced by the camper upon arrival. The loosely domesticated site requires the direct participation of the visitors who, importing their own equipment, such as tents, food, and sleeping bags, momentarily makes its full occupation possible, albeit briefly. By later taking care to pack up these belongings and clean the site before leaving, each camper unwittingly clears and prepares the site for the next occupant. This unending cycle preserves the impression that the camper is discovering a site for the first time and participating in its construction by temporarily staking claim to it—literally, with tent stakes, an immobilized trailer, RV, and other imported equipment—for the night. Hundreds of campers may lay claim to the same site, but all will remain unknown to the others who come after.

Spatial Coordinates: X Marks the Spot

It is an inspiring sight to go into…Denver and see several hundred cars parked in their allotted spaces and their happy owners, many of them with large families, enjoying the camp life or recreational facilities of their surroundings.[15]
—HORACE ALBRIGHT

In many ways, the assignment of specific campsites for individual camping parties constitutes a further refinement of the broad spatial enclosure found in early campgrounds. The idea originated with large

2017
Campsite Marker, Igloo Creek Campground, Denali National Park and Preserve in Alaska. Photographer unknown.

municipal facilities, such as Denver's Overland Park, in the 1920s. Occupying 160 acres along the Platte River, Overland Park built its national reputation by offering a wide range of attractions that became the envy of municipalities around the country and made it one of the largest and most significant automobile campgrounds of the period. Its reputation as the "Manhattan of auto-camps" owed perhaps as much to its broad range of service accommodations as its eight hundred individual lots, each measuring 25 × 35 feet, designed, collectively, to accommodate as many as six thousand autocampers each night.[16] This arrangement involved not only a higher degree of spatial organization but also increasingly sophisticated forms of control, including systems to collect fees, to keep track of individual camping parties, and to monitor the length of their stay.

This new spatial model superseded the open field campground with its loose amalgamation of vehicles, tents, and cables. Overland Park press releases in the 1920s reflect an obsession with precise statistics that only a refined spatial system of individual campsites could provide: "The total number of cars encamped at Overland Park from May 1 to October 20…was 7,874; the total number of passengers carried by these cars was 28,910….The visitors represented forty-seven state [sic], the Dominion of Canada and the district of Columbia. The only state not represented during the season of 1920 was that of Delaware."[17]

The demarcation of the campground into discrete plots, or campsites, produces a complex geography of individual and shared interests. Nowadays, this process of unitization is a useful way not only to physically untangle campers from one another but to fix the density of occupants within a particular territory, while grouping campers into like-minded communities (e.g., keeping noisier RVs and trailers from more modest tent sites). These relationships of individuals to the whole were later instrumentalized in the form of a unique visual document which will be discussed at length in the next chapter: the campground map.

➋ 1922
The Tent City at Overland, Municipal Facts Bi-Monthly, March–April 1922.

Camp scene in Overland Park, Denver's famous free automobile camp for tourists. The park will
accommodate more than one thousand automobiles at a time.

The Tent City *at* Overland

Attendance was forty thousand registered visitors last year

For current-day campers, the ritual of arrival to the campground typically begins with a handout of the facilities map; the visitor and attendant then agree on the precise location of the campsite. The live circling in ink of the agreed-upon location by the campground attendant ingeniously supports—as do the tent-pitching, cooking, and other rituals discussed earlier—the illusion of the cleared site. Like a signature, this simple personal gesture makes each copy of the map (and therefore each individual visit to the campground) seem at once fresh and original, as if each site is being claimed for the very first time.

Beyond its obvious locational benefits, the campground map possesses a peculiar kind of agency: as a visual diagram it employs graphic strategies that reveal little (if any) of the character of the surrounding natural environment. Indeed, a key aspect of this type of representation is that it produces an awareness of the campground as a self-sufficient spatial territory that is *independent from its natural surroundings*. Depicting numbered plots, roads, bathrooms, showers, water taps, woodbins, snack bars, boat launches, and the like, the map offers a lens through which the campground can be understood, used, and explored as an enclosed landscape; it reminds visitors of the campground's territorial limits and their place *inside* these limits.

Some campgrounds offer hundreds of individual campsites while other facilities are much smaller and intimate. With 432 campsites, for example, Bridge Bay Campground in Yellowstone National Park is one of the largest federally managed facilities, while Rough Canyon in Amistad National Recreation Area features merely four. No matter their size, campgrounds and the maps that reflect them are fairly generic and tend to resemble one another in many respects. Were it not for the title of Bruce Davidson's 1965 photo series, *Yosemite Campers*, the images would be impossible to trace back to one of the country's most iconic national parks.[18] In one image, a single camper has hung sheets

⊘ **1932**
Chief Ranger Lawrence Farwell (L. F.) Cook, field sketch for Firwood Camp, Sequoia National Park.

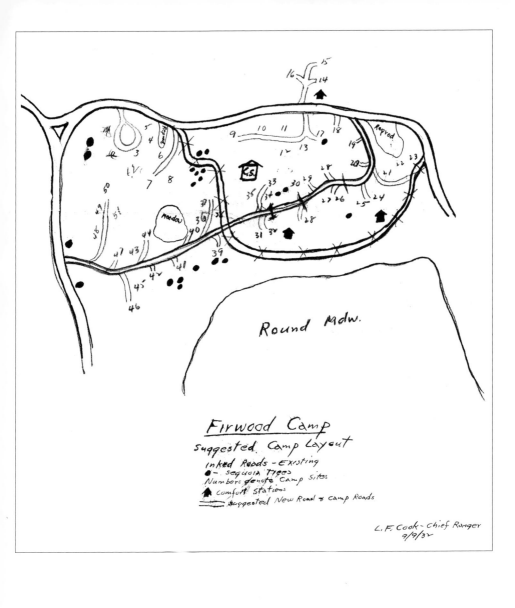

Round Mdw.

<u>Firwood Camp</u>
Suggested Camp Layout
Inked Roads - Existing
● - Sequoia Trees
Numbers denote Camp Sites
⚑ Comfort Stations
══ Suggested New Road & Camp Roads

L. F. Cook - Chief Ranger
9/9/32

and blankets between trees to demarcate her campsite from her neighbors', a strategy reminiscent of a back-yard fence. In another, a couple is relaxing at a picnic table behind their camper against a generic background of tall pine trees (page 93). In these images, the campsite is not defined by the unique character of its surroundings—in the way that perhaps early nineteenth-century recreation enthusiasts in the Adirondacks might have elected to set camp—but is an abstract spatial solution. This seems to be a key message of Davidson's subversive compositions: they purposefully downplay the iconic vistas featured in popular postcards of Yosemite. The photographed campsites could be anywhere. This reflects the choices and decision-making elements that visitors, presented with a map at any campground entrance, face: Near the bathroom or the water tap? Near the RV loop? Where are my neighbors?

X marking the spot on the map seems at once a direct challenge ("Please camp *here*") and the remnant trace of an event ("This is where I camped").

Physical and Virtual Access

A camp proper is a nomad's binding-place. He may occupy it for a season, or only for a single night, according as the site and its surroundings please or do not please the wanderer's whim.[19]

—HORACE KEPHART

The first act of camping is the act that initially lays claim to the site. The image of the camper pitching his tent constitutes an "inherited symbol of high adventure."[20] In fact, this gesture can rarely be construed as the very first sign of occupation. One might argue, for example, that the car—and not the camper—is the first resident of the cleared site: given its sheer bulk, the immobilized motor vehicle constitutes a powerful statement of intent that far eclipses the lightness of

⬆ **1965**
Bruce Davidson, *Child in Play Pen at Campsite*, from *The Trip West* series. It's impossible to avoid the irony of a toddler trapped in a nested set of enclosures, yet enjoying the presumed freedom associated with wilderness.

⬇ **1966**
Bruce Davidson, *Woman at Her Campsite*, from *Yosemite Campers* series.

the fabric tent. Others might point to the campground map and the fresh ink stain marking a recently claimed spot, or even the details of an online reservation made months in advance, as alternate evidence.

Access is a complex phenomenon that occurs both within and outside the site itself. To be sure, access involves the presence of a physical infrastructure (i.e., roads and motor vehicles) that leads the camper to the site's threshold. Expressing concern about overuse in ecologically sensitive areas of many national parks during the 1920s, the plant pathologist E. P. Meinecke was the first to codify the potentially lethal role of the automobile in wilderness areas: "Man injures only those smaller plants he actually tramples under foot. The car, much clumsier to handle, crushes shrubs and sideswipes trees, tearing off living bark and severely injuring them. Oil, a deadly poison to plants, drips from the parked automobile."[21] Meinecke's enduring contribution to campground design was to push beyond the notion of the individual plot and propose one-way loop roads that led automobiles to individual "garage spurs" next to each campsite.[22] In this regard, the plot as we know it today is as much about establishing a territory for the camper as about accommodating the automobile. The emergence of the trailer as a heavier, more sophisticated form of dwelling in the 1930s would require a yet more generous reengineering of Meinecke's original pull-off spur and the implementation of various infrastructural hookups (e.g., electrical, water, sewage) to make the trailer fully operational, as well as a progressive segregation of RV and tent sites. For the author John Steinbeck, trailers

are wonderfully built homes, aluminum skins, double-walled, with insulation, and often paneled with veneer of hardwood. Sometimes as much as forty feet long, with air-conditioners, toilets, baths, and invariably television....A mobile home is drawn to the trailer park and installed on a ramp, a heavy rubber sewer pipe is bolted underneath, water and electrical power

⊘ **1967**
Joseph O. McCabe, *Watchman Campground Completed from across Virgin River, below South Campground.*

connected, the television antenna raised, and the family is in residence.[23]

In proposing these new infrastructural guidelines, Meinecke was trying to put a contemporary spin on Horace Kephart's advice to take to the wild, "to pull up stakes" and move elsewhere at his own whim.[24] Kephart's advice proved popular with twentieth-century motor tourists, who rejected the tyranny of organization and the artificial trappings of late nineteenth-century railroad tours of the national parks:

> You are your own master, the road is ahead; you eat as you please, cooking your own meals over an open fire; sleeping when you will under the stars, waking with the dawn; swim in a mountain lake when you will, and always the road ahead. Thoreau at 29 cents a gallon.[25]

Kephart's original call had been about individualism as well as deep solitude, and one suspects that he would have become alarmed at the troves of automobile tourists flocking to the American road by the time Meinecke arrived on the scene—these new car campers had in fact created the need for another, highly regulated system. Railroad tours had once been the province of the wealthy, and the introduction of cheap automobiles like the Ford Model T in 1908 would open up recreational opportunities for the growing middle class. Despite Kephart's stirring rhetoric of what "lay beyond the horizon's rim," the emergence of autocamping immediately presented a series of challenges both internal and external to the campground: while Meinecke and Good sought to define the territory and organization of the campground, automobile travel also impacted camping prospects on a regional and even national scale: Where should I go? Will there be enough space? How long can I stay? Can I decide before I arrive?[26]

↑ 1965
Bruce Davidson, *Young Child Taking a Bath*, from *Yosemite Campers* series.

➲ 1938
Trailer Campsite Unit J, Albert H. Good, ed., *Park and Recreation Structures*, vol. 3—*Overnight and Organized Camp Facilities*.

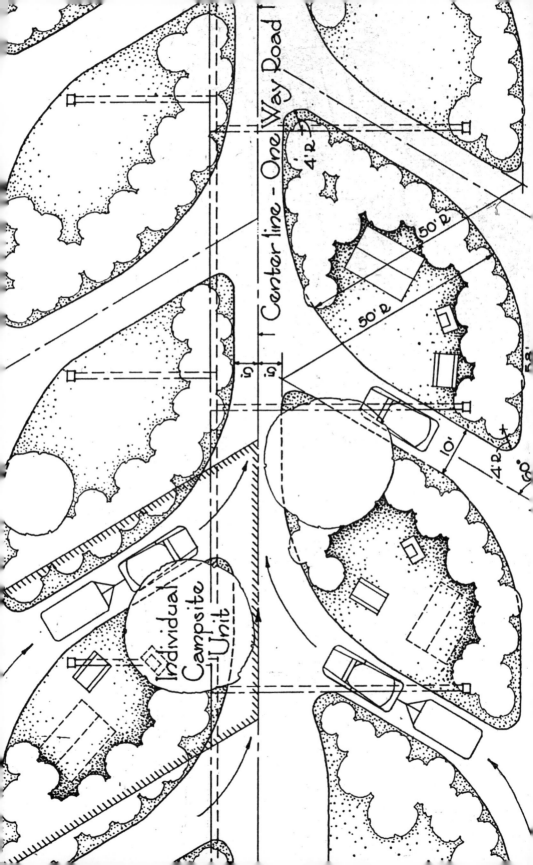
Center line – One Way Road

Individual Campsite Unit

50' R
50' R
4 R
4 R
5'
5'
10'
60'
58'

It is perhaps ironic, if not surprising, that these new freedoms would be accompanied by a deep sense of anxiety, which would in turn transform the campsite into a virtual commodity that could be compared, acquired, and traded outside the physical confines of the campground.

Chapter XIII of *Motor Camping* (1923) by John D. Long (1858–1931) and his son J. C. Long (1892–1980), stands out as perhaps the first true measure of the campground as placeless commodity. Consolidating information on over two thousand municipal, state, and federal facilities, the authors assembled the first campground directory ever published in the United States. Arguing that "the American motor camper has a continental range," the Longs sought to downplay the unique characteristics of individual facilities, such as location, surrounding natural context, and the like. Although Syracuse's municipal campground was located in Kirk Park along Onondaga Creek, for example, the authors would not mention this in their guide but adopted a more generic tone, opting simply to list the cities where camping facilities were available.[27] John D. and J. C. Long created a state-by-state, six-column matrix format that reviewed each facility using a rigid series of utility-based criteria (cost and the presence or absence of toilets, drinking water, fireplace or stove, lights, and bath or shower), the aim being to provide campers with the data needed to compare *in advance of arrival* the relative merits of several potential destinations.

An unexpected historical consequence of this comparative mode of description is that it would prove generative as well as archival: the campground matrix would act as both inventory record and an agent of change and transformation. Featured preeminently by the Longs in their book, Denver's aforementioned Overland Park was among the first campgrounds to take advantage of this utility-based descriptive style. Not only could it deliver all the services described (and expected), Denver's massive

⬆ 1925
Soda Fountain in the Clubhouse at Overland Park Auto Camp. Photographer unknown. A portion of the municipal automobile racetrack can be seen in the distance through the window.

➡ 1923
This directory page from J. C. and John D. Long, *Motor Camping*, highlights facilities in New York State.

NEW YORK—*Continued*

Town or City	Charge or Free	Toilet	Drinking Water	Fireplace or Stove	Lights	Bath or Shower
Corning	F	Y	Y	Y	Y	
Dunkirk	F	Y	Y	Y	Y	
Elmira	F	Y	Y	Y		
Fredonia						
Glens Falls	F	Y	Y	Y		
Hancock						
Ilion	F	Y	Y	Y		
Ithaca	F	Y	Y	Y		
Lake George						
Lake Placid						
Le Roy	F	Y	Y	Y	Y	
Lyons	F		Y	Y		
Medina	F	Y	Y			
Penn Yan	F	Y	Y	Y		
Oneonta						
Owego	F	Y	Y	Y		
Peekskill						
Perry	F	Y	Y			
Plattsburg	C					
Port Jervis	C					
Poughkeepsie						
Pulaski	F	Y				
Salamanca	F	Y	Y	Y		
Saratoga Springs	F	Y	Y	Y		
Schenectady	F	Y	Y	Y	Y	Y
Sherman	F		Y			
Syracuse	F	Y	Y	Y		

The New York State Conservation has laid out a number of marked routes in the State Forests, and along these has established a series of equipped camp sites.

campground could in fact provide far more, including a grocery store, lunchroom, soda and soft-drink parlor, barbershop, recreation hall, fueling station, garage, dance hall, movie theater, laundry room with irons and washing machines, and showers (with both hot and cold water), as well as several comfort stations separated by gender throughout the grounds.[28]

In energetically promoting this unparalleled range of services, which would secure its reputation as a popular destination throughout the 1920s, Overland Park served as a model campground for corporate operations like KOA in the 1960s. KOA's staggering growth from a single campground in 1961 to 829 nationwide by 1979 lay in promoting a corporate vision of camping based on a tightly packaged model operation like many others in the hospitality industry (e.g., McDonald's, Holiday Inn, Howard Johnson)—no longer a means of access to nature, camping was now big business.[29] KOA's founder and first campground operator, Dave Drum (1923–1994), of Billings, Montana, kept his ear to the ground, meeting nightly with visitors by the Yellowstone River, listening to their suggestions, leaving no stone left unturned. For him, camping needed to be inclusive of camper demands—whatever they might be. Over the years, the company has pushed the boundaries of innovation by offering such services as swimming pools, air conditioning, trailer rentals, cable television, phone hookups, prepared food, dog parks, wine-tasting socials, and even glamping. Echoing the 1920s camping expert Frank E. Brimmer's statement that "the right kind of outfit for motor camping will take out all the 'rough stuff,'" KOA's original motto, "Roughing it in luxury," suggested that camping could be redefined with modern comforts in mind.[30] After only six years of operation, the company surpassed the National Park Service in the number of individual campsites it offered nationwide.[31]

A crucial component of KOA's marketing was its annual directory of facilities. Unlike John D. and

⊘ c. 1920–1931
Grocery Store, Clubhouse, Overland Park. Photographer unknown. The shelves are stocked with canned, boxed, and fresh items, including Arm & Hammer Baking Soda, Quaker Corn Puffs, Herman's Dutch Cookies, Maple Leaf Bread, eggs, nuts, and cookies.

⊘ c. 1970
Kampgrounds of America convenience store. Photographer unknown.

J. C. Long's *Motor Camping,* the KOA directory focused exclusively on its own network of campgrounds, which then instituted and perpetuated its unique brand as a self-sufficient system of facilities. For the camper, the directory promised that the quality of the camping experience could indeed be duplicated at any of KOA's hundreds of locations: "Travel free from worry about where you will stay each night."[32] With this information at their disposal, campers could now plan their next stop well in advance or even call in a reservation to ensure availability. Why even bother looking elsewhere? By associating each franchise with an individual family of owner-operators, KOA put a friendly face on its corporate management model: the logistics might be highly organized and abstracted, but there would in fact be an actual person to speak to on the ground. This strategic combination virtually guaranteed repeat business from satisfied customers someplace down the road.

A close look at a series of yearly directory descriptions for KOA's longest-standing franchise in Cody, Wyoming, reveals shifting priorities in descriptions and style. Like the diagrammatic abstractions of the campground map and J. C. and John D. Long's early campground directory, the facility is here described through a complex shorthand of specifications:

1964
CODY
Open 1964 (June)
$2.00 per car up to four persons
25 cents for each additional person
53 miles from east entrance of Yellowstone National Park.
3 miles east of Cody on U.S. Hwys. 14 and 20.
Horseback riding, and at no extra cost, a beautiful view of our country.
Owners: Kampergrounds, Inc. M.C. Calkins, Pres., and E.J. Goppert, Jr., Secty.[33]

⬆ ➡ **1967**
Cover and sample page from KOA's June 1967 directory. KOA has published campground directories from 1964 to the present day; the 1967 edition was the first to include detailed maps featuring directions to each of its facilities.

TENNESSEE

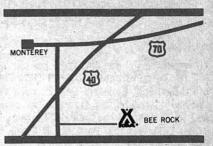

\[MO\]NTEREY   **APRIL 15 — NOVEMBER 1**

\[\$\]\.00 per car. ½ mile off I-40 at famous "Bee Rock" Natural \[Pa\]rk. Lake fishing and golf nearby. Bee Rock, one of nature's \[wo\]nders, stands at 2,000 ft. elevation and is crowned with hem\[loc\]k and pine and bordered with rhododendron and mountain \[lau\]rel. You will want to spend some time here. OWNERS: Cum\[ber\]land Properties, Inc.

BE ON THE SAFE SIDE . . . CALL
OR WRITE AHEAD FOR RESERVATIONS ! !

\[N\]ASHVILLE   **MARCH 15 — NOV. 15**

\[\$\]\.00 per car. 15 minute drive to downtown Nashville and 30 min\[ut\]es to "Hermitage". From Nashville take U.S. 31W and U.S. 41N \[ou\]t of Nashville to approximately 1½ miles past Goodlettsville. \[W\]e are on the left (west) side past the railroad underpass. \[Fr\]om the North we are located on U.S. 31W and U.S. 41, 200 \[ya\]rds past where they intersect on the righthand side. U.S. 31W \[an\]d I-65 intersect about 20 miles North. From Highway 31E \[(G\]allatin) inquire at Hendersonville or Madison. 615-839-4251.

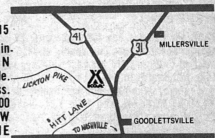

\[PI\]GEON FORGE   **MAY 1 — NOVEMBER 1**

\[\$\]\.00 per car for two persons. 25c each additional person. North \[en\]trance to Great Smoky Mountains 6 miles north of Gatlinburg. \[In\] the heart of Pigeon Forge, Tennessee. Turn east off U.S. 441 \[at\] the corner of the Steam Locomotives of Gold Rush Junction. \[G\]o 2 blocks across river. Building visible on left. OWNERS: Mr. \[an\]d Mrs. LaVerne Kelch. Telephone: 615-453-9606 or 615-453-\[9\]05.

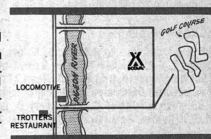

TEXAS

\[A\]BILENE   **OPEN ALL YEAR**

\[\$\]2.50 per car for two persons; 25 cents for each additional \[p\]erson. Maximum charge per family \$3.50. 800 feet east of \[S\]hirley Road, on the south side of U.S. I-20, and one mile west \[o\]f U.S. 277 Junction. Visit Old Abilene Town, Hardin-Simmons \[U\]niversity, Abilene Christian College, McMurry College, West \[T\]exas State Fair. OWNERS: Abilene KOA Kampgrounds. Route \[N\]o. 4, Box 179B. Telephone: OR 2-0139.

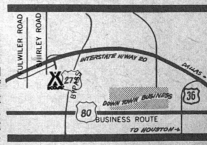

\[A\]MARILLO   **OPEN ALL YEAR**

\[\$\]2.50 per car for two persons. 25c for each additional person. \[M\]aximum charge per family \$3.50. One mile east of Amarillo on \[H\]wys. 60 and 66, between city and Amarillo Air Force Base. \[A\]pproximately 2 miles north of Hwy. 287 South. Easy access all

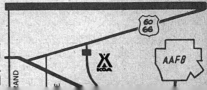

1972

CODY

June 1–Labor Day

$3.00 per night per camping unit, $3.50 with elec. hookup, $4.00 with water, sewer & elec. 53 miles from east entrance of Yellowstone National Park. Horseback riding, walkup restaurant, home of the Cody Night Rodeo. Cody Stampede, world famous Whitney Gallery of Western Art & Buffalo Bill Museum. Grigware Murals of Mormon Migration. Cody's Kampergrounds, 2513 Beartooth Drive, Cody, Wy. 82414. (307) 587-2369.[34]

1983

CODY

May 1–Sep 30 (307) 587-2369

Just 2½ mi East of Cody on Hwys 14, 16, 20. Htd pool, grassy sites, game rm, souvenirs, metered propane gas, horse & pony rides, plgrd. Good fishing, hunting, hiking, wtr skiing, golf & rock hounding nrby. Min to: famous Buffalo Bill Hist Cntr, Old Trail Town, Cody Mural, float trips, old time Melodrama, Cody Nite Rodeo, Cody Stampede Jul 4th wknd. Art galleries & beautiful scenic drives.

Rates: $9.50 for 2. $1.50 ea add'l person. $3 wtr & elec. $4 full hkups, $2 A/C or htr.

Cody KOA, 5561 Greybull Hwy, Cody, WY 82414.[35]

2013

Yellowstone National Park Area

Cody

5561 Greybull Highway

Cody, WY 82414

May 1–October 1

koa.com/camp/cody

Reservations (800) 562-8507

Info (307) 587-2369

—

If a vacation with Cody and Yellowstone National Park is in the cards, the Cody KOA is a sure bet. Just an hour away from the East entrance to Yellowstone, this

↑ 1967

Two KOA franchise salesmen await travel show attendees at the company's annual convention. Photographer unknown. At right is a physical model of one of the company's prototypical campgrounds.

➜ c. 1970

A KOA staffer proudly adds another pin to a map of the company's national network. Photographer unknown. From its inception, KOA's growth was propulsive: from a single campground in 1962, the company would expand to more than eight hundred franchises by the end of the 1970s.

campground makes a perfect base camp for your
Western adventures. Ride the free shuttle to Cody Nite
Rodeo every summer evening. Let KOA book your
Yellowstone guided tour. Buffalo Bill Historical Center
houses five museums featuring art, Native American
artifacts and exhibits. Fill up on free pancakes at KOA
before heading out on your own or with a guide to
whitewater raft or fly-fish on the Shoshone River. Don't
miss the spectacular views of Chief Joseph Scenic
Highway, climbing high into the Rockies. Swim in the
heated pool or soak in the hot tub while little ones
splash in a separate wading pool. The new Fun Zone
includes a Jumping Pillow, playground, giant chess/
checkers and fun-bike rentals. Fido will enjoy the Kamp
K9 dog park. Stick around for evening events including
Thursday bingo, Friday ice cream socials and Saturday
s'mores. Free Wi-Fi! Your hosts: Recreational
Adventures Co.

—

On U.S. 14/16/20: 3 miles E of Cody.
Past KOA Kampground of the Year[36]

In many ways, KOA's appeal lay in homogenizing
the camping experience and smoothing out the
endearing kinks that make each campground, each
campsite, and each camping experience unique. The
company's early telegraphic descriptions (characterized by abbreviations like *rm*, *wtr*, *nrby*, *plgrd*, and
hkups) underscore its standardization, the consis-
tency of utilities and the premium it placed on proximity to interstates, major roadways, and regional
attractions. As we can see in the Cody example above,
this initial approach contrasts significantly with the
company's recent (and rather sunny and optimistic)
practice of highlighting instead the range of unique
opportunities available both inside and outside its
individual campgrounds. "Remember. It's not
Camping. It's Kamping."[37]

During the 1960s and 1970s, KOA, like the hotel
chains it sought to emulate, supplied its directories

⦿ 1962
Earl Prevett, sketch map of
the first KOA campground in
Billings, Montana. This map was
redrawn from memory in 2002.
Prevett worked summers at the
facility between 1962 and 1967.

⦿ 1970
*KOA Development Plan, Laurel,
Montana.*

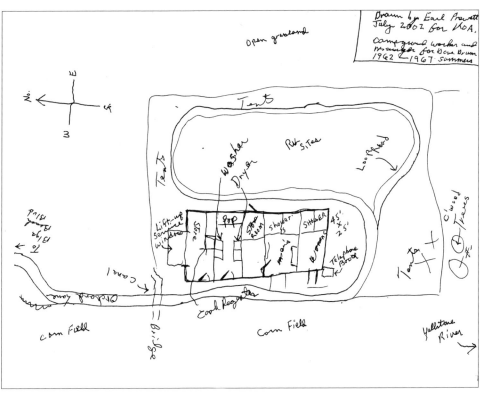

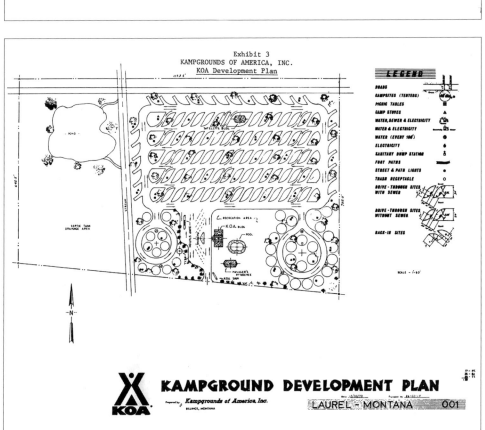

Exhibit 3
KAMPGROUNDS OF AMERICA, INC.
KOA Development Plan

KAMPGROUND DEVELOPMENT PLAN

LAUREL - MONTANA   001

with a range of additional innovative features— mass mailings of its annual directory , a toll-free 1-800 customer service phone system, and the ability to place credit card reservations—that played a large part in its financial success. Following in KOA's footsteps, third-party entities like ReserveAmerica sought to appropriate this technologically sophisticated model during the 1980s by offering to match campers and campgrounds (for a fee) through a revolutionary phone reservation service and later an online web-based one. The sale of ReserveAmerica to USA Networks Inc., later renamed IAC in 2001— a company whose portfolio has, at various times, included corporations in the entertainment and hospitality industries such as Expedia and TripAdvisor (travel) as well as a major stake in Live Nation (concerts)—suggests that camping had developed into a new form of mass recreation and could be bundled successfully with other forms of entertainment.[38] Originally managed under the National Recreation Reservation System (NRRS), Recreation. gov was one of many other websites to later enter the fray, providing access to all federally managed campgrounds (National Park Service, US Forest Service, Bureau of Land Management).

This increasingly pervasive and sophisticated virtual infrastructure has no doubt helped democratize the camping experience. Online information duplicates and, in most instances, enhances information previously only available on site. Campground maps on a variety of private and public facilities (often on the same website) can be browsed and clicked to reveal detailed specifications and photographs regarding individual campsites. Payments are transacted online. To ensure fair access, online advance reservations at some of the nation's most popular national park campgrounds are now accepted up to six months in advance. For the avid practitioner, camping has thus become a year-round activity, one continuous season, real and virtual, on the

⊙ 2013
A near-sixty-year timeline created by the author, illustrating the evolution of standard services and amenities offered at KOA campgrounds nationwide.

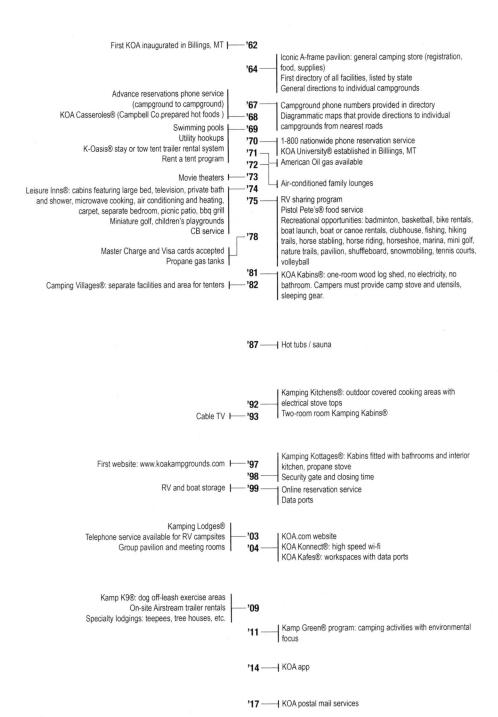

First KOA inaugurated in Billings, MT |—— '62

'64 —— Iconic A-frame pavilion: general camping store (registration, food, supplies)
First directory of all facilities, listed by state
General directions to individual campgrounds

Advance reservations phone service
(campground to campground) |
KOA Casseroles® (Campbell Co.prepared hot foods) |——
'67 —— Campground phone numbers provided in directory
'68 —— Diagrammatic maps that provide directions to individual campgrounds from nearest roads

Swimming pools |——— '69

Utility hookups |
K-Oasis® stay or tow tent trailer rental system |
Rent a tent program |
'70 —— 1-800 nationwide phone reservation service
'71 —— KOA University® established in Billiings, MT
'72 —| American Oil gas available

Movie theaters |——— '73

Leisure Inns®: cabins featuring large bed, television, private bath |——
and shower, microwave cooking, air conditioning and heating,
carpet, separate bedroom, picnic patio, bbq grill
Miniature golf, children's playgrounds
CB service |
'74 —| Air-conditioned family lounges

'75 —— RV sharing program
Pistol Pete's® food service
Recreational opportunities: badminton, basketball, bike rentals, boat launch, boat or canoe rentals, clubhouse, fishing, hiking trails, horse stabling, horse riding, horseshoe, marina, mini golf, nature trails, pavilion, shuffleboard, snowmobiling, tennis courts, volleyball

Master Charge and Visa cards accepted |
Propane gas tanks |
'78

Camping Villages®: separate facilities and area for tenters |———
'81 —— KOA Kabins®: one-room wood log shed, no electricity, no bathroom. Campers must provide camp stove and utensils, sleeping gear.
'82

'87 —| Hot tubs / sauna

'92 —— Kamping Kitchens®: outdoor covered cooking areas with electrical stove tops
Cable TV |——— '93 —— Two-room room Kamping Kabins®

First website: www.koakampgrounds.com |——— '97 —— Kamping Kottages®: Kabins fitted with bathrooms and interior kitchen, propane stove
'98 —| Security gate and closing time
RV and boat storage |——— '99 —— Online reservation service
Data ports

Kamping Lodges®
Telephone service available for RV campsites |
Group pavilion and meeting rooms |
'03 —— KOA.com website
'04 —— KOA Konnect®: high speed wi-fi
KOA Kafes®: workspaces with data ports

Kamp K9®: dog off-leash exercise areas
On-site Airstream trailer rentals |
Specialty lodgings: teepees, tree houses, etc. |
'09

'11 —| Kamp Green® program: camping activities with environmental focus

'14 —| KOA app

'17 —| KOA postal mail services

Glamping: tents with floor, electricity, storage, linens and furniture |——— '19

ground and in the imagination.[39] Web surfing, like camping, is at once a consequence and an ironic expression of the democratic ideal of access—nature commodified and à la carte. But in a 2022 opinion essay in the *New York Times*, the writer and climber Michael Levy expressed concern that online reservation systems are "disadvantaging the historically marginalized communities the Park Service has worked hard to attract in recent years to its more than 400 parks around the country."[40] Citing a recent study, Levy noted the importance of high-speed internet in competing for and securing reservations, something that lower-income groups are less likely to have access to.[41] For many prospective campers, making plans six months in advance of arrival is near impossible as well, for what does the future hold in store?

There is no question that the internet is altering the experience at the campsite as well. At the KOA Cody, for example, data ports were first introduced in 2000. Nowadays, cell phone reception is often available in the most remote parts of the country. While not inherently part of the campground infrastructure, satellites orbiting high above the earth make communication possible nearly anywhere; even in the most remote regions of the American West, for example, campers can link to the outside world and not only post their experiences to YouTube, Facebook, or Instagram but also send and receive email from their tent in the wilderness.[42] The growing presence—or intrusion—of ubiquitous media certainly takes us yet further away from the old idealization of the nature campground as a wild place.

◢ **1970**
"Free Reservation Service," ad in *KOA Kampground Directory, 1970–1971 Edition.*

◢ **2017**
Want to Camp? There's an App for That, 2017 *KOA Campground Directory.*

CAMPERS ENJOY FREE RESERVATIONS SERVICE AT ALL U. S. AND CANADIAN KOA KAMPGROUNDS

Conclusions

For John A. Jakle and Keith A. Sculle, the labor associated with making and maintaining the camp are necessarily tethered to both the familiar circumstances of domestic life and the unfamiliar challenges that make each new trip an adventure. But what happens when camping, overfreighted by the quotidian, blurs into an experience altogether too ordinary, too familiar? It is perhaps in this very situation that long-cherished ideals are tested most strenuously, that lines in the sand between what camping is and what it isn't are most forcefully revealed.

Drawing these lines might be largely an issue of perception for different campers. In looking at the case of Overland Park during the 1920s, it's clear that modern comforts have long been part of the camping experience. During this period, the installation of electric lights in municipal campgrounds allowed campers to stay on the road later into the day, no longer needing to set up camp in daylight. Nowadays, purists might gasp at the availability of flush toilets or of having neighbors a few feet away for the night, while others might gawk at the prospect of having to drive, as opposed to hike, to reach their campsite, or draw the line at the opportunity of overnighting an RV in a shopping mall parking lot. Indeed, Walmart's announcement in 2001 that it would open its parking lots nightly across the country to tourists in RVs suggests a financially vested interest similar to those of municipal campgrounds in the 1920s. Said one Walmart spokesperson, "We treat them as shoppers who take a long time to make up their minds."[43] The ability to watch a televised baseball game from the concrete pad outside a $200,000 RV using campground-provided cable (now a standard amenity at many RV campgrounds) or of sending emails wirelessly from the campsite picnic table suggests the near total elimination of boundaries between being home and being *away*. Is this the moment when the

↑ 1966
Bruce Davidson, *Television at a Picnic Table*, from *The Trip West* series.

➲ 2008
Eric Whitehead, internet at campsite, Ferry Island Campground, Terrace, British Columbia, Canada.

labor of camping—or, rather, the near *absence* of it—ceases to hold any of its old, almost mythical power? Or maybe denial has become a new form of labor, in the capacity to ignore, in the face of mounting evidence and increasing comforts, the parody that takes place at so many modern campgrounds. But *this*—well, this is camping too.

➋ 2007

Jim Bob Malone, Walmart, Whitehorse, Yukon Territory, Canada. The parking lot was a popular destination for overnighting campers. Since 2019, the company has enforced a parking ban at this location.

SEAWALL POND

EL. 31

S.W. HARBOR
ST. HWY 102

LOOP B

PRIVATE

TOILET
(PROPOSED)

CAMP GROUND

HEADQUARTERS

TOILET

LOOP A

TOILET

GRAVEL PIT

NAVAL RADIO BUILDINGS
(ABANDONED)

MAP

A camping area is a form, however primitive, of a city.[1]
—CONSTANT NIEUWENHUYS

The campground map has a very short shelf life. Once it passes from the check-in attendant to the arriving visitor, and once (and even if) it is used to orient the latter to their prospective destination—one of dozens or hundreds of similar campsites inside the facility—the map generally finds its way to the waste bin. Enterprising campers might save the scrap of paper a little longer to help ignite the evening campfire. For most, however, the map is not a keepsake: were it not for the thousands of identical copies of the very same map issued each year at a given campground, there might be no lasting memory of this document.

Anyone who's ever camped has received one. Printed in black and white and usually 8.5 × 11 inches, they show the location of individually numbered campsites, the network of roads within the grounds, and the facilities (e.g., restrooms, water taps). Campground maps are not merely cartographic

◐◑ 1941
National Park Service, master plan for Seawall Campground, Acadia National Park in Maine.

◑ 2012
Ranger Orientation for Visitors. Photographer unknown. A park ranger checks in newly arrived campers at Shenandoah National Park in Virginia.

illustrations—they often address restrictions like the maximum length of stay or the total number of occupants allowed per campsite. And the map represents a pact of sorts: the camper pays a usage fee, agrees to stated rules, and, in exchange, is allowed to occupy a designated spot, conveniently circled on the map by the park attendant in bright highlighter ink. First-time campers might take offense at the transactional nature of this experience: With signs posted at key intersections directing the visitor as they would in a hotel, aren't campground maps just a bit overkill? Because for many people camping represents a form of escape from the hustle of the city or town, from the confines of the home and the office, and from the predictable regularity of our work schedules, it seems ironic that freshly arrived inside a landscape rich with new possibilities (*hiking! swimming! s'mores!*), the camper would be met with still more rules.

How did it come to pass that virtually every single campground issues a similar document upon arrival? As was mentioned earlier, one of the keys to the map's rise in importance lies in the sheer number of copies in circulation. This only explains part of the story, however, since the map may derive its primary significance precisely *because* of its ephemeral character. With campers reaching a designated spot only hours after others have vacated the very same campsite, the map is generic enough and flexible enough to match the daily rhythm of arrivals and departures across the campground. Peeled off a thick stack at the registration desk, each copy is both the same as, but also different from, maps issued to other visitors.

As we will see, the generic character of these maps results in part from normative campground planning specifications implemented during the 1930s. It is therefore no surprise that campgrounds, and the maps that describe them, end up looking remarkably similar to one another. But when considering maps, it is also important to take into account their intended purpose and prospective audience. To this end, there

❷ 2014

Ten-X Campground map, Kaibab National Forest in Arizona. Photographer unknown.

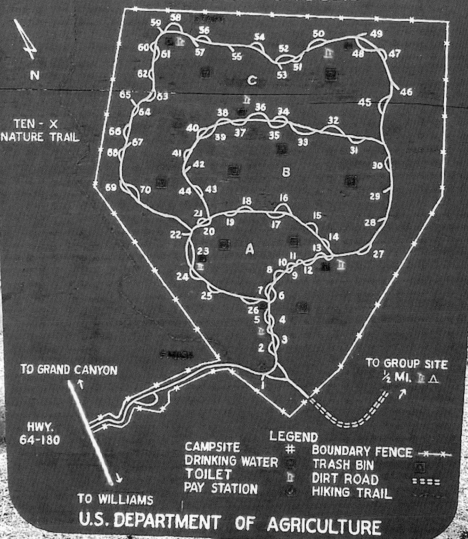

KAIBAB National Forest

TEN-X CAMPGROUND

N

TEN-X
NATURE TRAIL

C

B

A

TO GRAND CANYON

TO GROUP SITE
½ MI.

HWY.
64-180

TO WILLIAMS

LEGEND

CAMPSITE
DRINKING WATER
TOILET
PAY STATION

BOUNDARY FENCE
TRASH BIN
DIRT ROAD
HIKING TRAIL

U.S. DEPARTMENT OF AGRICULTURE

is no denying that maps have played an important role in preserving order among the campground's temporary residents. In effect, the graphic uniformity of these documents perpetuates standardized practices and codes of human behavior; maps look the same in part *because* campers are expected to behave in the same manner from one campground to the next. As the following history of campground maps also suggests, the evolution of graphic norms and standards has not, thankfully, come at the expense of visual artistry and craft.

Camping Grounds

For persons who prefer to make their stay in camps of their own, a ground has been set apart, with ample space for all, without interference with each other.[2]
— GEORGE GORDON MACKENZIE

In Yosemite Valley, the word *camp* first appeared on an 1888 map of the park published in *Yosemite: Where to Go and What to Do: A Plain Guide to the Yosemite Valley* by George Gordon MacKenzie (1849–1922), who wrote under the pseudonym of Lewis Stornoway.[3] The expression took its place among other verbal designations that included roadways (Wawona Road, Yosemite Ave., Hunt's Ave., Lake Ave., Sentinel Ave.), trails, summits (Half Dome, Sentinel Dome), natural landmarks (Merced River, Mirror Lake, Yosemite Falls), a small village, and two hotels (the Stoneman House and Barnard's).

MacKenzie's book provides a sense of the character of the valley during this period. Of the village, the author noted that it includes a "chapel and a school house, a postoffice [sic], a telegraph office, a general country store,…two photographers' rooms, a blacksmith shop, butcher shop, and that of a cabinet worker in woods."[4] Situated in isolation to the east of the village on the opposite side of the Merced River,

⊘ 2010
Moraine Park Campground, Rocky Mountain National Park in Colorado (detail).

Moraine Park Campground

NOTE: Loop A is a two-way road
        Loop B, C, & D are one-way

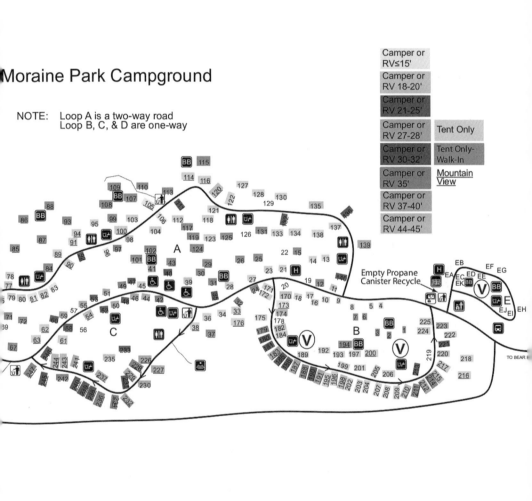

Camper or RV≤15'	
Camper or RV 18-20'	
Camper or RV 21-25'	
Camper or RV 27-28'	Tent Only
Camper or RV 30-32'	Tent Only-Walk-In
Camper or RV 35'	Mountain View
Camper or RV 37-40'	
Camper or RV 44-45'	

Empty Propane
Canister Recycle

TO BEAR L

the *CAMP* (both the word on the map as well as the campground itself) stands firmly apart from this nearby agglomeration. And while MacKenzie celebrates the prospective isolation the area could offer its visitors among "magnificent oaks to afford shelter from the sun, and thickets of young spruce and cedar trees among which a degree of privacy is obtainable," the author insists that the camp remains within easy access of the village's "general country store, where campers can obtain anything which they are likely to need."[5] From a reverse perspective, the geographer Stanford E. Demars noted that the new camp carried some appeal for hotel visitors as well, who recognized in this new type of facility a chance to experience Yosemite from a fresh perspective. The author goes on to provide a summary description of the area, observing that "the state purchased and erected a number of tents to provide accommodations for the Christian Endeavor Excursion into the Valley and thereafter began renting them to the general public."[6]

The facility described by Demars hardly resembled the controlled chaos of the modern campground. Rather it constituted a hybrid of sorts, which he described as a "hotel camp."[7] Such facilities had already proved successful in Yellowstone National Park, where concessionaires had been maintaining camps since the mid-1880s.[8] The 1910 edition of the Wylie Permanent Camp Company's Yellowstone brochure promised an experience that sounds remarkably similar to modern-day glamping, in which "all the savor and spice of 'camping out' are emphasized and all the characteristic annoyances are eliminated."[9] Of the many facilities it operated across the park, the company described the prototypical camp as a "village of 'tent-cottages'… erected on raised wooden floors, framed and double-topped to ensure dryness" and appointed with "a complete toilet set, a mirror, comfortable camp chairs, rugs, etc."[10] The brochure further noted that the tents are also "equipped with wood-heaters in which the 'camp boys' build fires when the mornings and

⬆ 1900

Croquet Ground—Noyo River Tavern, from the California Scenic Line collection. Photographer unknown. This illustration provides a sense of the character of hotel camps operated in Yosemite and Yellowstone National Parks during the same period.

➔ 1888

Map of Yosemite (detail), Lewis Stornoway, *Yosemite: Where to Go and What to Do: A Plain Guide to the Yosemite Valley.* The word *camp* appears above Glacier Point and Glacier Ave., at far right.

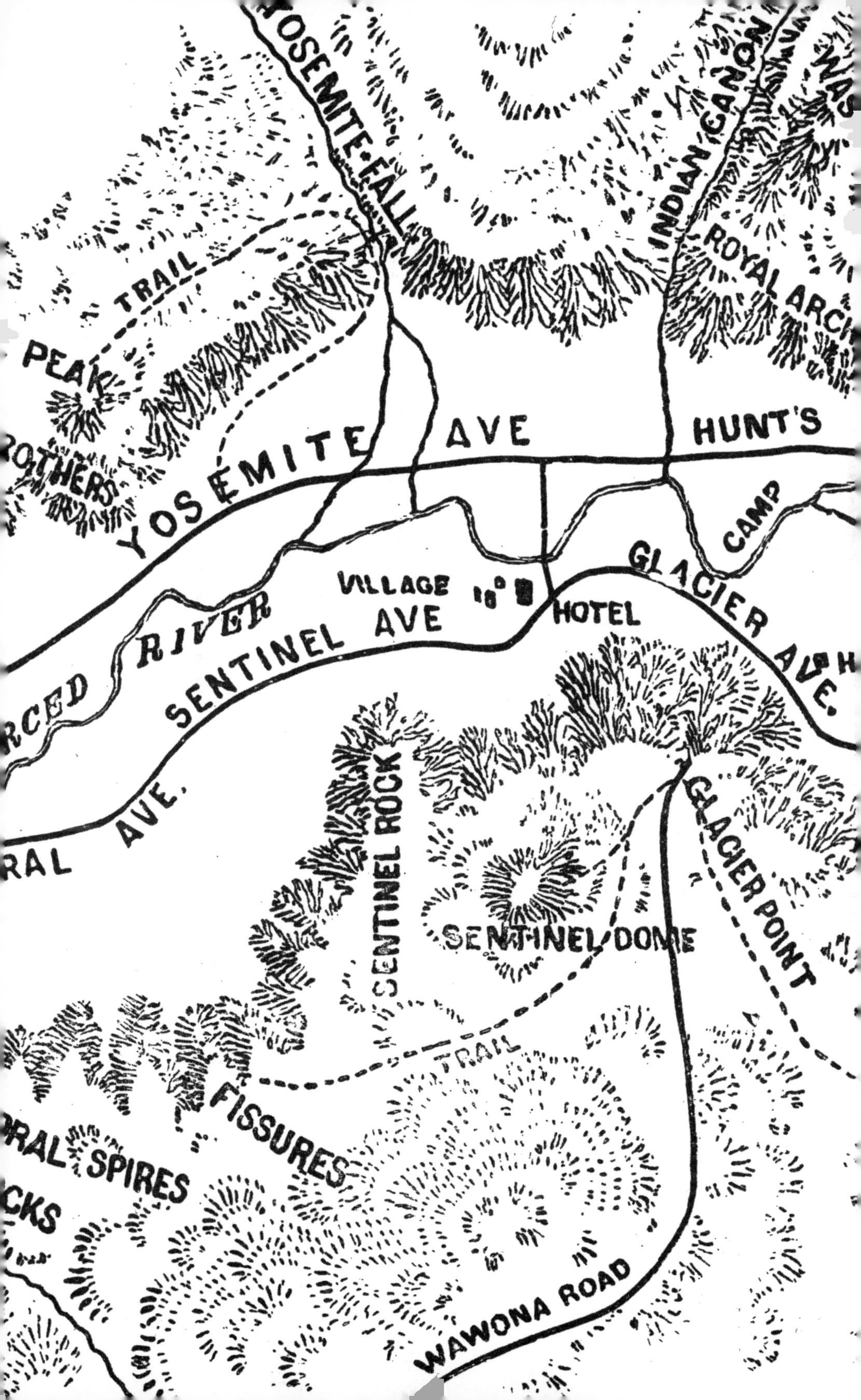

YOSEMITE FALL
INDIAN CAÑON
ROYAL ARCH
TRAIL
PEAK
BROTHERS
YOSEMITE AVE
HUNT'S
CAMP
GLACIER AVE.
VILLAGE
HOTEL
MERCED RIVER
SENTINEL AVE
RAL AVE.
SENTINEL ROCK
SENTINEL DOME
GLACIER POINT
TRAIL
FISSURES
RAL SPIRES
CKS
WAWONA ROAD

evenings are cool."[11] And as if to anticipate some of
the objections of its wealthier patrons, it concludes
of its beds that "they are the kind found in first-class
hotels—clean, comfortable and spacious."[12]

A large foldout map inside the Wylie brochure
highlights the company's network of permanent camps
and lunch stations across the park, all connected by a
loop road around the Central Plateau. This map persua-
sively reinforces the perception of a set of networked
facilities, sited near areas of touristic interest, which
in turn suggests a consistent touristic experience
throughout the park. Fifty years later, another private
concessionaire, KOA (Kampgrounds of America),
would employ the same strategy to promote its own
rapidly growing network of hundreds of campgrounds
across the country. From the pages of the company's
annual directory, which include a national map of
its entire network, prospective campers now travel
from state to state, choosing as their evening destination a nearby KOA with the certainty that their camping experience can be replicated at every stop.[13]

But the Wylie Company didn't simply choose to
make their case in print: of the "strong, spacious and
easy riding" horse carriages it deployed to shuttle
patrons between stops on a standard six-day tour of
Yellowstone, the company quite literally controlled
the end-to-end experience inside the park, with
"young men of experience and refinement" as drivers
and "uniformly courteous and intelligent" staff, as
well as hot, family-style meals prepared by "women
cooks exclusively."[14] And thrive it did. Wylie reported
a total of 7,700 visitors over the three-month 1909
season. These numbers suggest that the night camps
it operated at Swan Lake, Lake Camp, and Canyon
Camp could each accommodate roughly twenty campers per night, with a larger facility at Upper Geyser,
where Yellowstone's most popular attractions were
located.[15]

⬆ c. 1885–1910
Frank Jay Haynes, *Wylie Postcard Series #3: A Wylie Two-Compartment Tent Interior, Yellowstone National Park.*

➡ 1910
Yellowstone Campground map from Wylie Permanent Camping Company, *Yellowstone National Park*, 1910 ed.

Joseph Pk.
10400
Gray Pk.
10300
Little Quadrant
9900
Mammoth Hot Sprs.
Mt. Everts
7900
Undine Falls
Garnett Hill
Crescent Hill
Yanceys
GARNETT BRIDGE
RANGE
The Pocket
Quadrant Mtn.
10200
Terrace Mtn.
Glen Cr.
GOLDEN GATE
Rustic Fall
Bunsen Pk.
9100
Wraith Fall
Gardiner River
Junct. Butte
Bannock Pk.
10900
Swan L.
SWAN LAKE CAMP
ROOSEVELT CAMP
Tower Fall
G HORN PASS
atin L.
10400
Antlers Pk.
10200
Panther Cr.
WILLOW PARK
Lava Creek
Lupine Cr.
Blacktail
Prospect Pk.
9300
Folsom Pk.
9300
Tower Creek
Creek
Three Rivers Pk.
10400
The Dome
10400
Indian Cr.
Apollinaris Sprs.
Obsidian L.
Horse Shoe Hill
Storm Pk.
10000
Tower Creek
Mt. Holmes
10400
Trilobite Pt.
Beaver L.
Grizzly L.
Obsidian Cliff
The Landmark
8800
L. of the Woods
Carnelian Cr.
Mt. Washburn
10200
CHRISTMAS TREE PARK
Straight Cr.
Winter Cr.
Amphitheatre Sprs.
Roaring Mtn.
DEVIL'S FRYING PAN
Observation Pk.
9300
Dunraven Pk.
9700
Hedges Pk.
10000
Ink Pot
GRAND CAN
Twin Lakes
Grebe L.
SOLFATARA
Inspiration Pt.
Hot S
NORRIS GEYSER BASIN
WEDUZN TREES EAU
Pt. Lookout
Creek
Gibbon Hill
8600
Virginia Cascades
CAÑON CAMP
Lower Fall
308 Fall
Upper Fall
119
Mt. urz
Paint Pot Hill
Hot Sprs.
BRIDGE
Cr.
ent Geysers
Gibbon Cañon
Otter
Hot S
Cotton
Sour
SECRET VALLEY
Terrace Sprs.
Gibbon Fall
80
Cañon
Creek
Sulphur Mt.
Alum Cr.
HAYDEN VALLEY
Grass Cr.
Bluff
R.
Gibbon
GIBBON LUNCH STATION
Firehole R.
Mappin Cr.
CENTRAL PLATEAU
Trout Cr.
Cr.
Mud Volcano
Sentinel Cr.
FORD
Ne
Peres Cr.
Spruce Cr.
Mary L.
Jasper Cr.
Elephant Back
8600
7252
LAKE CAMP
LOWER GEYSER BASIN
win ttes
Great Fountain Geyser
Creek
Beach L.
NATURAL BRIDGE
Bridge Bay
MIDWAY GEYSER BASIN
Excelsior Geyser
Dryad L.
Bridge Cr.
YELLOWSTONE
R.
PPER GEYSER ASIN CAMP
Beehive
Giantess
Old Faithful
Mallard L.
CRAIG PASS
SHOSHONE PT.
Arnica Cr.
Sand Pt.
Rock Pt.
Kepler Cascades
8345
CARRINGTON ID.
Pumice Pt.
DOT ID.
Lone Star Geyser
Spring Cr.
Firehole R.
Lost L.
Duck L.
Lakeview
Lake Geyser
Bluff Pt.
Breeze Pt.
West Arm or THUMB LUNCH STATION
LAKE
Wolf Pt.
L.
NORRIS PASS
CONTINENTAL
Delusion L.
Lone Lake
7740
Flat Mountain Arm

Spatial Organization

*It was commonly joked—and not without some truth—
that the first camper to drive his automobile out of the
campground on a holiday morning was likely to dismantle
half of the campground in the process due to the common
practice of securing tent lines to the handiest object
available—including automobile bumpers.*[16]
—STANFORD E. DEMARS

The commercial success of private operators continued unabated until national parks were opened to
motor vehicles in 1916. While it meant a sharp decline
for the Wylie Company and its Yellowstone competitors, the decision also afforded prospective visitors
a welcome degree of independence. Free from the
tyranny of the scheduled tour, motor tourists could
now travel at their own pace and draw up their own
itineraries. As a result, not only did touring the parks
become more flexible but camping made the visit
more affordable as well. Automobile camping, or car
camping, as it came to be known, had far more in
common with modern-day camping than with the
plush hotel camps maintained by the Wylie Company.
For motor tourists equipped with their own tents,
bedding, food, and cooking gear, camping was considered less a curiosity than a way to avoid pricey and
more civilized accommodations. It was therefore no
surprise that demand for camping inside national
parks quickly intensified after 1916. Inside Yellowstone, the National Park Service appointed the Wylie
Company and its direct competitor, the Shaw &
Powell Company, to manage a new network of public
autocampgrounds under the aegis of the Yellowstone
Park Company.

Period photographs (page 97) offer a sense of the
informal character of these facilities. Unlike the
military-style organization of Wylie's permanent
camps, with rigid rows of tents set permanently in
place throughout the tourist season, these camping

⊙ 1931
Jo Mora, *Yellowstone*, detail
of map of Yellowstone
National Park showing public
campgrounds at Fishing Bridge
and Canyon Junction.

grounds offered large plots of open land, inside which campers were free to set up shop wherever they could find space. For twenty-five cents per night, visitors could expect a decent range of accommodations, including restrooms, showers, electricity, and clean drinking water.[17]

First published in the 1936 edition of the *Haynes New Guide: The Complete Handbook of Yellowstone National Park*, the map of the West Thumb campground captures the changing state of camping during this period. Originating during the 1890s, Haynes's guide had by this time become an essential part of the Yellowstone tourist experience. Based in St. Paul, Minnesota, Frank Jay Haynes (1853–1921) was granted a concession in 1884 at Mammoth Hot Springs to sell the photographs that would later become part of this celebrated annual guide. Unlike the thin brochures published by the Wylie Camping Company or Shaw & Powell, Haynes's guides were not mere ephemera but tomes to be cherished, consulted, and revisited periodically, even long after the return trip home. Haynes's son Jack (1884–1962)—to whom the West Thumb map is attributed—began producing reference maps of key areas of the park beginning in 1912. Among Haynes's most notable efforts was a 1936 map of the Upper Geyser Basin, which featured a dizzying number of landmarks competing for the reader's attention. Among the natural springs, pools, paint pots, and geysers (Catfish, Bijou, Spasmodic, etc.) were a growing number of commercial facilities, such as stores, overnight accommodations (Old Faithful Inn, Old Faithful Lodge, a public automobile camp), and a strategically located Haynes Picture Shop, where tourists could stock up on park memorabilia.[18]

Included in the same edition as the Upper Geyser map, Haynes's map of West Thumb was curious in many respects. The author took great care to articulate the network of routes passing through the area, differentiating between trails (dotted lines) and one- and

❯ 1936
Upper Geyser Basin, Jack Ellis Haynes, *Haynes New Guide—The Complete Handbook of Yellowstone National Park*, 1936 ed.

UPPER GEYSER BASIN

JUNCTION (MJ)

ROADS ▬▬▬
PATHS ▬ ▬ ▬
SCALE:

0   1/8   1/4   1/2 MILE.

CAULIFLOWER GEYSER
MIRROR POOL

MADISON

CALTHOS SPRING
GEM POOL
BENCH SPRING
IRON SPRINGS
ARTEMISIA GEYSER

N
19°

TRUE NORTH

MAGNETIC NORTH

NTINEL GEYSERS
FAN GEYSER
PS SPRING
MORTAR GEYSER
CHAIN LAKES
ROCKET GEYSER →

MORNING GLORY POOL

RIVERSIDE GEYSER
SPA GEYSER
GROTTO GEYSER
BIJOU GEYSER

BONITA POOL
R CONE
ER CRATER
Y GEYSER →

MASTIFF GEYSER
CATFISH GEYSER
GIANT GEYSER
← PURPLE POOL
OBLONG GEYSER
CHROMATIC POOL
BEAUTY POOL
WAVE SPRING
ECONOMIC GEYSER CRATER

SOLITARY GEYS

COMET GEYSER
INKWELL SPRING →

BASIN

ACK SAND
POOL
ME KILN SPRINGS
WITCHES CAULDRON
SAWMILL GEYSER
ORANGE POOL

CALIDA POOL

TURBAN GEYSER
GRAND GEYSER
BULGER SPRING
SPASMODIC GEYSER

GEYSER
HILL

CHIMNEY CONE
LIBERTY POOL
LION G.

BEACH
SPRING
DOUBLET POOL

CRESTED POOL
TORTOISE SHELL SPRING
TER GEYSER

CASTLE
GEYSER
LIONESS G.
DRAGON GEY.
BEEHIVE GEY.

GIANTESS GE
BUTTERFLY
SPONGE GEY.
SPUTTERER
CHINAMAN &

TLE GEYSER
N SPRING

THREE SISTERS SPRINGS
HAMILTON STORE
OLD FAITHFUL INN
MUSEUM
HAYNES PICTURE SHOP AND
PHOTO FINISHING
PLANT   CAFETERIA
STORE, POSTAL STATION →
PUBLIC AUTOMOBILE CAMP
BATH HOUSE

OLD
FAITHFUL
BATHS
OLD
STORE OF

GEYS

OLD FAITH-
FUL GEYSER

RANGER
STA.

OL
FL
LOD

Creek

FAITH
LOD

two-lane roads (solid lines), while also taking note of other landmarks (twenty-three miles to the park's south entrance, nineteen miles to Old Faithful) and parking areas. His generous graphic style also accommodated architecturally specific features. The reader will note, for example, the building footprints of important structures, like the Hamilton Store, the ranger station, the local cafeteria, and, of course, the ever-present Haynes Picture Shop. At nearly six acres, the West Thumb campground dwarfs any of these other facilities in acreage while presenting a curious lack of graphic specificity: on the map, all that we see is an empty rectangle fitted with rounded corners. And yet the high level of precision in the rest of the map suggests that Haynes could have portrayed the campground with greater detail. Indeed, the lack of graphic continuity between the campground's empty enclosure and the surrounding context reinforced the perception that the realm of the campground was disconnected from the outside world.

Despite the curious absence of specificity, Haynes's map was not entirely unusual for the time. Instead, it may have simply reflected a lack of attention to the spatial planning of campgrounds at the time. The landscape architect Charles Parker Halligan (1881–1966) offered in an early book on the design and planning of camping facilities titled *Tourist Camps* (1925) a standard plan that was indicative of a rather loose approach to spatial planning.[19] Featuring an area cleared of trees, a peripherical loop road, and one support building (presumably restrooms) at the back end of the site, Halligan's open spatial design represented a literal echo of Jack Ellis Haynes's depiction of the West Thumb auto campground. In other words, Haynes's campground may have amounted to little more in three dimensions than how it appeared on the map—a rectangular, open pen inside which visitors could set up camp wherever they wished.

The popularity of autocamping would push these informal facilities to a breaking point. Campgrounds

↑ 1924

Suggested Layout for Automobile-Tourist Camp with Equipment for a Large Volume of Traffic, from *Popular Mechanics Auto Tourist's Handbook No. 1.*

↗ 1936

West Thumb Area, Jack Ellis Haynes, *Haynes New Guide: The Complete Handbook of Yellowstone National Park*, 1936 ed.

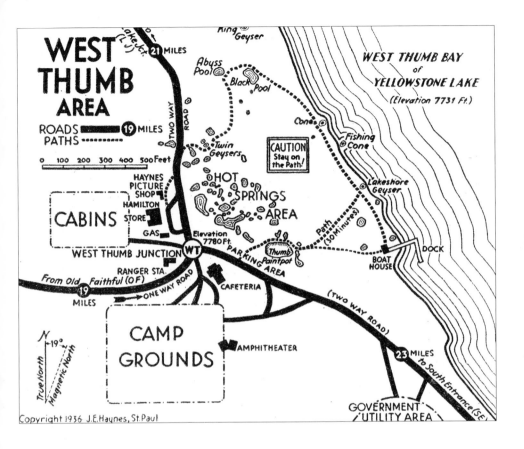

during the 1920s were characterized by overcrowding,
loosely arranged clusters of motor vehicles, tents,
and trailers. The directory of two thousand facilities
assembled by John D. and J. C. Long in *Motor
Camping* (1923) provides a concrete measure of the
wave of enthusiasm for camping that was then sweeping the country and, simultaneously, insight into the
national scope of the problem. As *Motor Camping*
also indicates, prospective campers could expect an
uneven range of amenities upon arrival: some campgrounds were properly equipped with basic services
like electricity, restrooms, showers, and running
water, while others merely offered the fellowship of
other campers confined to an empty baseball field
at the edge of town.

E. P. Meinecke, a plant pathologist for the US
Department of Agriculture, was the first to detail
the potentially hazardous impacts of motor vehicles
moving along the shady, tree-studded drives of new
autocampgrounds. And yet for all the problems the
automobile created, Meinecke recognized its presence
inside the campground as inevitable—camping may
have provided a form of escape from the drudgery of
modern life, but motor vehicles provided the means
through which this escape could take place. Unlike
the facility described, Meinecke felt it was not enough
for the car to shuttle the arriving visitor to the campground entrance, as Jack Ellis Haynes's map of West
Thumb suggested. He proposed that the movement of
vehicles be confined to a series of one-way loop roads,
along which individual campsites would be established. This solution was of a piece with larger planning strategies inside national parks, which employed
one-way roads to move traffic along a series of key
regional destinations. These vital campground arter-
ies could then be made narrower due to the lack of
incoming traffic and therefore less harmful to their
surrounds. If the camper missed his destination on
the first drive-by, he could simply loop back through
the circuit. Second, Meinecke equipped each campsite

⊘ 1925

*A suggestive plan of a tourists'
campgrounds*, Charles Parker
(C. P.) Halligan, *Tourist Camps:
Rural Landscape Series No. 2.*

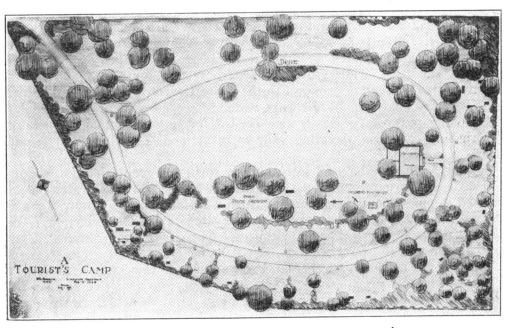

A suggestive plan of a tourists' camp grounds.

with a "garage spur" for parking the car, a fixed picnic table, and an outdoor fireplace.[20] An important departure from the open field campgrounds of the period, designated individual campsites helped establish a consistent density of occupants throughout the facility; further, the interplay between fixed, permanent components formed by the parking spur, the table, and the fireplace, and those introduced by the arriving visitor, such as the tent and the live fire, helped preserve the all-important illusion that she had played a key role in the construction of the campsite. The spatial features present at the individual campsites evoked the familiar domestic character and scale of a suburban development. As noted by the historical geographer Terence Young, this vision constituted a fitting, if somewhat ironic, endpoint to the camper's journey of escape. Directing their vehicle to the parking spur adjacent their designated site, the visitor had ended up right where they started—in a driveway much like the one they had left behind at home.[21]

Meinecke is now widely acknowledged as the father of the modern campground. His seminal sixteen-page pamphlet *A Camp Ground Policy* (1932)—its direct writing style and diagrammatic illustrations—gained considerable influence, in part because its publication coincided with the expansion of touristic infrastructure inside national and state parks during the Great Depression. We can glimpse the impact of Meinecke's recommendations only a few years later in a blueprint of Yosemite Valley published by the National Park Service in 1935. While still too small to reveal individual campsites, the map includes a pattern of looping roads along the Merced River and is instantly recognizable as his handiwork. Although not a widely available campground map, this representation is noteworthy because it seamlessly integrates Meinecke's vision of an end-to-end roadway network both throughout the park and inside the campground. Albert H. Good, an

↑ c. 1935
Longmire Village Campground, Mount Rainier National Park in Washington. Photographer unknown.

➔ 1932
Proposed layout of a camping ground under regulation, with system of one-way roads,
E. P. Meinecke, *A Camp Ground Policy*.

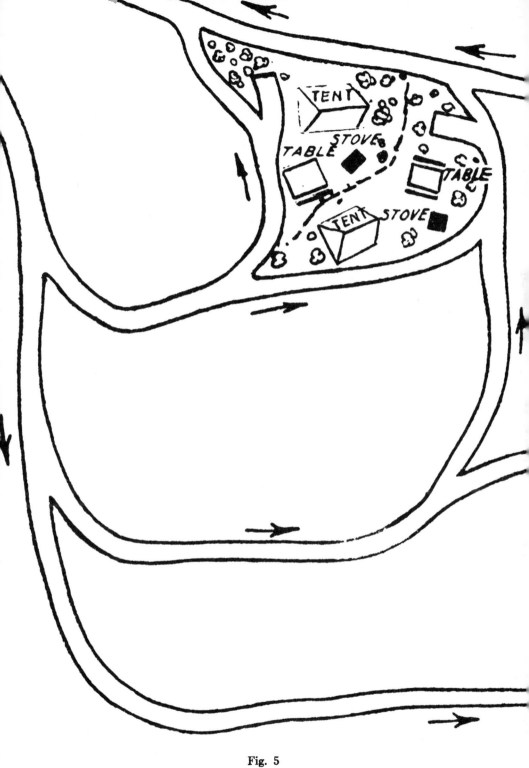

Fig. 5

Proposed layout of a camping ground under regulation, with system of one-way roads. Only one section is developed to show proposed car parking (garage spurs), tables, fireplaces and tents.

architectural consultant for the National Park
Service, would take the lead in articulating the next
scale of development. In the second edition of his
book, retitled *Park and Recreational Structures* (1938),
Good sought to provide general design specifications
for a wide range of structures to be erected inside
national and state parks, including maintenance
buildings, boathouses, picnic tables and shelters,
comfort stations, campfire areas, cabins, lodges, and
campgrounds.[22] Good's work constituted the most
definitive account of the age, with his lavish illustrations, superb line drawings, detailed dimensions, and
field photographs showing how general principles
were adapted to local sites' constraints, materials,
and building techniques. The US Forest Service produced its own campground design manual in 1935 for
the western regions of the country. It's easy to imagine that these two books functioned as field manuals
at Department of Interior branch offices and Civilian
Conservation Corps camps nationwide.[23]

For all their work on the subject, Meinecke and
Good never developed detailed master plans for individual campgrounds. They each proposed a series of
general guiding principles that could be scaled up or
down given the demands at a particular site. Two cases
stand as illustrative examples of this approach. A 1932
field sketch produced by Lawrence Farwell (L. F.) Cook
(1900–1966), chief ranger of Sequoia National Park in
California, for Firwood Camp (page 111), a fifty-one-
site facility near the park's Round Meadow, illustrated
the relative informality with which such specifications
were being implemented on a small scale. This back-of-
the-envelope sketch is notable for the way that it
numbers individual campsites: Did the numerals constitute a simple assessment of the campground's general capacity, or were these assigned designations or
addresses to specific campsites? At the other end of
the spectrum were detailed specifications issued for
larger facilities, such as the site plan for Blackwoods
Campground in Acadia National Park in Maine

❷ 1935
National Park Service, *Camp
Sites—Valley*, detail of map
illustrating the location of
camps #6, 7, 11, 12, 14, 15, and
16 in Yosemite National Park in
California. Highlight of Merced
River by the author.

❸ 1938
Trailer Campsite Unit K,
Albert H. Good, ed., *Park and
Recreation Structures*, vol. 3—
*Overnight and Organized
Camp Facilities.*

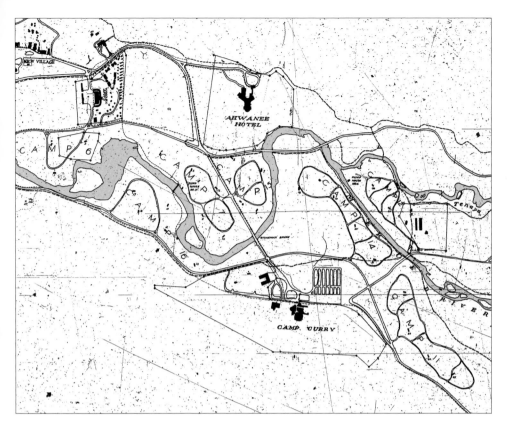

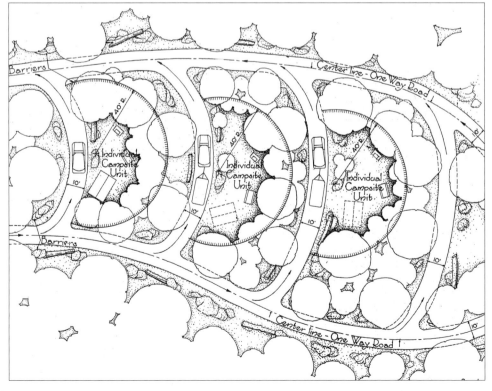

(published in 1941), a design featuring three clusters, labeled A, B, C and characterized by Meinecke's now-familiar pattern of loop roads and parking spurs he first detailed in *A Camp Ground Policy*.[24]

From Plan to Map

This light effort, not altogether truthful, so not altogether dull…[25]

—JO MORA

With approximately 450 proposed sites inside three major campground loops, Blackwoods and other similar master plans produced by the National Park Service during this period ushered in a whole new level of spatial complexity for campground planning. Could Meinecke's ideas be implemented on such a large scale? The issues were in part logistical— this meant hundreds of vehicles and trailers, some parked, others coming or going—and part spatial. How close could the campsites be located to one another without disrupting privacy? The placement of these individual campsites and the arc of looping roads required careful planning against the local terrain in order to produce level roadways and campsites. Planning a campground of this size could be no loose spatial diagram like the Firwood Camp sketch.

The master plans of the sort developed for Acadia National Park were technical, highly specialized representations created internally for the purpose of planning and construction. However, it is because of the increasing spatial complexity and scale of such campgrounds that reference maps were first offered to newly arrived visitors. To be sure, these new visual aids had much in common with detailed master plans issued by the National Park Service. Let's compare as an example the 1941 grading plan for Blackwoods Campground in Acadia National Park

⊙ **1941**
Black Woods [sic] *Campground, Part of the Master Plan for Acadia National Park* (detail).

U S DEPARTMENT OF THE INTERIOR · · NATIONAL PARK SERVICE
BLACK WOODS CAMPGROUND
PART OF THE MASTER PLAN FOR
ACADIA NATIONAL PARK
SCALE

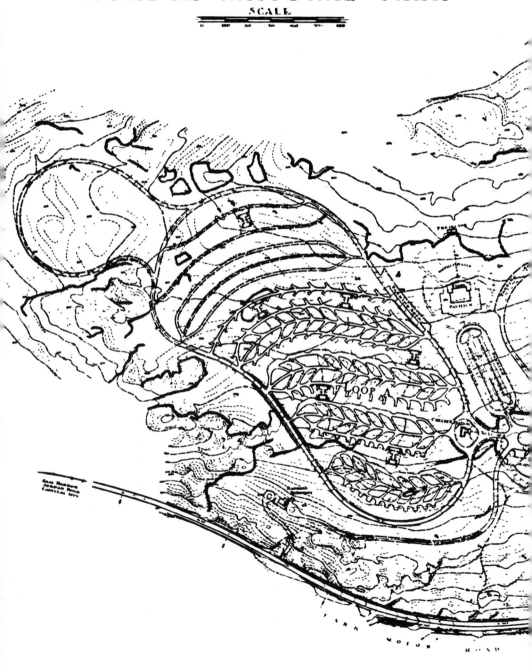

to a visitor's map of Dolly Copp Campground in New Hampshire from that same year.

The Dolly Copp map is one of the earliest examples of the kind of campground representation that has now become so familiar to visitors checking in at a new facility.[26] The Blackwoods and Dolly Copp maps both feature complex networks of looping roads and parking spurs that read as the backbone of the modern automobile campground. However, the two drawings also differ in important ways. The reader will note in the Dolly Copp map a complete lack of technical information, such as topographic contours and dimensions. As the modern camper knows, this is not unusual, since the mapmaker is generally concerned with capturing the internal complexity of the campground as a system of roads, campsites, and services, rather than representing the physical context in which the campground is located. As a result, campgrounds are represented against a flat terrain and devoid of trees, whether true or not. This visual sparseness constitutes an important graphic advantage since these maps could, unlike large, technical blueprints, be reproduced at a much smaller scale without suffering any loss of resolution. Another significant difference is that in the Dolly Copp map, individual campsites have been assigned a number. The practice of numbering tents had been in use at semipermanent facilities like Camp Curry in Yosemite for some time, and as the sketch for Firwood Camp (page 111) indicates, it's no stretch to see the advantage of putting in place a similar system for large campgrounds featuring hundreds of individual campsites. This practice also facilitated record keeping and a knowledge of the campground's various occupants at all times—everyone in their proper place.

An examination of a present-day map of Mather Campground on the South Rim of the Grand Canyon confirms that the basic visual strategies that characterized the Dolly Copp map have largely remained unchanged over the last seventy-five years. In

◗ **1940**
Dolly Copp Recreation Area, White Mountains National Forest in New Hampshire.

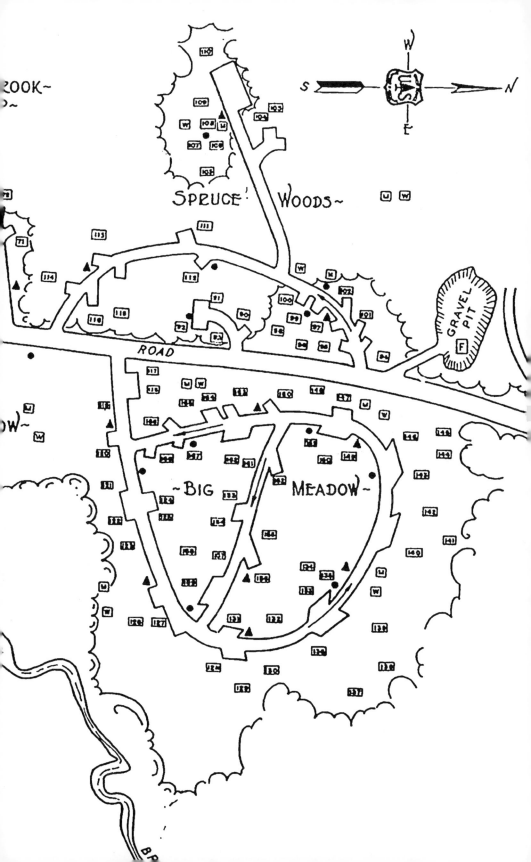

addition to the hundreds of individually numbered campsites on the map, the reader will note the flatness of the terrain and the importance attributed to the *territory* of the motor vehicle—roadways, parking spurs (tents), and pull-throughs (RVs and trailers)—all of which are captured in heavy, black strokes. Indeed, the repetitive loop pattern is so intense that it leaves virtually no room for any contextual features—like the Grand Canyon itself. And with each campsite address promising the same experience, the map completely internalizes the campground as a self-sufficient facility that is, in effect, fully disconnected from its natural surroundings.

Symbols and Standardization

A picture Esperanto.[27]
—OTTO NEURATH

The embrace of spare black-and-white graphics in campground maps made their mass reproduction cheap and straightforward, especially with the introduction of new techniques patented by the Xerox Corporation after 1959.[28] As ubiquitous as the Xerox machine would become in everyday life in the decades that followed, it's no surprise that campground maps end up looking remarkably similar to, in short, *copies of* one another. This is due to a number of factors: first, the normalizing effect of design specifications put in place by Meinecke, Good, and others during the 1930s, which collectively would have a profound impact on the standardization of automobile campgrounds; second, the increasing expectations of a camping culture that now demanded maps at every facility; third, the reproduction capabilities of modern-day copiers like the Xerox, which were partial to the ANSI (American National Standards Institute) letter (8.5 × 11 inches) format and a minimal, often grayscale color palette. These maps transcended both

➋ **2018**
National Park Service, *Mather Campground—South Rim,* Grand Canyon National Park in Arizona.

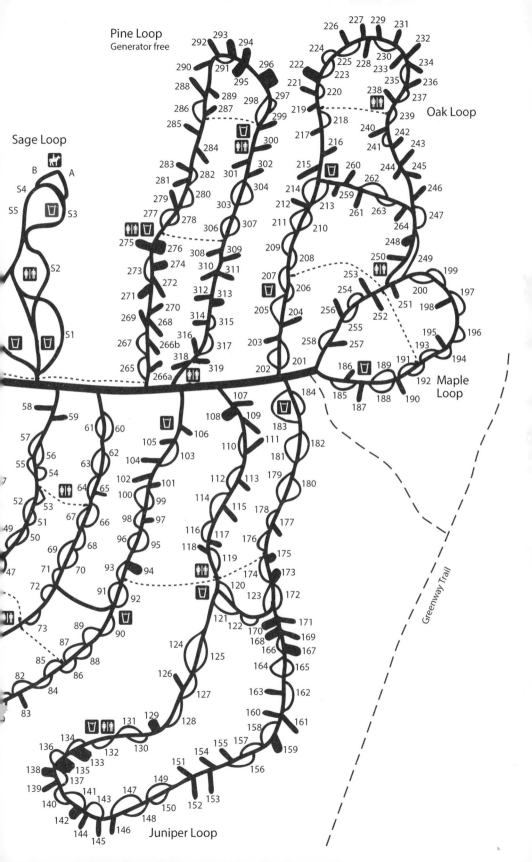

space and time: given this normative style, the experienced reader might have trouble distinguishing one campground, or one place, from another, or even be able to tell maps issued in the 1980s or 1960s from maps issued in the 1950s. Despite these facts, the execution of these representations remains in the best of cases a matter of skill and artistry.

Current maps of major campgrounds in Shenandoah National Park, including Big Meadows, Loft Mountain, and Mathews Arm, for example, are skillfully executed and truly beautiful in comparison to most others. But with its range of ten brightly colored bars indicating the maximum size of trailers and RVs that its various campsites can accommodate, the map of Moraine Campground in Rocky Mountain National Park (page 143) is crude and chaotic in nature. All four of these maps represent National Park Service campgrounds, and all four do the job, but functionality hardly seems like the only way to evaluate the quality of this visual output.

Jack Haynes thought enough of his maps of Yellowstone National Park to include his name at the bottom of each drawing. For decades, these distinctive representations achieved recognition both because of their skillful execution and the wide availability of these guides to patrons of Haynes gift shops located throughout the park. On the other hand, contemporary campground maps are rarely (if ever) credited to an individual or group of individuals; as was noted earlier, their use and availability is hyper-local, limited (and applicable only) to the single facility they serve.[29] Given the growing size of popular campgrounds nationwide, their distribution can be similarly (if unwittingly) impactful. The larger the campground, the larger the circulation. Fort Stevens State Park Campground in Oregon, for example, has 497 campsites. Imagine how many thousands of copies of their map are issued every month during high season?

As the comparison between Big Meadows and Moraine campgrounds makes plain, no official

➲ **2016**
National Park Service, *Big Meadows Campground Map*, Shenandoah National Park in Virginia.

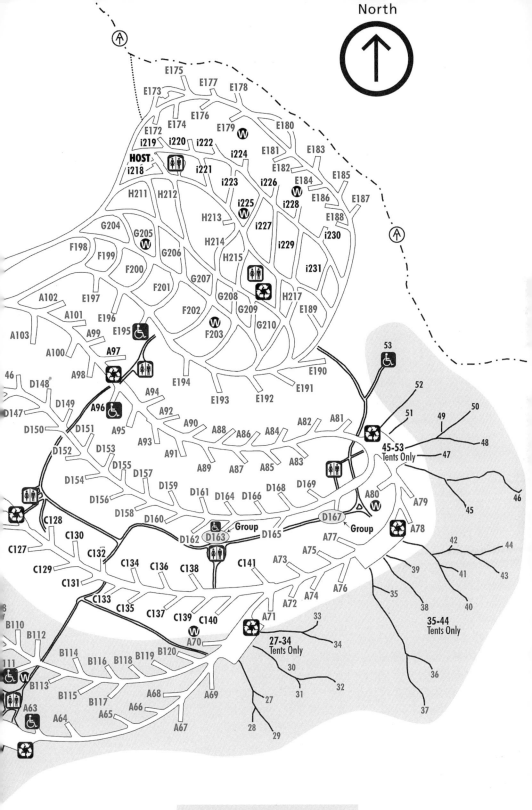

North

HOST

Generator-Free Zone

graphic standards governing the execution of campground maps in national parks exists. In fact, it was not until the 1970s that efforts were made to streamline the visual identity of general reference documents across the units of the entire National Park Service, which includes, in addition to parks, historic sites, recreation areas, historic battlefields, and historic trails. These graphic standards included a regular font type as well as various international symbols designating key services and amenities. Specifically, the use of such graphic shorthand helped lighten the visual clutter by ridding maps of excessive words and repetitive characterizations.

It may be hard to imagine a time when these distinctive symbols were not the norm, let alone a time when they didn't exist at all. In fact, the use of flat, highly contrasting black-and-white silhouette graphics was first promoted in the 1920s by the Viennese designer Otto Neurath (1882–1945). Neurath coined the term *isotype*, an acronym for International System Of Typographic Picture Education, to characterize what he described as a "picture Esperanto," a visual information system that he hoped could be read or deciphered in any language.[30] A version of those symbols was refined during the 1970s in a collaboration between the American Institute of Graphic Arts (AIGA) and the US Department of Transportation (DOT).

Because they represented familiar accommodations such as airports, escalators, toilets, hotels, taxis, restaurants, bars, and many others, these symbols have percolated very broadly into the modern landscape and, by extension, our daily lives. Camping is no exception: restrooms, tent sites, RV sites, water taps, and dumping stations have familiar icons recognized by the seasoned camper and the novice alike. The most recent list published by the National Park Service in 2018 shows no less than 265 standard symbols, including pictograms for highly specialized amenities such as bear spray rental stations, bear

➲ **1923**
This directory page from J. C. and John D. Long, *Motor Camping*, highlights facilities in Colorado.

by automobile and were prepared to camp." This number was exceeded in the season of 1922.

Much of the National Forest area is accessible to automobiles and more roads are being constructed all the time by State or National agencies. Owing to the activities of the Forest Service and the automobile clubs, California can now claim to have the best signed mountain roads in America.

The Forest Service has arranged a great number of camping places for motor tourists.

COLORADO

Municipal Camp Sites

Town or City	Charge or Free	Toilet	Drink-ing Water	Fire-place or Stove	Lights	Bath or Shower
Alamosa	F	Y	Y	Y	Y	
Arriba						
Ault	F	Y	Y	Y	Y	
Berthoud	F	Y	Y	Y	Y	
Boulder	F	Y	Y	Y	Y	Y
Brush	F	Y	Y	Y	Y	
Buena Vista ...	F	Y	Y	Y		
Burlington						
Canon City	F	Y	Y	Y	Y	Y
Castle Rock ...	F	Y	Y	Y		
Cheyenne Wells.	F	Y	Y	Y		
Colorado Springs	25c.-50c. a day	Y	Y	Fuel	Y	
Creede (2 parks)	F	Y	Y	Y	Y	
Cripple Creek ..	F	Y	Y	Y		
Denver	F	Y	Y	Y	Y	Y
Eagle						
Flagler						

spray disposal stations, cell phone charging stations, and dog kennels. To be sure, the richness of this list speaks to the increasing specialization of the camping experience—a far cry from the five services (toilet, drinking water, fireplace, lights, and bath or shower) listed in John D. and J. C. Long's *Motor Camping* (1923).

Most distinctive in this long list is the tent symbol, a solid isosceles triangle from which a smaller, similarly shaped and centrally located opening has been extracted. The near-universal practice of featuring the tent as *the* symbol for camping originated over a century ago. Early examples include Reau Campbell's depiction of Wylie Camp in the Upper Geyser Basin region of Yellowstone, which appeared in *Campbell's New Revised Complete Guide and Descriptive Book of the Yellowstone National Park* (1909). Here we can view the camp from an overhead perspective, and while the symbol for the tent is not quite the same as the one we know, it is self-explanatory. In 1931, the artist Jo Mora (1876–1947) created an extraordinary map of Yosemite National Park, employing a similar strategy to depict public campgrounds along the Merced River.[31] Mora's effort is chock-full of humorous situations, showing tourists (unsurprisingly for this period, all Caucasian) traveling across various parts of the valley—campers cooking around the live flame or fishing the river, couples frolicking, cars lazily crawling up steep inclines—resulting in a pleasure ground that appears safe, comfortable, and picturesque, and whose Indigenous history has been almost completely erased. In short, a wilderness defanged. Further, the overscaled figures place the various destinations on the map within a few footsteps' walk. Mora, who had first visited the area in 1904 and would retain a passion for the park throughout his life, sought to share his own deep knowledge of the area while adopting a tongue-in-cheek tone:

 Campfire

 Campground

 Electrical hookup

 Fire grate

 Firewood

 Firewood cutting

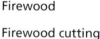 Food storage

 Generator

⬆ **2018**
National Park Service, "NPS Map Elements: Updated May 14, 2018."

➡ **1909**
Map of Upper Geyser Basin in Reau Campbell, *Campbell's New Revised Complete Guide and Descriptive Book of the Yellowstone Park.*

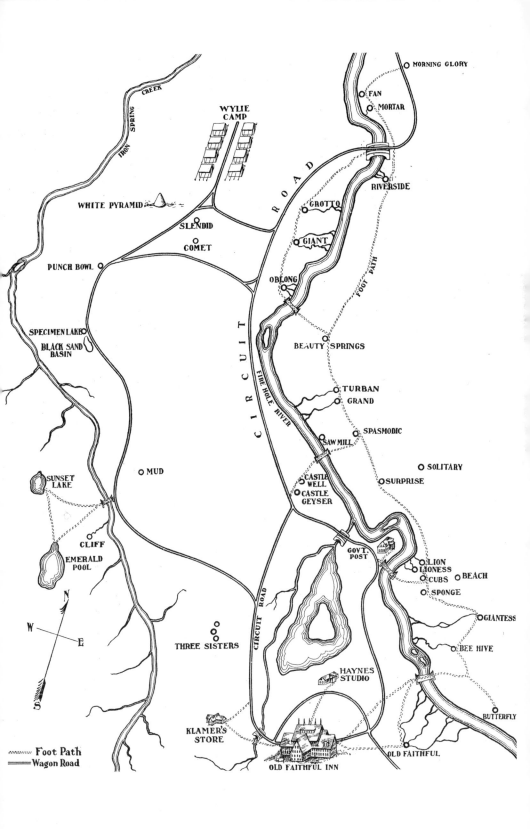

There is so much grandeur and reverential solemnity
in Yosemite that a bit of humor may help the better to
happily reconcile ourselves to the triviality of man....
Now, should this light effort, not altogether truthful,
so not altogether dull, afford you a tithe of mirth,
I shall feel I have added to your reverence of Yosemite.[32]

Like the best maps, Mora's work presents something to get lost inside of rather than simply a tool
for orientation, rewarding the viewer each time
it is consulted. In other words, his map achieved
the status of landscape in its own right.

Conclusions

*Campground Virtual Tours let you see, click and pick the
perfect campsite. Let the other campers go to the crowded
spots while you discover the hidden gems.*[33]
—CAMPGROUNDVIEWS.COM

Mora could not have known just how sustaining the
image of the canvas tent would become in representing the entire camping experience. For prospective
campers exploring campgrounds through websites
like Recreation.gov and ReserveAmerica.com, the
tent symbol now functions as a concrete point of
data. A single click of the mouse over one of the tent
icons delivers information on a particular campsite,
including photos, prices, and amenities (e.g., electrical service, water). And with dozens or even hundreds
of clickable tent symbols dispersed across the screen,
an online reservation map starts to look a great deal
like the real thing: the place is literally *filled* with
tents. Each tent stands for a single campsite, but it
might as well represent a single real tent erected
on the very same spot.[34]

Experienced campers know that popular campgrounds at national parks sell out quickly, so they
stand ready to claim their site precisely six months

◒ 1931 / 1941
Jo Mora, *Yosemite*, detail of
map highlighting camps 6
through 16 along the Merced
River. Like its Yellowstone
counterpart, the original 1931
map was conceived as a line
drawing; color was later added
in 1941 and 1949 editions
published by the Yosemite Park
and Curry Company, with slight
alterations. This map would
have been of limited use for
campers, however, since there
was no way of judging the size
and capacity of these facilities.

ahead of their planned arrival date. The clickable map is constantly updated to reflect availability in real time: a tent is represented in a solid color if available; alternately, the same icon is lighter when the campsite has already been claimed. Roads merely function as static reference points. Online campground maps feature the same green background, the same-sized tents all pointing toward the top of the computer screen. This standard of representation creates a continuous statewide or even nationwide digital territory, displacing the local campground map and its quirky graphics as the artistic expression of a unique place.

If the map served as a tool for orientation when first reaching the campground, it now helps the prospective visitor make informed choices before they even set foot on the campground. The negotiation that brought the visitor and campground attendant together in a brief moment of social interaction has now been disembodied over space and time. Rather than pointing and circling the campsite on a printed copy of the map, the camper points and clicks on the map on their laptop screen or phone, often from the comfort of home. The prospective visitor navigates this digital environment as one would reserve airline or stadium seats, days, weeks, or months before the actual event. Indeed, a simple "click" of the tent has come to stand for the entire process of erecting the campsite: Who knew camping could be so easy? And with innovative new features like those available at CampgroundViews.com—a system specifically designed for campgrounds that recalls Google Street View—it is possible to imagine navigation apps pointing the visitor directly to their desired campsite, altogether removing the social encounter with the campground attendant—as well as the paper map—from the carefully orchestrated ritual of arrival.

↑ 2022
Drive-by view of Site 6, Fruita Campground, Capitol Reef National Park in Utah, as seen on CampgroundViews.com.

➔ 2014
Recreation.gov reservation map, Big Meadows Campground, Shenandoah National Park in Virginia.

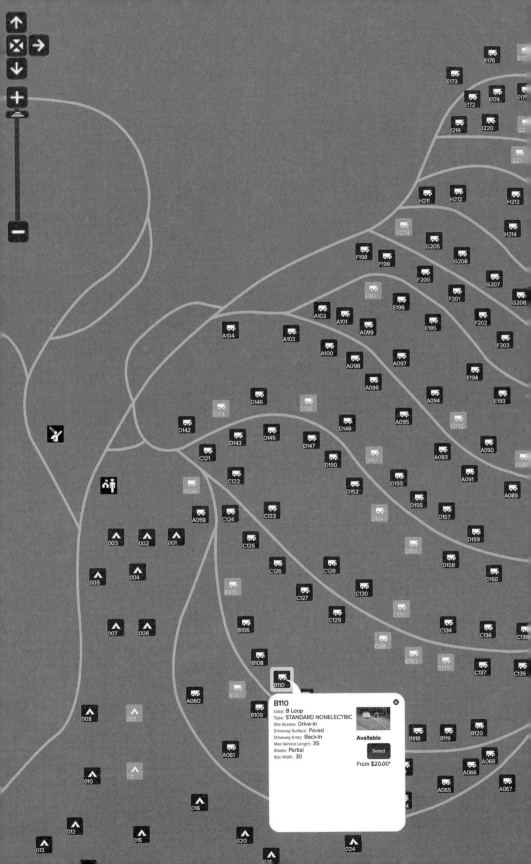

B110
Loop: B Loop
Type: STANDARD NONELECTRIC
Site Access: Drive-In
Driveway Surface: Paved
Driveway Entry: Back-In
Max Vehicle Length: 35
Shade: Partial
Site Width: 30

Available

Select

From $20.00*

PICNIC TABLE

Verging on chit-chat, or snip-snap, [Picnic is] an ugly word,…a busy, self-assertive mediocre word, that has sacrificed all dignity, but without attaining any compensatory sense of ease.[1]
—OSBERT SITWELL

The picnic table is an ingenious piece of design. Featuring a structurally bolted frame that unites bench seats and table into a sturdy package, its construction is so simple that it has not required any significant improvements for nearly a century. It is safe to say that there are picnic tables in every park, every campsite, and, seemingly, almost every suburban backyard in America. And yet its ubiquity has also made it largely unremarkable, to the point of invisibility.

Having transcended the event it was originally intended to accommodate, the picnic table is now the ideal setting for any outdoor event that compels us to face one another squarely across a shared surface. A 2009 photograph by Pete Souza featuring then President Barack Obama and Secretary of State

◐ ◑ **2012**
Edward Norton as Scout Master Ward in Wes Anderson's *Moonrise Kingdom*.

➋ **1911**
Picnic grove at Cedar Point, an amusement park opened in 1870 in Sandusky, Ohio, on a peninsula along Lake Erie.

Hillary Clinton meeting at a massive picnic table on the White House grounds seems to bring new meaning to this ordinarily mundane experience. Though off-limits to the general public, there is something intensely familiar about this table—as if we had all sat there ourselves. Indeed, the table seems to humanize its powerful occupants, if not also curiously diminish them with its outsized components.[2]

These qualities of familiarity and abundance have made the picnic table an American icon. On the Home Depot website, buyers can choose from among hundreds of models, priced between $120 and $3,700.[3] How can we possibly select from such a broad array of choices? And how can there be such disparity of pricing, given that all such tables are structurally alike? For decades, we have occupied picnic tables chosen by others, by the operators of car washes and rest stops and hospital cafeterias—and because their design remains almost flawlessly the same, they rarely disappoint.

This Is the Spot

Nature has provided no comforts at all, and she launches her armies of insect life or her legions of chilly particles of air and water against the poor body without respite and without pity.[4]
—WARREN H. MILLER

For all its weight, bulk, and permanence, the historical antecedent of the picnic table is clear. For Professor Walter Levy, the classic image of the picnic is that of a daytime meal "typically eaten on a blanket on a fine patch of grass."[5] Iconic representations include the 1846 painting by Thomas Cole (1801–1848) called *A Pic-Nic Party,* an increasingly common scene for the period that is imbued with the Victorian flair of "a day in nature for feasting, amusements, privacy amid the masses, and freedom."[6]

➋ 2009
Pete Souza, photograph of President Barack Obama and Secretary of State Hillary Clinton seated at a picnic table on the White House grounds.

➋ 2018
Mahershala Ali (right) as the jazz pianist Dr. Donald Shirley and Viggo Mortensen as his driver Tony Lip in a scene from Peter Farrelly's *Green Book.*

As with the pitched tent at the campsite, spontaneously putting down the blanket on the ground is the first act of laying claim to the picnic site. Before any of the picnic supplies have been unpacked and laid out or the occupants seated, someone declares: "This is the spot!" Despite its decisive character, the gesture is also temporary. Once the provisions, plates, and utensils have been packed up after the picnic, the blanket can easily be hoisted off the ground by a single pair of hands, shaken free of crumbs, and folded back into the provisions basket—the last act before participants leave.

Historian Mary Ellen Hern noted in "Picnicking in the Northern United States, 1840–1900" that "nineteenth century etiquette writers recommended 'canvas camp chairs, mats and pieces of carpet…to give people easy seats…[and to] prevent the damp striking through thin dresses.'"[7] And the blanket or piece of carpet serves an additional utilitarian role, mediating revelers' contact with nature. This attitude toward the ground reflected not only a desire for comfort but also a fear of disease and a growing concern for hygiene and sanitation that characterized the nineteenth century. More recently, Stanford University biologist Deborah M. Gordon noted that "the observation that where there is a picnic, there will be ants, rests on the notion that there is an ant lurking everywhere, all the time, ready to mobilize its nest mates when a picnic appears."[8] In its attempt to recreate the formality of the indoor table setting outside, the blanket also represents an act of domestication of the ground surface: it functions as a tablecloth, an area over which the meal can be properly laid out and consumed.

In the film *Powers of Ten* (1977), written and directed by Charles (1907–1978) and Ray (1912–1988) Eames, we meet a young couple picnicking on a near-perfect square of carefully arranged blankets whose colorful textures and rectilinear edges contrast sharply with the surrounding grass. The area forms

⊘ 2005
Sheila Bridges, *Harlem Toile de Jouy* (detail). For Bridges, an African American interior designer who was inspired by the late eighteenth-century French toile and its pastoral motifs, this scene, and five others repeated throughout the pattern, "lampoon some of the stereotypes deeply woven into the African American experience."

⊘ 1846
Thomas Cole, *A Pic-Nic Party*.

an island of sorts—a place on which to lie and dispose food over. Unlike Cole, whose work was shaped by a Romantic perspective of nature (note the tree stump in the foreground, page 183), the Eameses are interested in the setup of the picnic itself. The occupants, their provisions, and their entertainments are all carefully arranged—even the clothing has been artfully chosen to complement the colors and fabrics of the rest of the scene. The overhead shot is clinical: if the blanket is hovering slightly over the ground, we too are hovering above the components of the picnic, the edges of the blankets nearly parallel to the image frame. To be sure, this perspective is now familiar to anyone who has operated or viewed video from a small drone equipped with an internal camera, but this visual perspective was quite radical for the 1970s and in the decades that predated the arrival of Google Earth in 2001. As the camera pans away, the picnic rapidly shrinks in size against the sea of grass before the edges of the park and other major urban landmarks along the Chicago lakeshore begin to appear.

A Piece of Equipment or a Destination?

Dining in nature is elementally savage in otherwise ordinary people.[9]
—OSBERT SITWELL

In many respects, the modern-day cooler has supplanted the checkered blanket and the provisions basket as the single most important piece of picnic gear. Packed with ice, food, and refreshments, the cooler is usually so heavy that it is impractical to transport over long distances—from the kitchen to the trunk of the car, and from there to a nearby designated outdoor spot. It seems only natural then that picnic tables, which we now recognize as the ultimate destination for the event, are often situated near parking lots in state or national parks. A piece of

➔ 1977
Film still from Charles and Ray Eames, *Powers of Ten.*

infrastructure designed for heavy usage, the picnic table can be shared over time by many groups in areas specifically designed for daytime use.

If the picnic table has become a ubiquitous part of public landscapes, then the introduction of tables in the outdoors may have appeared equally natural during the late nineteenth century. Indeed, for the Victorians the idea of moving an entire meal from the indoor confines of the dining room to the out-of-doors seemed a logical extension of the traditional picnic: Why not move the entire food-consumption apparatus—tablecloth, utensils, dishware, tables, and chairs—along with the food itself? In the circa 1855 painting *A Pic Nick in the Woods of New England*, the artist Jerome B. Thompson (1814–1886) depicted a conventional meal with indoor furniture that had been temporarily moved outdoors. While this arrangement no doubt increased the level of comfort of the participants, transportation of bulky chairs and tables for a single daytime meal would have been highly impractical, unless the picnic site was located near the home. Later on, the commercialization of leisure activities and the emerging market for portable recreational gear like the Coleman picnic table would be introduced into the growing market of motor camping equipment. As we will soon see, some of the first patents to which modern-day tables can be traced were designs that were meant to be folded up and transported to the picnic site. During this period, the table was conceived as a piece of equipment on par with the provisions basket and the blanket.

As picnics became more popular during the late nineteenth century, high demand led to the creation of designated areas known as picnic groves: areas furnished with rudimentary tables and benches like those found at Cedar Point, an amusement park located in Sandusky, Ohio (page 179). For Mary Ellen Hern, picnic groves were "a tidied up natural landscape,…neither a constructed landscape like an urban park nor a developed pleasure ground,

↑↑ 1900
Arthur Wigram Allen, photograph of Allen and his brother Boyce on a picnic in Sutton Forest, Australia. Ingeniously, their provisions basket opens up to support a tabletop.

↑ 1924
Advertisement for the Lincoln Folding Furniture Company in *Motor Camper & Tourist*, March 1925.

⊃ c. 1855
Jerome B. Thompson, *A Pic Nick in the Woods of New England*.

although it may have provided such passive recreation facilities as pavilions, tables, benches and hearths."[10] Made from rough-hewn boards and designed for heavy usage, the tables in these early picnic groves were fixed in place, their posts deeply embedded in the ground. Long benches without backs stood in lieu of individual chairs. As the illustration on page 179 indicates, tables became an integrated function inside the grove—less accessory than destination. Dense arrangements of tables and benches that could accommodate several parties at once were the norm. Hern noted that these picnic grounds were later emulated outside the city, in places like the Mohonk Mountain House in New Paltz, New York, as well as in the national parks. For all the daytime pleasures they offered, such picnic grounds were not exempt from racial prejudice in the decades before the Civil Rights Act became law in 1964. A 1938 map of Shenandoah National Park, for instance, indicates that picnic grounds were highly segregated: its daytime facility at Elkwallow, for example, was for the use of white persons only, while another at Lewis Mountain had been set aside for African Americans visitors as early as 1935. Regrettably, even after it expanded into a fully functioning campground, Lewis Mountain remained the only overnight destination for Black visitors in the park between 1939 and 1950.

Walter Levy noted that the picnic was always conceived as a one-day affair that did not require an overnight stay.[11] More serious recreation enthusiasts of the period were drawn to the wilds far beyond the city. The Adirondacks experienced its first tourism craze in 1869 after the Reverend William Henry Harrison Murray published *Adventures in the Wilderness* (1869) following his own camping adventures there. With an enthusiasm verging on hyperbole, the author trumpeted the restorative properties of a few weeks spent roughing it in the outdoors, noting the case of a young man whose health was ailing:

⬆ 1938
H. S. Teller, *Guide Map of the Shenandoah National Park, Virginia, 1938*. This detail highlights the "LEWIS MTN. Picnic Ground for Colored People."

➡ 1924
Victor Anderson, *Stribley Park, Stockton, California* (detail). Emphasis on the picnic grounds at far right by the author.

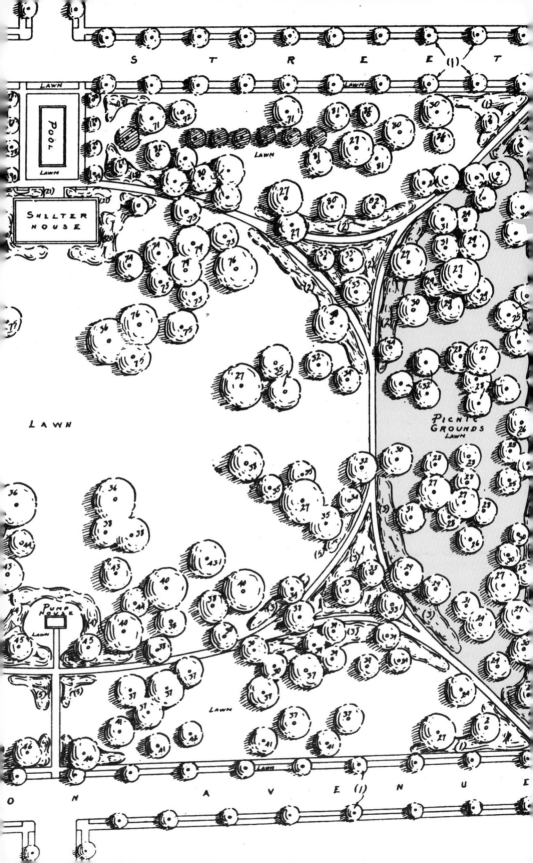

The second day his cough was less sharp and painful. At the end of the first week he could walk by leaning on the paddle. The second week he needed no support. The third week his cough ceased entirely. From that point on he improved with wonderful rapidity. He "went in" the first of June, carried in the arms of a guide....In five months he had gained sixty-five pounds of flesh, and flesh, too, "well packed on", as they say in the woods.[12]

A 1886 photograph by George Bacon Wood of Camp Colden in the Adirondacks would have been illustrative of the period: it features a pair of sportsmen seated at a table constructed from a framework of posts planted in the ground, two additional men preparing a meal on the open fire, and a rustic shelter made from branches and bark in the background. Commenting on this type of improvised furniture, Warren H. Miller observed in *Camp Craft: Modern Practice and Equipment* (1915) that "the necessity of an eating table of some sort has been given much study by veteran outfitters, so important it is in the long run. For the permanent camp the log and plank tables...solve the problem amply and, with a log bench by each side, make for comfortable, happy meals."[13] Similarly, the explorer and author A. Hyatt Verrill offered that such tables could be made "very easily by driving forked sticks into the earth and then lashing a rectangular frame to them and which should then be covered by birch and bark....In place of the bark, rods or withes may be lashed close together, or cords may be stretched across the top and wattled with willow, withes or other materials. Chairs or benches may be constructed in the same manner."[14] Made from unmilled lumber collected around the campsite—the very same wood used to construct shelters or keep the daily campfire going—these tables were designed for intensive usage, presumably for the duration that the party remained at the site. On the last day, they would break camp (literally) and throw the table straight into the fire, leaving few traces.

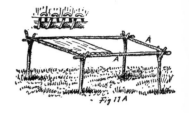

⬆ 1917

Illustrations from A. Hyatt Verrill, *The Book of Camping*, depicting methods for creating rudimentary furniture at a campsite.

⮕ 1886

George Bacon Wood, *Camp Colden*, Lake Colden, New York.

The Design of the Table

There is in this specimen a remarkable appearance of being braced against overturning.[15]
—ALBERT H. GOOD

Two key features distinguish the modern-day picnic table from those found in picnic groves at the turn of the twentieth century: the combination of seats and tabletop into a single unit and the design's near-unshakable stability. Dating from 1904, US Patent 769,354 by Charles H. Nielsen (1872–1945) constitutes the first clear antecedent to this design. The author characterized his invention as a "table capable of being cheaply made, which is portable and equipped with seats, preferably on both sides…particularly designed and adapted for use at picnics and other gatherings of a similar character where temporary use only is required."[16] Although it was the first to combine seats and top, Nielsen's chief concern seems to have been the table's portability.[17] In particular, a drawing of the collapsed table suggested a level of flatness close to its distant counterpart, the nineteenth-century picnic blanket.

In hindsight, the portability of Nielsen's table was less consequential than its innovative frame. The inventor's concern for stability indicated a clear lineage to an earlier tradition of American furniture-making, the eighteenth-century sawbuck table and its pairs of legs crossing in X-shaped structural frames. As with most new ideas, unexpected challenges emerged: the integral seating gave rise to a potential weight imbalance between the two sides of the table, as shown in a hilarious illustration in *The Family Flivvers to Frisco* (1927) by the journalist Frederic Van de Water (1890–1968), a book that relays his personal journey from New York to San Francisco along the Lincoln Highway. To guard against this issue, Nielsen proposed to support the ends of each bench with vertical posts. This meant there were in

➔ 1927
W. J. Enright, illustration in Frederick Van de Water, *The Family Flivvers to Frisco.*

WE WERE LYING ON OUR BACKS PINNED DOWN BY THE CA-
REENED TABLE, WITH OUR EVENING MEAL UPON US

fact eight points of contact with the ground—
a redundant approach. This awkward combination
of vertical and diagonal posts could be seen in similar
tables produced throughout the 1920s, including
those found at Overland Park, Denver's famed municipal automobile campground. Each of its eight hundred campsites was marked by a sturdy table whose
long benches were supported by such vertical posts
and braced diagonally to the ground.

The ultimate refinement of the modern-day design
would lie in the elimination of these redundant vertical supports. The improvement can be traced to two
separate sources: dating from 1918, US Patent
1,272,187 by Harold R. Basford (1873–1954) represents
the closest antecedent to the picnic table as we know
it today.[18] Like Nielsen's, Basford's design was collapsible and meant to be portable, so that motor campers
roaming the countryside in a new age of mobility
could pack the table along with their tents, bedding,
cooking stove, and other assorted gear. As leisure
activities were further commercialized throughout
this period, suppliers like the Coleman Company,
Lincoln, and their competitors rushed in to define
an emerging market for portable recreational gear.

Was Nielsen the first to integrate seating, tabletop, and diagonal structure into the spare, utilitarian
form we know today? Or was he merely adapting an
earlier, undocumented design so that it could be
transported? There is evidence that similar picnic
tables were in use as early as 1916 in the US Forest
Service campground at Eagle Creek, the first developed facility on public lands in the country.[19] Unlike
Nielsen's patent, the Eagle Creek design featured no
hinged components, but period photographs showing
a disassembled table suggests that portability was in
fact an important concern. This made a great deal of
sense: components could be mass-produced in distant
woodshops, then transported on a flatbed truck to
remote sites like Eagle Creek, deep in the Oregon
National Forest, and later assembled at individual

↑ **1925**
Picnic table at Overland
Park Campground in Denver.
Photographer unknown.

↘ **1904**
Diagrams from Charles H.
Nielsen, US Patent 769,354,
illustrating how the table can be
collapsed for transport.

No. 769,354.

PATENTED SEPT. 6, 1904.

C. H. NIELSEN.
TABLE.
APPLICATION FILED SEPT. 28, 1903.

NO MODEL.

2 SHEETS—SHEET 1.

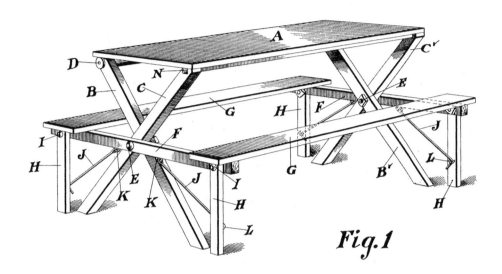

Fig.1

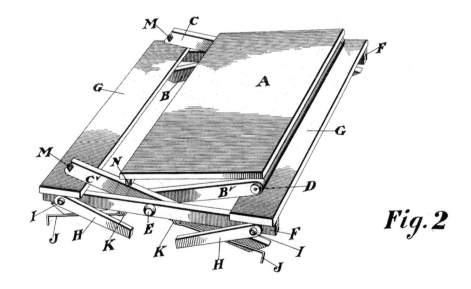

Fig.2

campsites. Conversely, the same sturdy tables could be easily broken down and stored during the off-season. Anyone who has purchased a wooden picnic table at a local hardware store knows that this ingenious "flat packing" of partially assembled components is still how tables are sold today.

Proliferation

The camper is really furnished with a roofless cabin in which the essential commodities are the garage, the kitchen stove, the dining table and the sleeping quarters with enough space to move around without inconvenience.[20]
—E. P. MEINECKE

By 1935, Albert H. Good, an architectural consultant for the National Park Service, would note in *Park Structures and Facilities* that "an average of the dimensional limits of the human frame and uniformity of sorts in the distribution of hinges thereof, have long since determined certain basic dimensions for the picnic table."[21] Inasmuch as he was referring to the widths of the tabletop and seats, the spacing between them, and their respective heights above the ground, Good was, in a limited sense, correct. However, his statement omitted the role that drawings and specifications had played in normalizing these dimensions in the first place. There is no question that Nielsen's and Basford's respective patents established the primary design principles of the picnic table, but the attentive reader will note that their drawings feature no specific dimensions. In the interval of time between the Basford patent and the publication of Good's *Park Structures and Facilities*, a 1922 blueprint issued by the National Park Service titled *Table for Public Autocamp* would lay down these key dimensions for the first time. Recorded in this document is one additional structural improvement: two diagonal braces positioned along the main axis of the table to

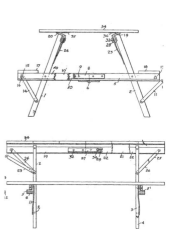

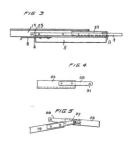

⬆ **1918**
Diagrams from Harold R. Basford, US Patent 1,272,187. Though he meant his design to be collapsible, Basford's patent contains all the elements of the contemporary picnic table.

➡ **1919**
US Forest Service, Pacific Northwest Region, picnic tables for Mount Hood National Forest in Oregon. Photographer unknown.

I-Studies-Mt. Hood
Historical Information
General.

Type picnic table used on Mount Hood National Forest before 1930.
After 193ʘ rustic tables were constructed by the Zig Zag CCC Camp.
Negatives No. 43960 & 43961A.

provide additional stability. The drawing was also unique for the fact that it broke down the table into its individually dimensioned components: in all, fifteen pieces of milled lumber were required, including boards measuring 2 × 12 inches for the tabletop and seats, as well as boards measuring 2 × 4 inches and 2 × 6 inches for the structural frame. The drawing even specified the location of holes to be drilled for the structural bolts.

It is hardly a surprise that the first technical drawing for a picnic table would be issued by a government agency rather than a private inventor like Nielsen or Basford. A note on the drawing indicated that the design was "Adapted from a Forest Service Table"—perhaps the very same tables first documented at Eagle Creek? Indeed the National Park Service, the US Forest Service, and the Civilian Conservation Corps would take on leading roles as major developers of campgrounds and picnic areas throughout federal and state parks during the New Deal era in the 1930s. As these facilities gained in popularity and size, it is easy to see why these widely disseminated specifications would prove more influential than comparable designs at independent municipal campgrounds across the country, even facilities as large as Overland Park.[22]

Published by the US Department of the Interior and the National Park Service, Good's *Park Structures and Facilities* (1935) and subsequent *Park and Recreational Structures* (1938) would become the authoritative standards during this period. Beautifully illustrated and laden with the author's own delightful commentary, the books included specifications for a broad range of infrastructural components, including picnic tables, fireplaces, shelters, comfort facilities, and campsites. Like other chapters, the section on picnic tables featured several different designs, some more rustic than others, as well as examples of their adaptation in different parks across the country. Made from milled lumber,

❷ 1922

Table for Public Autocamp (Adapted from Forest Service Table).

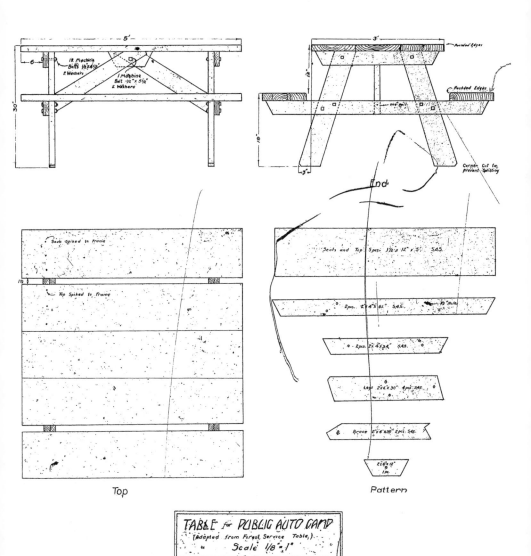

5'

6

30"

1R Machine
Bolts 1/2"x4 1/2"
2 Washers

1 Machine
Bolt 1/2" x 5 1/2"
2 Washers

3'

Rounded Edges

Rounded Edges

18"

one bill

3'

Corner Cut to
prevent Splitting

End

Seat Spiked to Frame

Top Spiked to Frame

1 1/2

Top

Seats and Top 5 pcs. 1 1/2 x 12" x 5' S.4.S.

2 pcs. 2"x 4" x 6' S.4.S.   2" Holes

2 pcs. 2"x 4"x 34" S.4.S.

Legs 2"x 6" x 30" 4 pcs. S.4.S.

Brace 2"x 4"x 28" 2 pcs. S.4.S.

2"x 6" x 12"
1 pc.

Pattern

TABLE for PUBLIC AUTO CAMP
(Adapted from Forest Service Table.)
Scale 1/8" = 1"

roughly sawn logs, or massive stone slabs, these tables were imposing structures, and their immobility had by now become an important design feature.

With the utmost concern for the impact of automobiles, E. P. Meinecke's ideas had a tremendous impact on the design of campsites and campgrounds such that his recommendations would come to form the backbone of contemporary campground planning. He proposed the "definite fixation" of the automobile, the firepit, the tent, and the table at the campsite, allowing an informal network of trails to develop between these key infrastructural components. Of the picnic table in particular, Meinecke wished that "only tables of very heavy construction involving considerable expenditure can be considered."[23] Echoing this perspective, Good observed in *Park Structures and Facilities*: "The fixed position, if a good one, is desirable, and is achieved by means of the right of the picnic unit or table, or better still, by anchoring."[24]

The historical geographer Terence Young astutely observed that for Meinecke, this vision of the campsite as a *roofless cabin* "included many of the same essential commodities that were found in a suburban home: the garage, the kitchen stove, the dining table and the sleeping quarters, with enough space to move around without inconvenience."[25] Only a hundred years before, the Victorians had shared in this vision, moving the meal from the interior confines of the dining room to the out-of-doors. So their disorientation would not be quite complete, they tried to lend a measure of formality to the occasion by using proper dishes, silverware, and blankets as tablecloths, creating a space around which the meal could be set and consumed. By the 1930s, the entire apparatus of domestic life—not only eating, but cooking and sleeping as well—had been moved outdoors. Hundreds of families would be going through the same motions inside a single campground, many within sight of one another.

○ **1938**

Two illustrations from *Picnic Unit, Bonham State Park, Texas* (top) and *Picnic Unit, Guernsey Lake State Park, Wyoming* (bottom), Albert H. Good, ed., *Park and Recreation Structures*, vol.2, *Recreational and Cultural Facilities*.

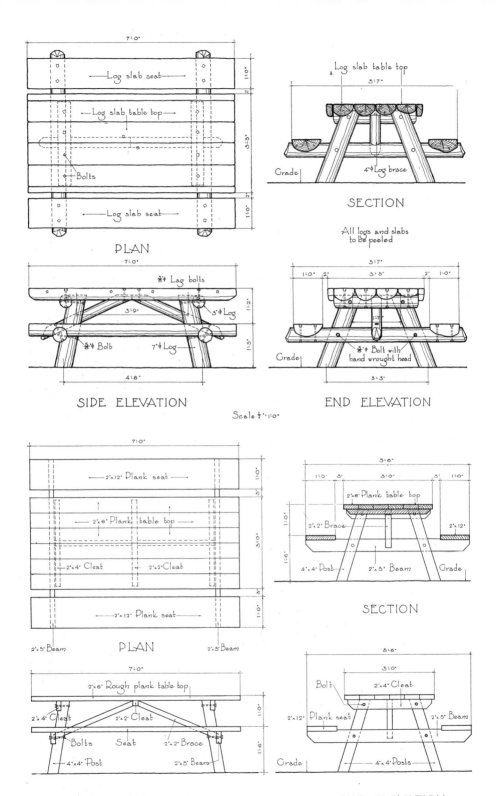

Log slab seat

Log slab table top

Bolts

Log slab seat

PLAN

7'-0"

1'-0"

3'-5"

1'-0"

Log slab table top

SECTION

3'-7"

Grade

4'-4" Log brace

All logs and slabs
to be peeled

7'-0"

⅜"ø Lag bolts

3'-9"

5"ø Log

⅝"ø Bolt

7"ø Log

1'-2"

1'-5"

4'-8"

SIDE ELEVATION

Scale ½"=1'-0"

END ELEVATION

3'-7"

1'-0" 2"   3'-5"   2"   1'-0"

1'-7"

⅝"ø Bolt with
hand wrought head

Grade

3'-5"

2"x12" Plank seat

2"x6" Plank table top

2"x4" Cleat   2"x2" Cleat

2"x12" Plank seat

2"x5" Beam

PLAN

2"x5" Beam

7'-0"

1'-0"

5"

3'-0"

5"

1'-0"

2"x6" Plank table top

2"x2" Brace

4"x4" Post   2"x5" Beam

3'-6"

1'-0"   3"   3'-0"   3"   1'-0"

1'-0"

1'-6"

2"x12"

Grade

SECTION

2"x6" Rough plank table top

2"x4" Cleat   2"x2" Cleat

Bolts   Seat   2"x2" Brace

4"x4" Post   2"x5" Beam

SIDE ELEVATION

7'-0"

1'-0"

1'-6"

Bolt

2"x4" Cleat

2"x12" Plank seat

2"x5" Beam

4"x4" Posts

Grade

END ELEVATION

3'-6"

3'-0"

Scale ½"=1'-0"

Conclusions

All picnics might be structurally similar, but the
preferences are idiosyncratic.[26]
—WALTER LEVY

While their basic features are essentially the same,
each picnic table, just like each picnic, can often be
distinguished by a range of details large (extending
the length of tabletop past the seats to achieve
ADA compliance, for example) and small—an
additional cleat, narrower boards, bigger bolts, and
chamfered corners on the ends of the table and
seats, to name a few.

In these subtle differences we begin to recognize
the table's cohesive essence, the aspects that make
this design both unique and simultaneously unremarkable. Tracing the design history of a culturally
significant yet nearly invisible object is a curious
process: drawings and photographs are collected,
dated, their attributes compared. Moving back in
time, its once key features become less and less clear,
until the moment when they no longer exist: *this* is
the beginning of the history.

Now let's eat!

⬆ 1965
Bruce Davidson, *Woman in
Boots Sitting at Picnic Table*,
from *Yosemite Campers* series.

➡ 1932
*Proposed Plan of Regulated
Development on a Newly
Laid Out Camp Ground*, E. P.
Meinecke, *A Camp Ground
Policy.*

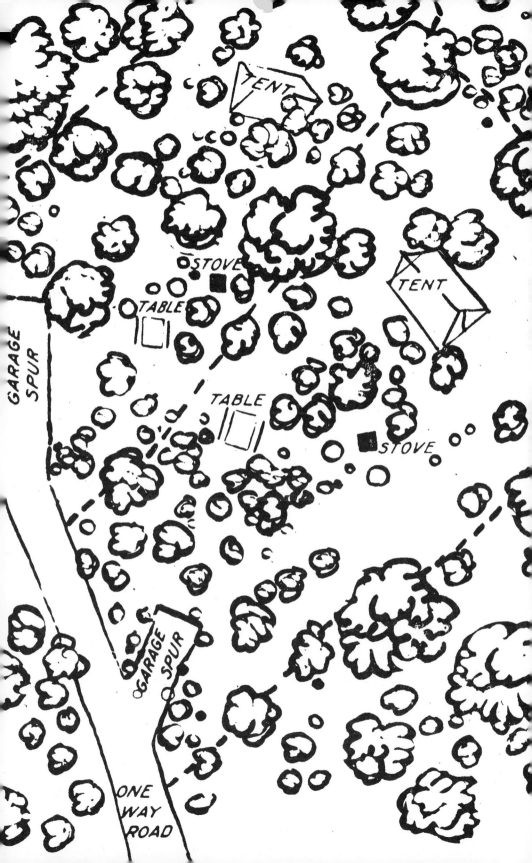

TENT

How big and open the camp site seems before the tent is pitched.[1]
—S. H. WALKER

One of the great joys of camping is laying claim to the campsite. Describing the rough shanty tent, fashioned from sheets of duck cloth stapled to hemlock poles he had cut down nearby, the legendary Adirondack outdoorsman George Washington Sears (1821–1890), better known as Nessmuk, boasted that "the affair…takes a skillful woodsman about three hours of easy work to put it in the shape described."[2] One hundred years later, all that remains of this "easy work" is a series of streamlined, well-rehearsed procedures: parking the car at the edge of the designated campsite and taking out the cooler, the lawn chairs, the box of firewood, the cooking stove, the pots, the pans, the plates, the duffel bag full of clothes, the sleeping bags, the mattresses, the pillows, and the tent. The sturdy, weather-beaten picnic table and the rusty firepit that first greet the camper at the site

↩ ↩ **1916**
John Singer Sargent, *Inside a Tent in the Canadian Rockies.*

➡ **1920**
Shanty-Tent and Camp-Fire, George Washington Sears, *Woodcraft*, 14th ed.

SHANTY-TENT AND CAMP-FIRE.

function as conspicuous, permanent spatial markers on an otherwise bare patch of land, beckoning the camper forward. The place is unoccupied, the proper fees have been paid, the number on the wood post by the parked car matches the information highlighted on the map—there is, in other words, no doubt that *this is the place*. And yet, can a legitimate claim be made to the site until the tent has been erected?

As the largest structure on the campsite, the tent performs a number of important functions: rising tall and wide from its compact and sturdy rucksack, its colorful surfaces signal the occupants' presence in camp while acting as a shelter from the wind, sun, rain, and bugs. And because the tent itself is made of constituent parts (i.e., stakes, poles, guy lines, insect screen, and rain fly) that require some assembly, the raising of the tent functions as a ritualized process that connects the camper to the practices and labor of forebears like Nessmuk: "pitching," or erecting, the tent is the symbolic gesture that helps reset the clock on each new occupation of the campsite. Later, "striking," or taking down, and stowing away the very same tent helps put an end to the stay while setting the stage for the next occupants. Even Nessmuk would grudgingly admit that the umbrella-like design for the 1955 Pop Tent (US Patent 2,953,245) by designer Bill Moss (1923–1994), which could be fully deployed to a diameter of seven feet at the press of a single button, does fulfill this basic need.[3] For all the innovative claims that characterize and drive the development of modern camping gear—lightness and size (the largest tent for the smallest bulk), efficiency (fastest set-up time), and predictability (its form never changes from site to site)—those precious few minutes "assembling" the Pop Tent suggest that the camper is not quite ready to give away the entire game just yet.

Peg out to exact rectangle

Erect front pole first

Attend to pegging out of side-guys and walls las

↑ 1947
Drawings from S. H. Walker, *The Way to Camp*, illustrating how to pitch a lightweight tent.

➋ c. 1960
Pitching the Pop Tent.
Photographer unknown. With a hub that deploys like an umbrella, the tent springs to life in a few minutes.

Attached/Detached

A tent for tentativeness. The gift of portable roots.[4]
—GAIL SHEEHY

In *A Hard Blow* (1881), the artist Charles (Carlos) J. Hittell (1861–1938) captured an unsettling sight in the nineteenth-century California wilderness. Needless to say, things are not going well. A man on the right side of the drawing is desperately pulling on the upright pole beneath the tent canvas in order to prevent the structure from blowing away. Feet firmly planted on the ground, and leaning down slightly to his right, he is exerting a certain amount of resistance that is helping provisionally stabilize the structure. If only he can hold on for a little longer.

Yet even in fair weather the system of forces that keep the tent in place are complex, though perhaps not quite as dramatic as in this drawing. Derived from the Latin adjective *tentus* (stretched), the shelter embodies dueling ideals held under a state of tension: the structure is assembled from a range of components, some soft and diaphanous (fabric, guy lines), others rigid and bulky (poles, stakes); it can be easily compacted for transport, yet becomes spatially expansive at the campsite; it is firmly connected to the surface of the earth while pushing off into the sky; and the stakes that stabilize the tent against internal tensions and high winds also serve to provisionally and symbolically *resist* the daily tide of arrivals and departures that characterize the modern campground. On the last morning, the stakes are easily pulled out of the ground, the tent folded up and stuffed back into its matching sack; no trace remains of its past occupants, their claim to the site relinquished. We can almost imagine the patch of land by the picnic table and the firepit riddled with holes: "the gift of portable roots." Similarly, the British researcher and felt expert Stephanie Bunn posits that the term *yurt,* used to describe Central Asian nomadic

➋ **1881**
Charles (Carlos) J. Hittell, *A Hard Blow.*

tents, probably came into use through a misunder-standing of the word *jurt*, which in Kyrgyz and Kazakh means "tent site," "homeplace," or "motherland."[5]

While tents have remained relatively unchanged for several millennia, the key to important design innovations over the last century has been to recognize that the balance between these ideals could, in ways large and small, be modulated, often with surprisingly radical results. Describing a Chinese military tent from the early eighteenth century, for example, Godfrey Rhodes (1815–1897), who would one day become president of the legislative assemblies of the Kingdom of Hawaii, observed that no less than eighty individual ground pins were required to hold the shelter in place.[6] In many ways, this was the mirror opposite of the tent in Hittell's illustration—a highly stable tent in any weather. But was anything lost in the balance? For one thing, there is no getting around the idea that pitching this structure would have been a time-consuming affair, running counter to its nature as a provisional shelter in the field. Like the land surveyor who plants flags in the ground to demarcate the limits of a property, the soldiers were, with each stake, further committing themselves to the location of their encampment: the structure was so completely and safely grounded that it could not be moved about the campground without being entirely struck down. Finally, the design failed to take into consideration changes in the surface tension of the tent. As the sun moves about the site and the structure is pelted by rain and wind and exposed to changing temperatures, the fabric is naturally given to contraction and expansion, rips and sags. All to say that to evaluate these two very different tents along a sliding scale defined at one end by failure and at the other by success is to miss the broader point: between them lies a fascinating continuum that has propelled design innovation forward.

3. *tie rope around behind rock*

rock in here

4. *pull out & tie down to stake*

⬆ **1976**
Margot Apple, *Pullouts*, in Steve Futterman and Margot Apple, *Soft House*.

➡ **1920**
How One Man May Put Up a Tent, Daniel Carter Beard, *The American Boys' Handybook of Camp-Lore and Woodcraft*.

HOW TO PITCH AND DITCH SINGLE HANDED

HOW TO ANCHOR A TENT IN SANDY OR WET SOIL

SURFACE OR TOP EARTH

SECTION OF EARTH

Guy lines and sliders introduced during the nine-teenth century let the occupant regulate the tension on the fabric without altering the location of the stakes—indeed, the very term *slider* suggests that the tent's stability needs to be constantly regulated. Bill Moss's 1957 design for a Flexible Hyperbolic Paraboloid Shelter (US Patent 3,060,949) is another great example. Choosing to abandon the overde-signed safety that characterizes Rhodes's illustration, Moss proposed instead to largely free the structure from the ground.[7] Held down at four anchoring points, which saved precious installation time and made the structure more flexible to changes in loca-tion, Moss created a revolutionary model that chal-lenged the rectilinear geometries of the traditional tent through an elegant set of catenary curves. Later commercially licensed as the Parawing, even its name implied flight.

The single most important and surprising inno-vation of the last century, however, is the idea of a tent that could be *completely* unmoored from the stakes that hold it fast to the ground while remain-ing, in every sense of the word, a fully pitched tent. Interestingly, the incremental improvements that led to this advance weren't driven by the kind of structural considerations that yielded the Parawing. Rather, a key development lay in engaging the ground not as merely a surface to sit or sleep on, but as an integral tent surface all its own. The Forester Tent is an interesting starting point. The minimalist design was first introduced by Warren H. Miller, who at the turn of the twentieth century was widely recognized as one of the leading writers and recreational camping advocates in the United States. Commercially sold by Abercrombie & Fitch in the 1910 edition of their catalog, the Forester had walls that were pinned to the ground, but the ground itself inside the tent was left bare. The lack of a proper floor was typical for the period since it saved campers a lot of weight and bulk—a reasonable feature that probably applied to

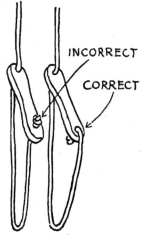

FIG. 9.—**Fixing a guy-rope in the slides.**

↑ 1940
Fixing a Guy Rope in the Slides, Druce Raven, *Let's Go Camping*.

❷ c. 1720
Chinese Soldiers Tent, Godfrey Rhodes, *Tents and Tent Life*.

❸ 1962
Charles W. (Bill) Moss, Flexible Hyperbolic Paraboloid Shelter, US Patent 3,060,949.

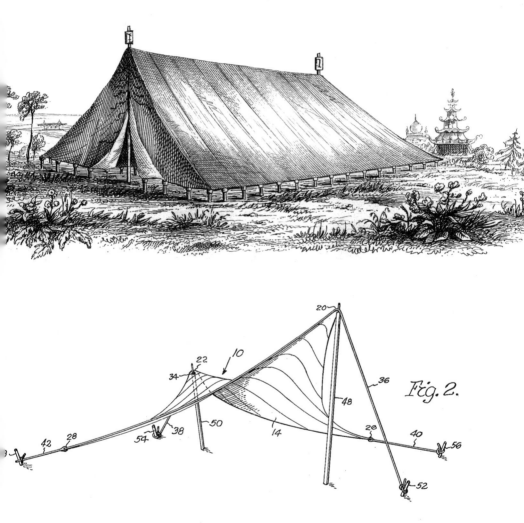

Fig. 2.

INVENTOR.

Charles W. Moss

BY Barthel + Bugbee

Attys

tents like those described by Godfrey Rhodes. Generally writing about tents from a military perspective, Rhodes could easily have been referring to recreational campers in the Forester tent when he observed that "to oblige them to seek [shelter] with the damp ground as their bed, or to bury themselves in the moist earth…is, to say the least, a most pernicious and destructive proceeding."[8] To remedy the situation, many enterprising campers customized their tents with a separate cotton ground tarp treated with paint to reduce humidity. Alternately, they padded the ground with a bed of pine branches, which was referred to during the period as *mountain goose*.[9] As for affluent campers staying overnight in relatively permanent camps like those maintained by the Wylie Permanent Camp Company in Yellowstone National Park, they could expect spacious and generously furnished tents built on wooden platforms, creating the illusion of a real hotel room absent the discomforts of the typical tent. Without such sturdy floors, however, tents from this period remained highly susceptible to leaking rain, wind drifts, bugs, and snakes that would infiltrate the gap where structure met ground. Attempts to address these shortcomings included sod cloths, typically twelve-inch wide strips of fabric that were sewn to the lower edges of the tent. Weighed down with rocks, they produced a "wind- and bug-proof seal at the juncture of the ground and walls."[10] If sod cloths helped turn the corner, so to speak, in addressing this critical interface, then the 1913 patent belonging to Ferdinand Eberhardt (1869–1956) and titled *Combined Tent and Ground Floor Cloth* (US Patent 1,057,628) took the idea to its logical conclusion, an integral, fully sewn-in floor.[11] But with greater security came less comfort. With the Forester, a tent with no floor and no front door, Miller had doubled down on economy of weight as a driving feature; what Eberhardt proposed was virtually a sealed fabric cocoon that would have been extremely hard to illuminate and cross ventilate.

↑ 1910
"Tanalite" Waterproof Forester's Tents, Abercrombie and Fitch Co. catalog, 1910 ed.

↗ 1933
Illustration from Frank H. Cheley, *Camping Out*, featuring a tent equipped with sod cloths.

→ 1913
Ferdinand Eberhardt, Combined Tent and Ground Floor Cloth, US Patent 1,057,628.

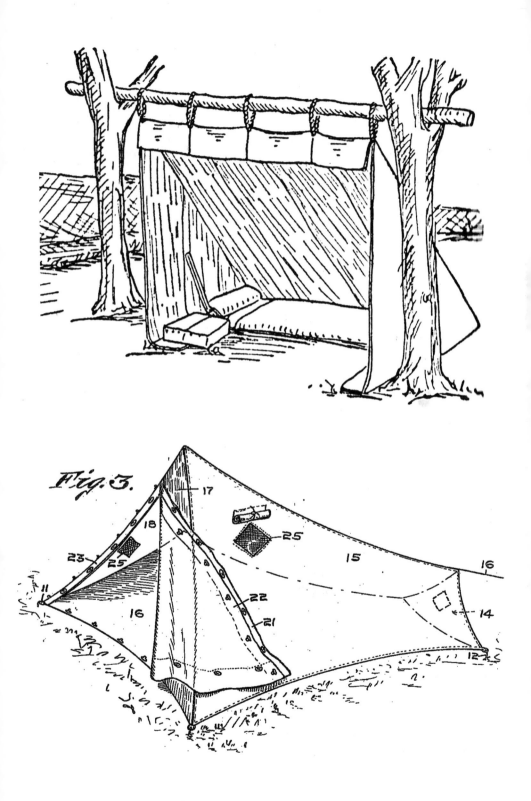

Fig.3.

Claiming a tent in which "the covering is stretched solely by the framework without the necessity for staving it by means of ropes and pegs," Jarl Reinhaldt Lönnqvist (1896–1972) was the first to recognize the structural potential of the sewn-in floor. The Finnish inventor first patented his design in Great Britain in 1932 (GB Patent 377,831) and later commercialized his operation as the Sopu Tent (*Telttaliike Sopu*) in Helsinki that same decade.[12] The Sopu is perhaps the oldest direct descendant of the contemporary dome tent: its arching form was innovative in an era where rigid A-frames still dominated the market, though it was still not entirely new for the period. At the time, similar profiles could be achieved by using permanently curved bentwood poles, as was the case in the tents designed by George Marston (1882–1940) for the famed 1914 Shackleton Antarctic expedition; alternately, bent forms could be obtained by planting the ends of a thin, flexible pole into the ground, as had been observed, for example, by Sir Francis Galton (1822–1911) in English gypsy tents in *The Art of Travel* (1855) as well as in the 1924 edition of the *Popular Mechanics Auto Tourist's Handbook*.[13] Lönnqvist understood that bending tent poles was like stringing a bow—a simple rope could provide the tensile strength required to resist the arc's tendency to straighten back to its original state. The shorter the string, the tighter (and higher) the arc. Imagining as an analog for his design a four-sided, domed tent held by a pair of tightly strung bows crossing at the tent's apex, Lönnqvist proposed connecting the ends of these structural arcs directly to the corners of the square floor; substituting for the resistance offered by the bowstrings, the heavy cotton floor would be naturally stretched taut as a result of its four corners being pulled away from the center of the tent. Further, the tensile capacity in the cotton duck ensured that the exact profile of the arcs remained consistent with each installation. Finally, Lönnqvist

⬆ 1957
Demonstrating the assembly and structural integrity of the Sopu tent. Photographer unknown.

➔ 1932
Reinhaldt Lönnqvist, An Improved Tent, GB Patent 377,831.

Fig. 1.

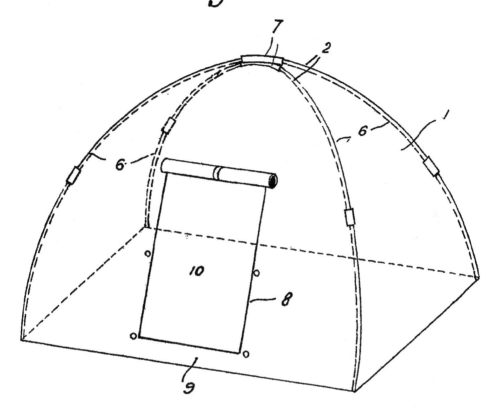

Fig. 2.

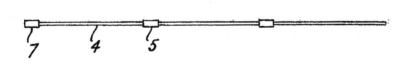

Fig. 3.

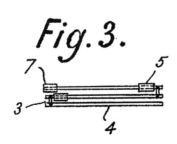

suggested guiding the two arching poles through long and narrow fabric sleeves on the outer surface of the four tent walls, producing the now-familiar dome shape.

With the Sopu's internal tensioning system, Lönnqvist had achieved something miraculous— a tent that could be easily moved about the campsite without first being struck down. Taking a cue from the gypsy camps depicted by French architect Eugène Emmanuel Viollet-le-Duc (1814–1879) and the nineteenth-century Conestoga wagons known as prairie schooners that roamed the Western prairies, it was only one more step to imagine a mobile version of the tent that could be placed on wheels, towed by cars, and easily transported across great distances.[14] Thus the hybridization of the tent and the automobile had begun in earnest. Spurned by several midcentury editions of *Popular Mechanics*, nearly three-quarters of the reported 160,000 trailers roaming the American landscape during the 1930s were home-built by weekend tinkerers.[15] By the end of the decade, there were several factory-built options on the market. Some, like the trailer proposed by W. B. MacDonald Jr. (US Patent 2,481,230), could be compacted during transport and partially unfolded at the campsite; others, like the Kozy Coach and the aerodynamic Airstream, were hard-shelled and included amenities like a fully functioning kitchen, a toilet, and a shower.[16] Soon, the Hollywood motion picture cameraman J. Roy Hunt (1884–1972) envisioned an iteration of the modern house trailer that could be self-propelled; he designed and crafted a limited number of vehicles built on a Ford chassis, known as Hunt House Cars (1935–1945), that count among the first antecedents of the modern RV.

⬆ c. 1930
Rooftop camping tent on a 1930s Fiat. Photographer unknown. The ladder at the front of the vehicle provides access to the elevated tent.

➡ 1949
W. B. MacDonald Jr., Vehicle Trailer, US Patent 2,481,230.

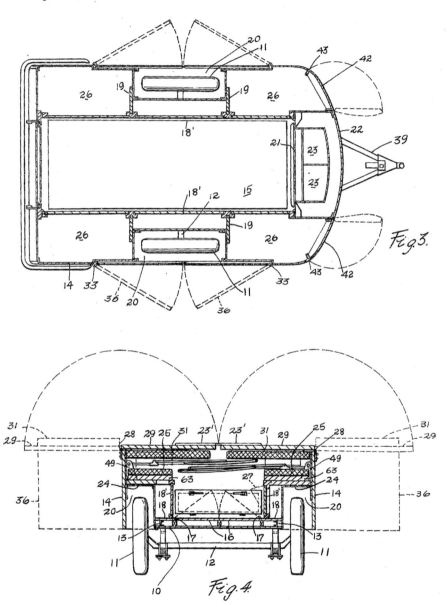

Fig.3.

Fig.4.

INVENTOR.

William B. MacDonald, Jr.

BY

Hrs Attorney.

Smaller, Lighter, Faster

The less a man carries in his pack, the more he can carry in his head.[17]
—HORACE KEPHART

Despite their central claim to mobility, tents remained large and cumbersome affairs until the very end of the nineteenth century. There was the heavy cotton duck, to be sure, but the poles tenting the fabric off the ground were often the single most critical feature in determining the portability of the structure. Designed in 1867 by Confederate general Henry Hopkins Sibley (1816–1886), the spacious twelve-man, conical Sibley tent (US Patent 14,740) required an impressive center mast no less than twenty feet tall.[18] Similarly, E. M. Hatton observed in *The Tent Book* (1979) that the hunting encampments of seventeenth-century Indian sultans were reportedly so extravagant that they involved caravans led by as many as sixty elephants, two hundred camels, one hundred mules, and one hundred men.[19] To this end, the author notes that transport operations were divided up into two separate convoys, each called peiche-kanés (houses which precede), in which one such deployment kept "a constant distance of one day's journey in advance of the other." This was done so that at day's end a fully prepared camp was ready for the sultan as he and his entourage stopped for the night.[20] This, of course, brings to mind the way KOA (Kampgrounds of America) promised the same normative experience at any one of its hundreds of facilities across the country.

Ironically, as tents like the Sopu became increasingly lighter, more compact, and easier to install, so grew the capacity of the automobile to transport greater amounts of cargo. For the modern camper pulling up to the campsite in their sport utility vehicle, bulky camping gear hardly seems a concern in the way it would have been one hundred years ago. Indeed, late

❷ 1921
Illustration from Elon Jessup, *The Motor Camping Book*, depicting the hybridization of vehicle and tent that would become the precursor of the modern RV.

Two single lean-to tents of the Stoll type, one with bed attached and the other to serve as a living room.   (See Chapter X.)

nineteenth-century recreational campers traveling deep into the woods on foot put a premium on portability. Warren H. Miller encouraged enthusiasts of the period to "never carry anything into the woods that you can easily make with the materials ready at hand."[21] A thick rope could be strung between two large trees, for example, and function as an improvised ridgepole; stakes could be made from dead branches lying about the campsite; and small trees could be felled and used as supports, as illustrated in the 1916 watercolor *Camp and Waterfall* by John Singer Sargent (1856–1925). Describing the structure needed to pitch the Forester tent, Miller offered that "I never saw yet, in the U.S.A, a country where these 3 poles could not be had in any thicket in five minutes."[22] For his part, Horace Kephart suggested that in a pinch, campers could use their rifles as tentpoles.[23] A paragon of minimalism, Kep's own pyramid-shaped George Tent could be suspended from a single tree.[24]

Fig. 43.—George Tent

It should come as no surprise that the most revolutionary technological breakthroughs in twentieth-century tent design were led not by stodgy commercial outfits like the Coleman Company or some of its midcentury peers, but by young, fearless climbers who went on to establish leading brands like The North Face, Sierra Designs, A16, and JanSport during the 1960s. These adventurers faced conditions far more extreme than those described by Miller and Kephart. In addition to confronting fast-changing weather and brutal winds sweeping narrow, exposed rocky shelves, climbing expeditions require careful planning for forward ascents in which all supplies (e.g., tent, sleeping bags, clothing, food, fuel) have to be packed in en route for the summit. In fact, this trend toward minimalization had begun a full century before those leading brands were ever established. The British mountaineer Edward Whymper (1840–1911), best known for leading the first ascent of the Matterhorn in 1865, should be properly credited among those leading innovators.

⬆ **1957**
George Tent, Horace Kephart, *Camping and Woodcraft*, 18th ed.

➡ **1916**
John Singer Sargent, *Camp and Waterfall*.

In *Scrambles Amongst the Alps in the Years 1860–'69* (1871), Whymper recalled the four-person tent he devised specifically for the expedition: the wedge-shaped structure was supported by four long ash poles, arranged in pairs at both ends of the tent to form inverted *V*'s, or shears. An important aspect of the alpinist's design was its ease of installation. Connected by a single bolt near its highest point, each pair of poles could be easily hinged open or closed; as for the fabric, it was permanently stapled to these same poles. The result was a tent that "could be unrolled and set up by two persons in three minutes, a point of no small importance during extreme weather."[25] Here again, the length of the poles proved a critical factor: an illustration of Luc Meynet, the local porter from Breuil who proved "invaluable as a tent-bearer" during the Matterhorn expedition, suggested the relative length of the rolled-up tent was about six feet.[26] Given contemporary expeditions in which a comparable structure would list as three to five pounds, the twenty-three pounds shouldered by Meynet were far from inconsiderable and a good example of the hidden costs associated with such prestigious expeditions.

Thomas Hiram (T. H.) Holding (1844–1930), a British tailor and cycling enthusiast, is perhaps the most important early standout and innovator in addressing heft and compaction. In 1897, he embarked on a three-day bike tour of Ireland. Thanks to Meynet, Whymper never experienced for himself the true weight of his invention. Holding prided himself on self-reliance, however—everything had to fit on *his* bike. He devised an eleven-ounce wedge tent made of Japanese silk that was held by two thin uprights situated at the front and end walls.[27] Holding's most important and enduring contribution lies in segmenting these structural poles to make them easier to transport, such that they "are almost imperceptible when hitched to the off fork of a bicycle."[28] The first ingenious system he proposed functioned like a folding rule, its wood battens secured

⬆ ⬆ ⬆ 1871
My Tent-Bearer—The Hunchback, Edward Whymper, *Scrambles Amongst the Alps in the Years 1860–'69*.

⬆ ⬆ 1926
Illustration in Stoll Outing Equipment, *Practical Camp Equipment*: "A bag for the arch supports, as well as a carrying bag for tent, are included with all sizes of Clear Space Tents."

⬆ 1969
A camper on the move, his tent affixed to the top of his "packbag." Photographer unknown.

⬀ 1871
Alpine Tent, Edward Whymper, *Scrambles Amongst the Alps in the Years 1860–'69*.

ALPINE TENT.

to one another with copper rivets and rings to form a pole that stood "as firm as if in one piece."[29] Later, Holding proposed breaking down the pole into short bamboo segments strengthened with steel ferrules that fit together end to end. Advertising a system of thirty-inch telescoping segments made from hollow tubing that, incredibly, was designed to reach lengths of up to twelve feet, the 1910 edition of the Abercrombie & Fitch catalog suggests that Holding's ideas had taken hold and would soon become the industry standard.[30]

This is not to say that the process of compacting the tent did not bring about its own set of challenges. In fact, putting components back together was just as important as breaking them down. More parts made them likelier to get strewn about the campsite or lost altogether. In addition, there was the puzzle of fitting so many loose components in the right order. The Canadian James H. Blair (1881–1955) faced a similar challenge when trying to devise a compact rod to clean his shooting rifle: he ingeniously proposed running a continuous chain through the hollow tubular components forming the rod.[31] As such, the instrument would remain whole at all times and more compact when not in use. A few decades later, it was Harry H. Harsted's (1897–1945) posthumous 1945 patent for the Foldable Antenna (US Patent 2,379,577) that established itself as the true forebear of the modern tent pole.[32] Working, as Blair had, with multiple segments, the Chicago inventor used a long, spring-loaded coil and turnscrew system to regulate tension of the internal cable. A tighter fit would bring the segments together into a rigid upright, and loosening the cable rendered the pole more flexible to the point that it could be bent. Completely releasing the cable provided enough give to allow the camper to pull the segments apart and compact the pole for storage or transport.

These dual properties of compactness and flexibility are key to understanding contemporary tent specifications. As explained earlier, poles like those

↑ **1897**
Thomas Hiram (T. H.) Holding's *Cycle and Camp in Connemara* describes the first camping trip that Holding and two of his friends took in 1897

↗↗ **1908**
Illustration from Thomas Hiram (T. H.) Holding, *The Camper's Handbook*, depicting disassembled tent poles packed in their carry bag.

↗ **1908**
Folding of the Battens, Thomas Hiram (T. H.) Holding, *The Camper's Handbook*.

↗ **1945**
Harry H. Harsted, Foldable Antenna, US Patent 2,379,577.

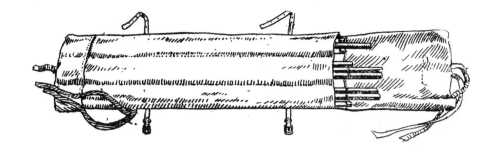

N.° IV

FOLDING OF THE BATTENS.

Diagram V is the battens as they fold up flat, making a total of 27-ins. when folded.

N.° V

Plan for Joints to provide compact folding

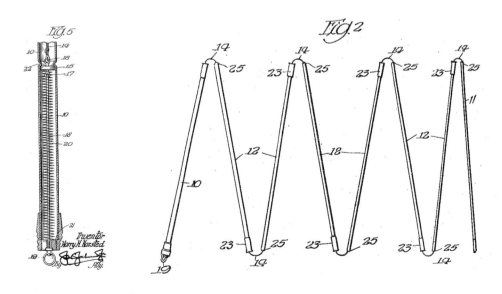

used for the Sopu were no longer simply required to
span the distance from floor to ceiling, as Holding
himself had demanded, but rather the height *and* the
length of the tent in a single, leaping arc. Derived
from an internal, highly elastic nylon and rubber
bungee cord stringing hollow tubes made of aluminum, carbon fiber, or fiberglass, modern poles are as
long, light, and compact as they are flexible. A case
in point: the revolutionary Oval Intention, a tent
inspired by the geodesic domes of the architect R.
Buckminster Fuller (1895–1983) and commercialized
in 1975 by The North Face, is a mountaineering tent
framed by three sets of aluminum alloy poles or
"wands," the longest of which is fifteen feet long and
can be bent to a height of three and a half feet.[33]

Fabric, Environment

*It should be possible to make an artificial, glutinous
composition, much resembling, if not full as good, nay
better, than that excrement, or whatever other substance
it be out of which the silkworm wire-draws his clew.*[34]
—DR. ROBERT HOOKE

For all the unique insights he contributed to the
compaction of camping gear, Holding was foremost a
tailor by trade. The parallels between tents and clothing are fascinating and bear further consideration.
There are, of course, the materials and tools they
share—the fabric, the thread, the snaps, the zippers,
the sewing machines, and the like. In *The Camper's
Handbook* (1908), Holding even provided campers
with a pattern, similar to one for a piece of clothing,
to realize his lightweight tent. Just like with a garment, the tent was broken down into its constituent
parts, flat shapes that could be set down onto a roll of
fabric, traced, cut, and sewn together. While larger in
size than any garment, Holding's instructions were,
in fact, far easier to execute than even the simplest

⊙ c. 1970
Bruce Hamilton, photograph of
The North Face sewing room,
with the company's famed Oval
Intention tent attached to the
wall (top, center).

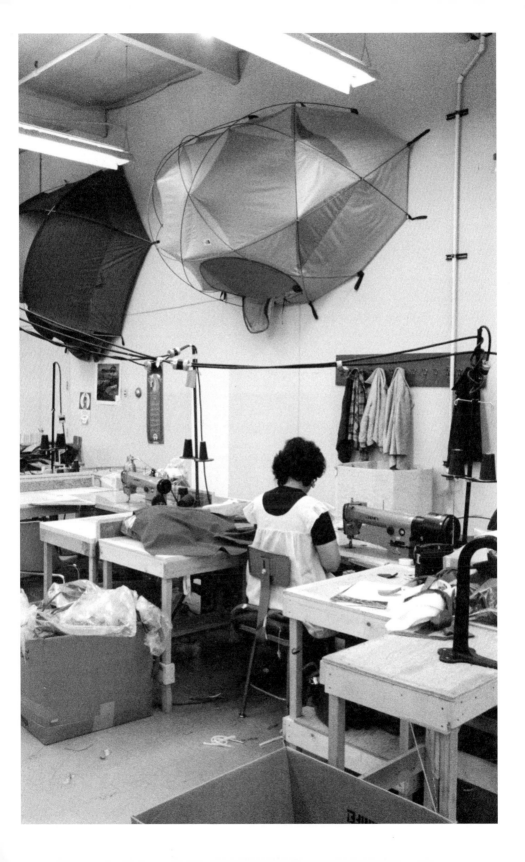

shirt or pair of pants, resulting in a single surface that could later be hemmed and reinforced with a few long strips of thick fabric tape.

For the modern camper considering these instructions, it is plain to see how tent technology has evolved over the past one hundred years: modern dome tents are complex, three-dimensional structures. They are designed using cutting- edge architectural modeling software and assembled with exacting precision by the most experienced seamsters. To be sure, little remains of the DIY ethos celebrated in Holding's book. In the span of fifty years, even the four sagging walls of the first dome-shaped Sopu tent, a design that would have seemed out of this world to Holding, were supplanted by the crisp, taut surfaces of The North Face's Oval Intention, a similar volume realized with no less than thirty-one individual pieces of fabric.[35] Hinting at the complex three-dimensional puzzle of stress distribution posed by his revolutionary Geodesic Tent (US Patent 2,914,074), R. Buckminster Fuller explained that he was "tailoring the several pieces which go to make up the tent."[36] In putting these elements together, the prolific inventor was using the term *tailoring* (and, by extension, the techniques of the trade) to convey both the process of breaking down the dome into a set of discrete surfaces and the assembly of these respective parts—a process akin to architectural tectonics. It is indeed interesting to consider tentmaking as having architectural merit: Bill Moss, designer of the famed Pop Tent, was certainly channeling the celebrated German architect Frei Otto (1925–2015) when he offered that "the seams became sculptural drawings in space, completely spontaneous and poetically descriptive."[37] At the same time, the entirety of the tent is subjected to the seamster's meticulous handiwork, with the poles of the most high-tech, lightweight backpacking tents now remade as inflatable fabric tubes.[38] In penetrating this new and exciting realm, these architectures of fabric, we are far away indeed from a flat pair of pants.

⬆ **c. 1970**
Bruce Hamilton, photograph of R. Buckminster Fuller under an early prototype of the Dome tent on a visit to The North Face.

↗ **1908**
A flattened "A" tent pattern from Thomas Hiram (T. H.) Holding, *The Camper's Handbook*.

↗ **1959**
R. Buckminster Fuller, Geodesic Tent, US Patent 2,914,074.

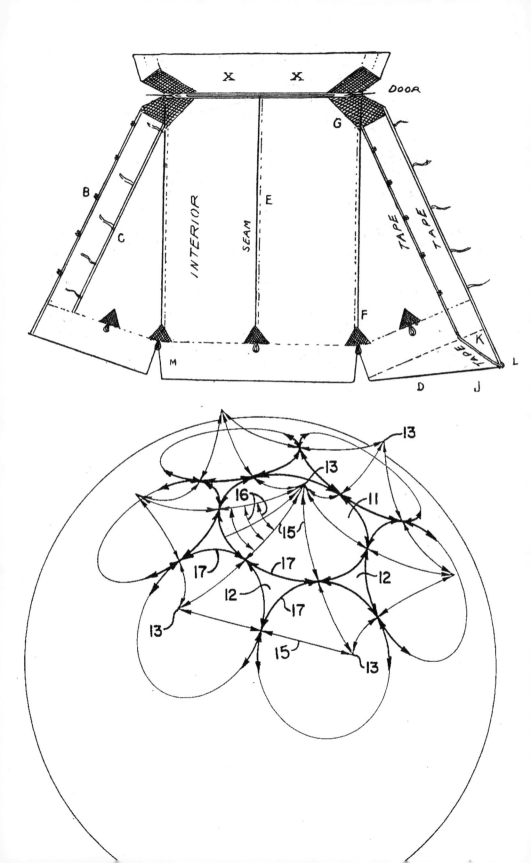

Moving beyond the parallels in execution, the analogy between tents and clothing had already begun to capture the imagination of many of Holding's peers at the turn of the twentieth century. Instead of packing the tent into a tight roll and strapping it down for transport, could the shelter be *worn* as clothing when it was not deployed on the ground for the night? Doing so would help reduce both redundancies and weight. The 1902 patent (US Patent 703,245) proposed by William S. Faulkner (1868–1945) provides an early illustration of this concept: here is a tent that could pull double duty as a poncho.[39] In the proposed design, a small aperture fitted with a flap at the side of the tent functions as a window through which the head passes when the camper sets out on the trail. A careful review of patents from this period reveals that Faulkner's proposal was but one of a growing obsession in the genre, each one as silly and impractical as the next. For his part, the Austrian industrial magnate Isidor Mautner (1852–1930) proposed to convert his shelter into an overcoat (US Patent 535,066), its sleeves protruding awkwardly at either side of the tent like venting ducts.[40] Similarly, Frank H. Gotsche (1864–1951) proposed a conical Sibley tent whose ten triangular panels, edged with buttons and buttonholes, could be detached and reconfigured into either a low-lying ground tent or, alternately, worn as a poncho (US Patent 901,802).[41] If none of these ideas ever found commercial success, Faulkner and his peers would be comforted to note that they were at least right in one respect: the camper browsing a large-surface REI store will likely find products designed by tent manufacturers like The North Face in just about any area of the store. Some will attribute this fact to the global reach of the brand, but from a material standpoint, there is virtually no difference between a tent and a raincoat. In fact, the parallel extends to most camping gear: tents, jackets, shirts, pants, shorts, sleeping bags, backpacks, stuff sacks—even shoes—are all now largely made from synthetic fibers.

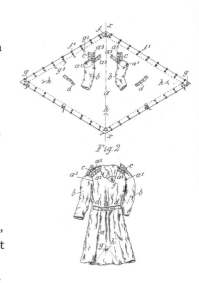

Fig. 2

⬆ **1895**
Isidor Mautner, Tent, US Patent 535,066.

➲ **1902**
William S. Faulkner, Shelter Tent Half and Poncho, US Patent 703,245.

No. 703,245.

Patented June 24, 1902.

W. S. FAULKNER.
SHELTER TENT HALF AND PONCHO.
(Application filed July 16, 1901.)

(No Model.)

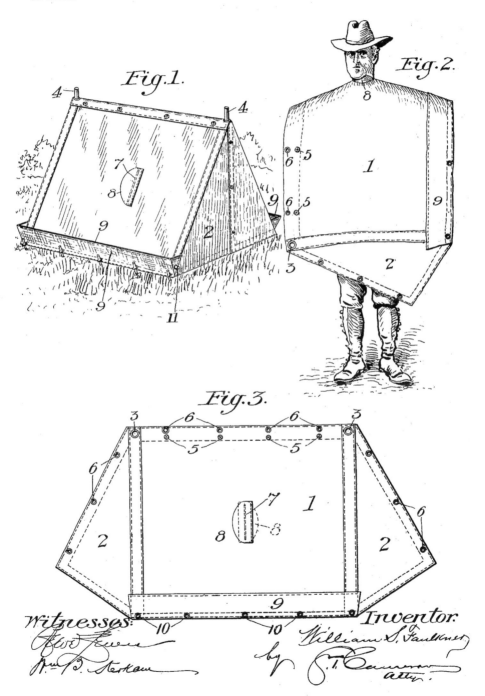

Fig.1.

Fig.2.

Fig.3.

Constructed for centuries from natural fibers like goat's hair, wool, silk, or cotton, tents had a long-standing reputation for being dark and dingy spaces. The watercolor *Inside a Tent in the Canadian Rockies* (1916), by John Singer Sargent (pages 204–5) is one of those rare illustrations that captures the interior atmosphere of this important camping space at the turn of the century. Outfitting the tent with door ties, window flaps, sod cloths, and fully surfaced floors had undoubtedly helped secure the interior from pesky bugs and snakes. Further, the use of wax, paint, and other chemicals—useful agents in fireproofing the heavy cotton duck and increasing its resistance to rain and rot—added considerable weight to the fabric, further rendering it incapable of venting the excess moisture exhaled from the breath of sleeping campers. Indeed, a thickened ambience seems to leap out of Singer's watercolor study. Sealed against outdoor views and light, its air damp and pungent with the smell of infrequently washed bodies and smelly clothes, the tent would surely have been a miserable place to rest.

The architectural historian Reyner Banham invites us to reconsider this unfortunate paradigm. For him, the tent was a dynamic environmental system in which a delicate balance among many competing objectives—providing shade, deflecting wind, excluding rain, retaining internal heat, and maintaining privacy—remained open to careful modulation.[42] Here again, a comparison between tents and clothing offers useful insights. The experienced hiker approaches each outing tactically, setting out with a wide range of clothing articles: a wicking base layer for sweat, a series of heavier garments for warmth, a water-resistant outer shell for wind or rain. As the weather improves, these items are progressively shed and returned to the day pack. A veteran of the trail will tell you it is better to have three or four thin layers at the ready than a single thicker insulating garment, since layers allow a camper to carefully calibrate her comfort in response to changing temperature and weather conditions.

⊘ **1969**

Environmental Behaviour of a Tent, Reyner Banham, *The Architecture of the Well-Tempered Environment*.

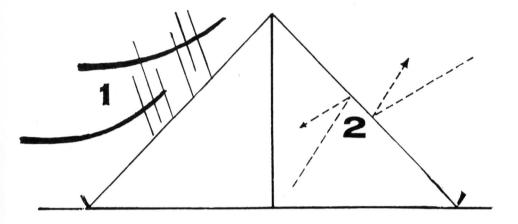

Environmental behaviour of a tent.

1. Tent membrane deflects wind and excludes rain
2. Reflects most radiation, retaining internal heat, excluding solar heat, maintaining privacy

Similarly, synthetic fibers created an opportunity for designers to set aside the static and largely *defensive* heavy, dark, dingy prewar cotton duck tents in favor of a dynamic system of complementary layers. The introduction of nylon by the chemist Wallace Hume Carothers (1896–1937) and the DuPont Company in 1938 (US Patent 2,130,948) would have a tremendous impact on all aspects of daily life—from toothbrushes to clothing, from drapes and carpets to camping gear.[43] After the initial nylon stockings craze of May 1940, the company shifted its entire synthetics operation to supply the war effort. Early applications of nylon for essential military gear included parachutes and tents. Dr. Susannah Handley wrote in *Nylon: The Story of a Fashion Revolution* (1999) that DuPont expanded its usage to a range of equipment including "ropes, tyre cord, tents, uniforms, mosquito netting, tarpaulins, hammocks, webbing, bomber noses and shoelaces."[44] The advantages of synthetic fibers were many. Nylon was strong, resistant to rot, slow to ignite, fast drying, shrink proof, and far lighter than cotton or silk. The material did not breathe well, however, so to simply remake an old-fashioned tent out of nylon would bring about serious problems.

Based on what we can glimpse in a 1943 edition of the *DuPont Magazine*, the use of nylon in early military tents resulted in designs that looked much the same as they had before the war. Early applications of the synthetic fiber to postwar models like Bill Moss's Pop Tent and the popular Draw-Tite model—from the company Eureka! based in Binghamton, New York—followed the same trajectory.[45] It would take innovators like Åke Nordin (1936–2013) to address these potential shortcomings and bring a new paradigm to market. Following in a long line of outdoor enthusiasts like Whymper one hundred years before, Nordin, a Swedish hiker who founded the outdoor gear company Fjällräven in 1960, found early commercial success with an innovative hiking

↑ 1943
A US solider in his nylon tent. Photographer unknown. *The DuPont Magazine*, April–May 1943.

⊘ 1957
Gear at the campsite, in Franklin M. Reck and William Moss, *The Ford Treasury of Station Wagon Living* (partial view). Photographer unknown. According to Reck and Moss, the gear includes "seven tents, five boats and forty-five other items designed for camp comfort and outdoor fun!"

backpack he helped develop. In 1964, the company released its Thermo tent, believed to be the originator of the modern two-layer tent.[46] Nordin ingeniously proposed delaminating the functional needs of the tent into separate pieces of equipment: first, a highly breathable nylon bug screen is combined with an impermeable floor to form the permanent inner core of the tent.[47] On most clear summer nights, this first layer can stand alone, since pesky mosquitoes and morning dew are the only real obstacles to comfort; under cold or rainy conditions, Nordin proposed suspending a thicker nylon rain fly a few inches above the inner envelope to shield the camper from the elements while simultaneously facilitating the passage of air and keeping the interior dry. The Thermo was met with immediate commercial success and tested under extreme conditions with a Scandinavian expedition to Greenland later that same year.

Conclusions

The story of synthetics is the story of the eternal competition between nature and artifice.[48]
—SUSANNAH HANDLEY

The two-layer, all-season tent merely represents the outermost manifestation of a much larger system designed to insulate the human body from the elements. We begin with intimate layers of clothing, move to the warm cocoon of the down sleeping bag, the inflatable air mattress, the impermeable floor of the tent. We imagine the clicks of long zippers as campers gingerly move in and out of the layers of this system. Before we reach the bug screen, we encounter the bodies of other campers, for the role of the tent is not only to insulate but to bring occupants together. It is here that the social dimension of camping begins.

↥ ↥ **1923**
A tent made from screen netting. Photographer unknown.

↥ **1910–1913**
Edward Adrian (E. A.) Wilson, *Sledging in April, Camping After Dark*. Executed during the British Antarctic Expedition of 1910–1913 (also known as the Terra Nova Expedition), Wilson's sketches were retrieved after he perished on the Ross Ice Shelf.

❷ **1967**
Promotional illustration featuring the Fjällräven Thermo G66 tent. Note the external rain fly (the gray area bounded by dashed lines) and the internal nylon bug screen.

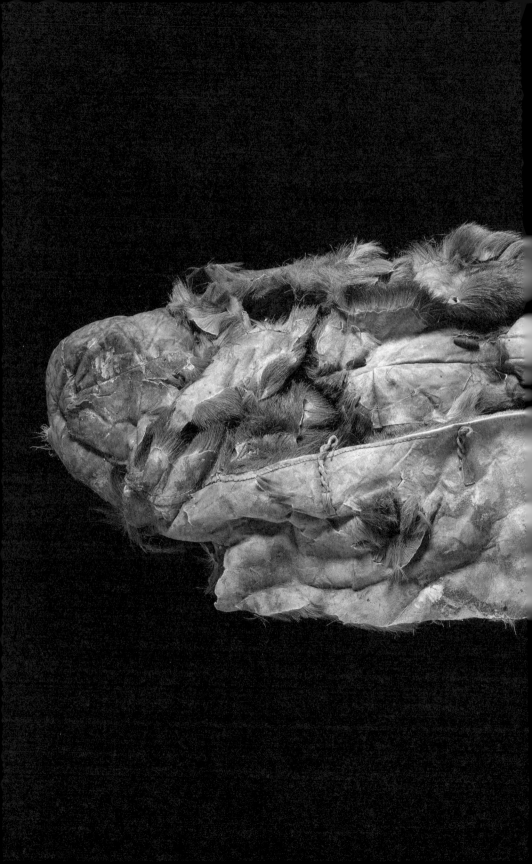

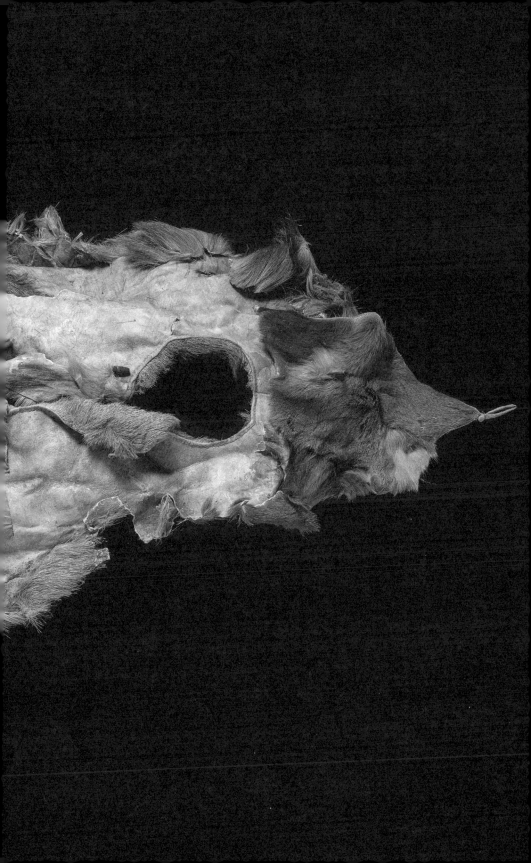

SLEEPING BAG

Let us have one more whack at the sleeping-bag—
that accursed invention of a misguided soul.[1]
—EMERSON HOUGH

Though we can precisely date the emergence of the term *sleeping-bag* to the mid-nineteenth-century memoirs and speeches of the Arctic explorers Sherard Osborn (1822–1875) and Sir Robert McClure (1807–1873), we do now know that the expression did not immediately catch on.[2] Throughout that period and well into the twentieth century, authors and experts circuitously referred to the familiar implement of gear in different ways, calling it a *sleeping-sack* (1856); a *drugget bag* (1860); a *blanket-bag* (1871); a *strong linen sack* (1872); a *knapsack bag* (1872); a *peasants' sack* (1872); *a traveling rug* (1876); *a sleeping valise* (1903); a *sleeping-pocket* (1908); and a *quilt bag* (1918).[3] The interchangeability of these terms suggests that the sleeping bag's function, design, and—to believe certain hearty woodsmen—its sheer necessity, were not yet fully settled matters. Even a century later, writer

c. 1881–1884
Reindeer skin sleeping bag used during the Greely Expedition to Ellesmere Island on the northwest coat of Greenland.

1871
The Blanket-Bag, Edward Whymper, *Scrambles Amongst the Alps in the Years 1860–'69.*

THE BLANKET-BAG.

John Steinbeck remained unconvinced: "Anyone who doesn't prefer a good bed in a warm room to lumpy pine boughs and a sleeping bag that feels like a plaster cast is either insane or an abysmal liar."[4]

It's in the Bag

If you wish to "rough it," spread your blanket for one night on the ground beneath the starry sky. The next night you will have a bed made.[5]

—FRANK A. BATES

Steinbeck certainly had a point, but it hardly seems fair to compare the comforts of an indoor bed to a sleeping bag. Horace Kephart called the problem "of a good portable bed" the most important issue facing the camper.[6] For Kephart, a leading expert in the field, tying the prospect of outdoor sleep with one of the heaviest and bulkiest components of the modern home suggests that many campers were still trying to recreate the domestic conditions they had left behind. The folding chest "bed" presented by General Peter Gansevoort to George Washington in Schuylerville, New York, during the American Revolutionary War, is an early case in point. One can scarcely imagine that its wafer-thin mattress would have been comfortable in warm or cold weather, let alone portable.[7] Adirondack campers in search of a more rustic experience improvised cots by planting heavy sticks into the ground, tying crossbars between them, and lacing a supporting trellis from thin rope. For their part, wealthier nineteenth-century tourists who sought to escape the comforts of leading national park hotels in favor of a slightly edgier experience did not have to go to any such extremes. Permanent camps like those maintained by the Wylie Company in Yellowstone or Camp Curry in Yosemite presented patrons with an opportunity to sleep in real beds supported by real mattresses inside large canvas tents erected on sturdy

◑ c. 1885
Henry Patrick Marie, Count Russell-Killough (1834–1909), an early enthusiast of Pyrenean exploration. Photographer unknown.

➋ 1908
Sleeping Bag, Back and Front, Thomas Hiram (T. H.) Holding, *The Camper's Handbook*.

➌ 1903
William Pascoe, *The Wolseley Sleeping-Bag*, in Harry Roberts, *The Tramp's Hand-book*.

SLEEPING BAG, BACK AND FRONT.

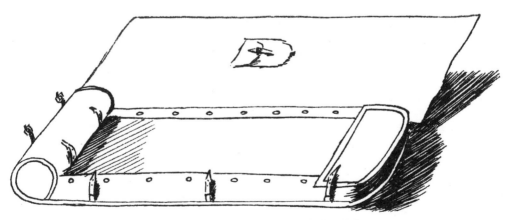

THE WOLSELEY SLEEPING-BAG

wood platforms and furnished with wood stoves and reading chairs, as well as, sometimes, desks and dressers. With these new facilities functioning more like the roadside motels they would soon inspire, there was no need for these visitors to pack in anything but their travel clothes.[8]

Today, the modern sleeping bag has replaced Kephart's portable bed as a staple of the overnight camping experience. There is something about wriggling into a dusty old sleeping bag that provides even young children bivouacking on the hardwood floor of their living room a feeling of excitement unlike that of slumbering in their own beds. How did this come to pass in such a short period of time? Like Osborn and his men, who "rolled up [their] beds, or rather sleeping- bags" on a cold mid-nineteenth-century morning, we must imagine a time immediately before the words themselves were uttered and the idea thus conceived—only then can we begin to glimpse why taking the restorative function of "sleep," detaching it from the space of the "bed," and placing it inside a "bag" may have seemed like an idea worth pursuing. [9]

For all the originality their new idea represented, Osborn and McClure were not suggesting that sleeping outdoors represented a new challenge. Social anthropologist Stephanie Bunn, specializing in Central Asian felt, observed that nomadic animal herders in the Middle East, Afghanistan, Central Asia, the Caucasus, and Eastern Europe had, since the Middle Ages, worn long, woolen cloaks known as *kepeneks*.[10] Fashioned from a single piece of boiled wool, the implement functioned as both full-length coat and a sleeping space. Noting their use in extreme weather, the author and researcher Marlene Lang observed that "when a shepherd wants to sleep, he puts a shoulder or the hood over his head and rolls the cloak around him. 'Only the dog and the donkey know you are there!'"[11]

The kepenek's carefully tailored measurements evoke the snug fit of a modern mummy bag—with

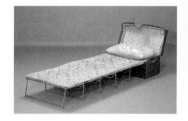

⬆ c. 1775
A folding camp bed used by George Washington during the American Revolutionary War. According to the Henry Ford Museum of American Innovation, the bed was made of linen, cotton, iron, steel, leather, and brass.

➋ 1915
Wylie Way tent interior, Yellowstone National Park. Photographer unknown.

one important difference. Shepherds cloaked in
a kepenek can continue to walk around and tend to
their flock, but the camper entering the cozy and
comforting cocoon of his sleeping bag is willing to
temporarily sacrifice his ability to propel himself
forward. The 1920s autocamping writer Elon Jessup
said it best when he suggested that "when you get
into a sleeping bag, you are in for keeps; you can't roll
out."[12] An implement prized for its portability, lightness, and minimal bulk is ultimately one from which
it is hard to escape. The French alpinist Pierre Allain
(1904–2000) might have had immobility in mind
when he introduced the pied d'éléphant, or elephant's
foot (note the singular), a large down "sock" that
evokes children hopping forth in an old-fashioned
potato sack race. A minimalist for whom a few ounces
represented the difference between a failed and a
successful climb, Allain was intrigued by the way the
upper portion of the traditional sleeping bag was
designed to protect the very same parts of the body
as the down jacket, which had first been introduced
by the Australian chemist and mountaineer George
Finch (1888–1970) on Everest in 1922. Imagining that
the climber could wear their jacket both day and
night, he proposed instead a half-length sleeping
bag to keep the immobilized feet and legs warm.[13]

The pied d'éléphant reminds us how much our
own contemporary perspectives regarding sleeping
bags are entrenched. It is hard nowadays to conceive
of a scenario in which a bag isn't designed to accommodate the entire body. If Allain's innovation led
to critical savings in weight and bulk, then the
Norwegian explorer Fridtjof Nansen (1861–1930)
can be credited with another, equally unusual effort
as he prepared for the first crossing of Greenland in
1888. Side by side, Allain and Nansen's bags would be
a sight to behold given their relative differences in
size and weight. Fearing that popular woolen models
offered by the likes of Dr. Gustav Jaeger (1832–1917)
and his Sanitary Woolen System Company would

⊕ 2013
Seyit Konyali, photograph of
a shepherd in Beyşehir, Turkey,
warming a newborn lamb inside
his kepenek.

not be warm enough, Nansen conceived of two large bags made of reindeer skin that could each fit three men (page 254). By forgoing individual sleeping bags, the explorer achieved two simultaneous goals: he reduced the overall weight of the gear per individual while increasing the comfort of his men "because the three [occupants] mutually profit by each other's heat."[14] Designed by a well-known furrier in Bergen, Norway, each bag was so large that it became a room all its own, swallowing its occupants whole so they could brave temperatures that dipped as low as −49°F/−45°C.

Inside/Outside

Being sack-like the sleeping bag retains the heat within and keeps the cold out.[15]
—CLAUDE P. FORDYCE

Once they had retired for the evening, Nansen and his team would have undoubtedly been in for a rough night's sleep on the ice. The heavy flaps and ties that secured the entrance to the bags ensured minimum heat loss throughout the night. The pelts were so thick they were nearly airtight, preventing any moisture from the occupants' breathing from being expelled outside the bag. Apsley Cherry-Garrard (1886–1959), who participated in Captain Robert Falcon Scott's (1868–1912) British Antarctic Expedition to the South Pole, also known as the Terra Nova Expedition (1910–1913), noted of his own equipment that "the trouble really began in your sleeping-bag, for it was far too cold to keep a hole open through which to breathe. So all night long our breath froze into the [animal] skins, and our respiration became quicker and quicker as the air in our bags got fouler and fouler."[16]

Reading these dramatic lines, we can imagine that Nansen faced a similar dilemma: fully sealing the bag against the outdoor elements made sense at first

↑ c. 1930
P. Dalmais, photograph of Pierre Allain's full-body weatherproof shell, known as the Système Intégral, in Raymond Gaché, "Le matériel de bivouac," *Alpinisme*, 1935.

➜ c. 1930
The down elements of Pierre Allain's Système Intégral include a jacket, the pied d'éléphant, and slippers. A thin inflatable mattress and an external waterproof shell complete the system. Photographer unknown.

since it quickly warmed up the interior cocoon. Over time, however, the occupants might suffocate since they would be forced to breathe in the very carbon dioxide their lungs had just exhaled. On the other hand, opening the flaps to some much needed (but glacially cold) fresh air would cause the bags, damp from sweat and heavy breath, to freeze. For Cherry-Garrard, "those obstinate coffins…were all our life to us," a perplexing remark that manages to sum up these early sleeping bags' curious amalgam of properties. They could be life-sustaining devices and deadly traps all at once.[17]

In a much-publicized spat with the outdoor gear supplier Gerry Cunningham (1922–2010) in *Summit* magazine in the late 1950s, the writer and outdoor enthusiast Harvey Manning (1925–2006) tried to tackle these challenges head on (quite literally) during the decade following World War II. With images of fighter pilots still fresh in his mind, Manning proposed hooking up the sleeping bag occupant to a snorkel/gas mask assembly that carried the camper's breathing exhalations to a bag of anhydrous calcium chloride designed to absorb excess moisture.[18] While technologically sound in many respects, the idea represented a sheer affront to the physical and emotional benefits of sleeping outdoors—something Adirondack Murray called forth in *Adventures in the Wilderness* (1869): "And then the waking! The air fresh with the aroma of the wilderness. The morning blowing its perfumed breezes into your face. The drip, drip of the odorous gum in the branches overhead, and the colors of russet, of orange, and of gold streaking the eastern sky."[19] Even with the greatest warmth assured, would camping still be worth it if there was nothing left to smell?

For Manning, president of the Washington State–based Cougar Mountaineers, a group of friends and enthusiasts who considered the "Issaquah Alps" their home base, the experiment was no doubt rhetorical, a hoax that likely never took place.[20] In a close reading

❷ **1888**
Half the Expedition in Its Sleeping Bag, Fridtjof Nansen, *The First Crossing of Greenland.*

❷ **1988**
James G. Phillips & Gordon K. Scott, Sleeping Bag With Snorkel Hood and Draft Curtain, US Patent 4,787,105. The patent recalls the snorkel/gas mask assembly that Harvey Manning first proposed in the pages of *Summit* magazine.

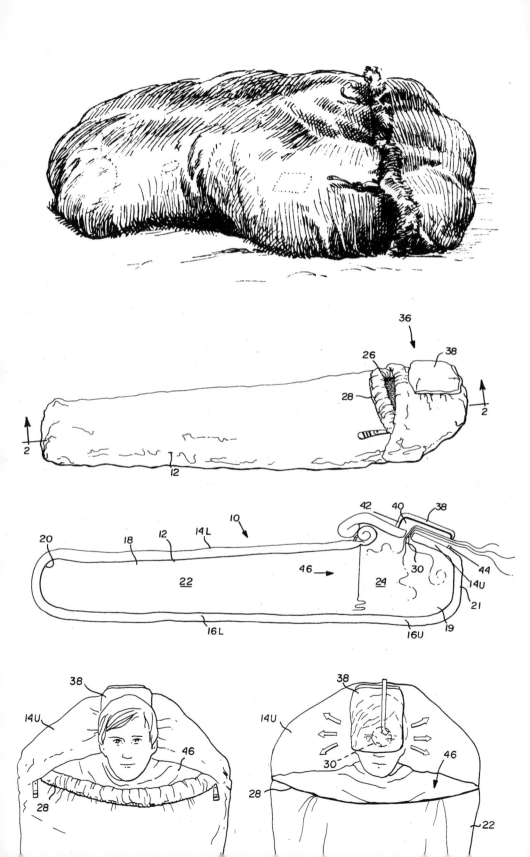

of the exchange between the two men over several issues of the magazine, Manning seemed in effect bent on challenging Cunningham's "very scholarly" technical expertise and goading him into legitimizing preposterous scenarios like this new bag.[21] However, the design did prove an important point: modulating the complex atmospheric interactions inside and around the sleeping bag represented, and would continue to represent, a critical and continuing factor of design innovation. Archived at the Scott Polar Research Institute at the University of Cambridge, England, is a touching photograph of the ill-fated Terra Nova Expedition to the Antarctic, in which Petty Officer Edgar Evans (1876–1912) and Tom Crean (1877–1938) are carefully mending their fur bags.[22] Looking at the image now, it is easy to see how their careful stitching would have resulted in an overly hermetic design. Damp from sweat and breathing, the insulating value of the thick pelts they had fashioned together was significantly diminished—in other words, too much of a "bag" may not be much of a good thing after all.

Let's think outside the bag, so to speak, and consider a different paradigm in which the body doesn't simply wriggle inside and out of a static envelope. Instead, let's imagine the same body engages the insulating material in a dynamic and reciprocal process of enclosure. The alpinist Edward Whymper, who long preferred the simplicity and minimal bulk of wool blankets when he camped at high altitudes in the nineteenth century (page 245), would surely have scoffed at Horace Kephart's ridiculously dry and technical instructions for achieving what on the surface may have seemed like a simple task: wrapping himself into a blanket. Kep's 208-word account is in fact so convoluted that it may take longer to read in full than to achieve:

To roll up in a blanket in such a way that you will stay snugly wrapped, lie down and draw the blanket over you like a coverlet, lift the legs without bending at the

⬆ **1911**
Herbert George Ponting, photograph of Petty Officer Edgar Evans and Tom Crean mending their sleeping bags during Captain Robert Falcon Scott's British Antarctic Expedition of 1910–1913, also known as the Terra Nova Expedition. Evans perished on February 17, 1912, during the return journey from the South Pole.

⬇ **c. 1890–1918**
Inughuit sleeping bag. According to the Smithsonian Institution, the item was probably acquired by Mink Wallace after 1910, when he returned to Greenland from New York City, where he was brought with his family in 1897 by Arctic explorer Robert E. Peary. Photographer unknown.

knee, and tuck first one edge smoothly under your legs then the other. Lift your hips and do the same there. Fold the far end under your feet. Then wrap the free edges similarly around your shoulders one under the other. You will learn to do this without bunching, and will find yourself in a sort of cocoon. This fold being turned under, stand with your back toward the blanket and draw its right-hand corner snugly up under the right armpit so that the triangle hangs down in front of you, and hold it firmly there. With left hand then draw the blanket up over left shoulder from behind, tight against nape of neck, and down in front. That leaves the left corner trailing on the ground before you. With a quick flirt throw this corner up over right shoulder and let it hang down your back, where it will stay of its own weight. You are now wrapped up but with right arm free. The blanket can be cast off in an instant.[23]

The fact that Kephart was still writing about blankets as late as 1917 suggests that sleeping bags had not yet fully taken hold as a key implement of camping gear, and this, nearly fifty years after they were first introduced. Did this mean that sleeping bags remained the exclusive province of fearless explorers? Would ordinary campers find any use in them? To be fair, an important advantage that traditional wool blankets had over sewn-up bag models like the popular Euklisia Rug, developed by the Pryce Jones Company of Newtown, Wales in 1876, was that they could be hung flat to dry during the day; alternately, the same blanket could be compacted into a bedroll that doubled as a rudimentary rucksack to carry gear and supplies. During this period before they finally went mainstream, experienced outdoorsmen began placing a higher premium on flexibility with respect to this critical implement of gear. They recognized that a good sleeping bag was also one that would be easy to get into, get out of, aerate, and modulate with respect to interior temperatures. With this goal in mind, they

⊙ **1947**
Folding double-bed blankets,
S. H. Walker, The Way to Camp.

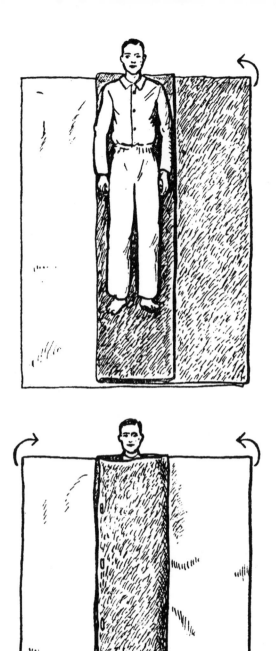

Folding double-bed blankets

proposed incorporating a range of temporary fasteners to convert folded blankets into secure bags that would not come undone if the camper rolled around the tent at night. Dr. Gustav Jaeger, for example, gained early notoriety for producing a camel-hair fleece bag edged with a series of buttons, the whole of which could be stored inside a solid protective case that doubled as a head support during the night. For his part, Warren H. Miller proposed a hybrid model equipped with eye loops, snap hooks, and buckles that he documented in his book *Camp Craft* (1915). A similar model put forth by Elon Jessup in his book *Roughing It Smoothly* (1923) featured a blanket folded lengthwise and equipped with series of opposing straps that could be tied together.

Consider the serendipitous fact that these important alterations were introduced at the very same moment that the zipper was first patented and commercialized. Robert Friedel, author of *Zipper: An Exploration in Novelty* (1994), noted that the earliest closure system was patented by Whitcomb L. Judson (1846–1909) as far back as 1893.[24] However, the device in its current form is attributed to Gideon Sundback (1880–1954), founder of the Hookless Fastener Company of Meadville, Pennsylvania, who described the Separable Fastener (US Patent 1,219,881) as "two flexible stringers…locked and unlocked by a sliding cam device mounted on both members, the locking being effected by movement in one direction and unlocking by an opposite movement."[25] Sundback envisioned that the device could replace buttons, snaps, buckles, ties, laces, and other temporary fasteners in a range of garments, such as pants, coats, gloves, and shoes, yet he could not foresee the ubiquity and impact of his invention over the next century. How many zippers does the average person operate in a single day, from backpacks to computer cases, trouser flies to jackets? Shortly after Sundback's patent was issued in 1917, the James Field Company was already marketing the Field Autokamp

⊘ 1907
Pure Camelhair Sleeping-Bag,
Gustav Jaeger, *Health-Culture.*

⊘ 1923
Drawing from Elon Jessup,
Roughing It Smoothly,
illustrating a sleeping bag made
from a blanket folded in thirds
and secured with ties.

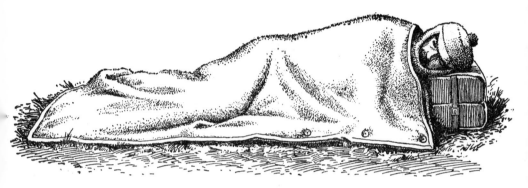

PURE CAMELHAIR SLEEPING-BAG.

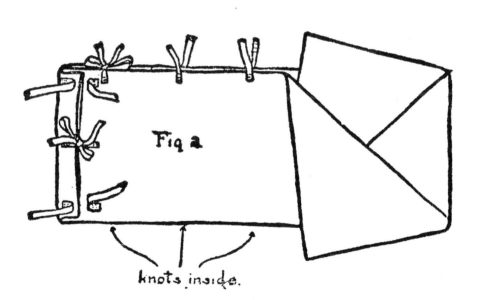

Fig a

knots inside.

Tent (1925), a model whose screen doors were secured with the help of the Hookless Fastener. A few years later in 1927, the Ideal Bedding Company began marketing sleeping bags outfitted with the same device (page 265).

In retrospect, it is safe to say that the success of Sundback's groundbreaking invention was due at least in part to the catchy new name *zipper*, conferred upon the device by the industrialist B. F. Goodrich (1841–1888), who was drawn to the clicking sounds it made as each row of protruding teeth met the cam. To be sure, using the original name of Sundback's invention in a sentence would have been a mouthful ("Psst—the Hookless Fastener on your jeans is open!"). Shouldn't something so effortless to use also be quick and easy to pronounce? Converting a series of hundreds of individual mechanical operations into a simple, buz-z-z-z-zing sound, the zipper matched the extraordinary tensile resistance of the best-stitched seams and could be magically pulled apart in an instant by holding the cam with two pinched fingers guiding it in reverse along its entire length. While we have long ceased to pay attention to the miraculous nature of the operation, early commercial advertisements sought to explain the process in detail. In the Field Autokamp Tent, for example, the Hookless Fastener pulled "the bob netting together as though it were sewed."[26] Shortened to the even more colloquial *zip* we use nowadays, the expression manages to embody the full range of properties facilitated by the device. Because the zipper sounds just the same on the way down as it does on the way up, the term characterizes both opening and closure (we store food in Ziploc bags, we instruct others to "Zip it!"); the geometrically fluid direction of its movement (zipline); and the speed with which the operation takes place (zipping through).

It is no exaggeration to say that the zipper was the most important innovation visited upon the sleeping bag, marking the moment when this

➲ 1917
Gideon Sundback, Separable Fastener, US Patent 1,219,881.

1,219,881.

Patented Mar. 20, 1917.

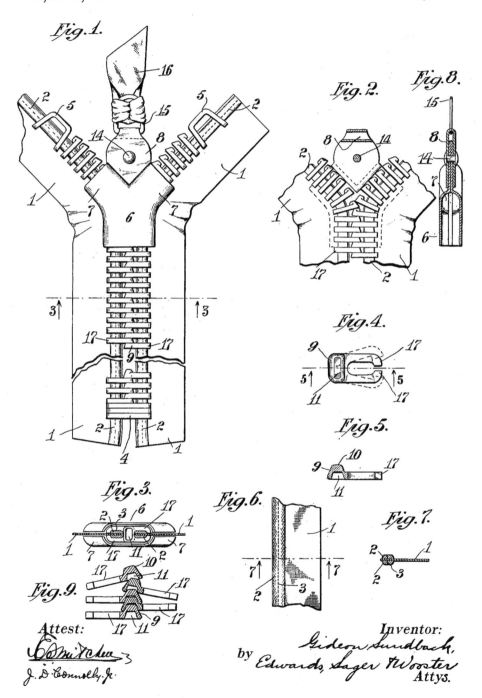

Attest:

Inventor:
Gideon Sundback.
by Edwards, Sager & Wooster
Attys.

now-familiar implement of camping gear finally went mainstream. Who had time to operate the myriad of loops, laces, and buckles that populated Warren H. Miller's sleeping bag? For the Ideal Bedding Company of Rochester, New York, there was "no crawling into an IDEAL Bag. It's like going to bed…then you close [the bag] tight with one movement as you slide the fastener up to your neck."[27] It is hard to now imagine any bag not equipped with at least two long, nonconductive nylon zippers—one along the edge that holds the tubular enclosure in place and one at the lower end to facilitate air circulation (in a pinch, the camper can operate this lower zipper to expose their feet, stand upright, and hobble toward the bathroom during the night). Nowadays, state-of-the-art deep-winter expedition sleeping bags are mummies outfitted with two additional zippers from which the camper's arms can easily emerge and retract. This is the case of the Nemo Canon -40, which retailed for $840—its hood fully covers the head of the camper except for a stovepipe vent around the mouth, nose, and eyes; much like the collar of a turtleneck sweater, the vent projects upward from the surface of the bag, helping pre-warm the cold air before it is breathed in.[28] Arms extended from the opened zippers, the occupant can sit up inside their bag and go about basic daily tasks like reading or tending to the portable stove without ever having to step out of their cozy cocoon.

⬆ ⬅ 2020
Nemo Canon -40 sleeping bag. This sleeping bag was discontinued in 2020.

⬀ 1927
Why Not Have a Convenient Sleeping Bag, in *The Mountaineer*, December 1927.

Insulation, Padding, Cushioning

The forest is the poor man's jacket.[29]
—OLD SWEDISH SAYING

Anyone who has ever taken a rake to the backyard during a late fall afternoon knows how hard it is to resist: there is something about jumping into a pile of leaves, something about the prospect of a soft landing and the enveloping sense of warmth that follows that are simply too good to pass up. Hours of labor are undone in a matter of seconds for a single leap into the pile, which ends up so flattened by the encounter that it can rarely sustain another go. In *The Art of Travel* (1856), Sir Francis Galton recognized in this type of yard waste the makings of an important survival technique for warding off the cold and humidity throughout the night. He noted the smarts of early eighteenth-century Highland poachers:

> They cut quantities of heather, and strew part of it as a bed on the ground; then all the party lie down, side by side, excepting one man, whose place among the rest is kept vacant for him. His business is to spread plaids upon them as they lie, and to heap up the remainder of the heather upon the plaids. This being accomplished, the man wriggles and works himself into the gap that has been left for him in the midst of his comrades.[30]

The nineteenth-century Adirondack outdoorsman, author, and guide George Washington Sears, better known as Nessmuk, noted that a bed fashioned from such branches and boxed in by four logs featured many distinct advantages. The layer of boughs formed a soft cushion for a body made weary at day's end from labor and travel; the layers of branches further prevented direct contact with the "bone-searching chill" of the ground while insulating against the cold air above.[31] The rustic bed's thermal properties and the padding it provided constitute different forms of

⬆ **2013**
Robin-Bliss Wagner, photograph of the camping author Dan White demonstrating a fast debris shelter developed during a workshop in Santa Cruz County, California.

➲ **1860**
Illustration from Francis Galton, *The Art of Travel; Or, Shifts and Contrivances Available in Wild Countries*, 3rd ed., depicting a makeshift bivouac improvised by early eighteenth-century Highland poachers.

cushioning against the elements—something that modern-day sleeping bags are expected to provide not on their own but in conjunction with inflatable mattresses and pillows. On an especially cold night when even a thick bed of branches could not do the trick, Galton recommended the more drastic approach of burrowing among the ashes of a recently extinguished campfire.[32]

These low-tech methods differed from the traditional expedition sleeping bags of the period in one important respect: they improvised rustic comforts from materials found around the campsite. Arctic explorers like Fridtjof Nansen and Robert Falcon Scott or alpinists like Edward Whymper and Pierre Allain had little choice but to transport significant amounts of expedition gear since they could not hope to find in situ the resources on which their survival depended. In lieu of wood and wild game, for example, they traveled with portable Primus stoves and food rations. In this regard, the sleeping bag is to the tent what the rustic bed Galton described is to the overnight shelter built from scratch out of branches, slabs of sod, and bark.

Galton, a British polymath who is considered the father of eugenics and was knighted in 1909, estimated that the real precursor to the modern-day sleeping bag was in fact not the heavy deerskin expedition models that McClure, Nansen, and their peers had made to order. Instead, he pointed to a simple sack made of linen that early nineteenth-century German peasants filled with leaves or hay before "putting their feet into it [and pulling] its mouth up to their armpit."[33] This unusual contraption served the same range of critical thermal and padding functions described above. In addition, the sack facilitated the gathering of leaves around the campsite and prevented their dispersal, like so many bags of lawn clippings left by the side of the road. On the morning of departure, the "insulation" was dumped from the bag and provisionally returned to the site. What

⊘ 1960
A man (standing) stuffs down feathers into the open walls of a sleeping bag, while others stand ready to seal each tube. Photographer unknown. *Summit*, June 1960.

⊘ 1925
Kapo Camp Equipment, *Motor Camper & Tourist*, May 1925.

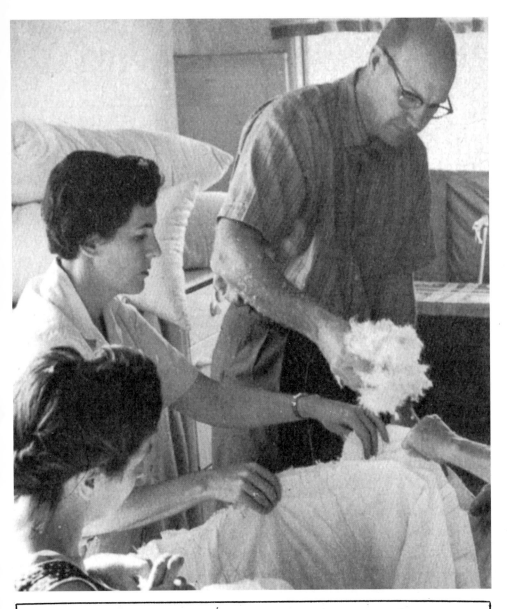

KAPO CAMP EQUIPMENT

Filled with Kapo "Ceibasilk." Moisture proof, vermin proof, light
in weight, easy to pack. Repels both heat and cold.

Outdoor Sleeping Equipment
Life Saving Devices
Boat Pillows and Cushions
Automobile Cushions
Toboggan Cushions
Chair Cushions, etc.

Camp Mattresses 30x78, 36x78, 18x78. Quilted to roll easily. O. D. Cloth. Weight 5 to 9 lbs. Endorsed by National Recreation Society.

Sleeping Roll 30x78. Outside Rubberized Cloth, inside O.D. Cloth. Contains removable padding of Ceibasilk, padded pocket for feet. The end flap protects against shower or wind.

KAPO PRODUCTS CO., 80 Traverse Street, BOSTON, MASS.

Send for catalogue, Price List and the name of our nearest dealer.

remained was just that—a thin pouch or shell that was easily rolled up and transported to the next encampment.

Galton could not have known just how closely this rudimentary prototype approximates the modern item. By treating the bag's portability, enclosure, and thermal performance as separate features, early sleeping bag manufacturers discovered they could do away with heavy pelts and wool blankets in favor of a slate of lighter and far more compact insulating materials. This was the case of the 1890s Norwegian textile manufacturer Ajungilak, for example, a company that introduced a revolutionary new model lined with kapok, a cottonlike fiber harvested from the fruit of the kapok tree. Then, in 1892, the British alpinist Albert Mummery (1855–1895) proposed using the down feathers of the eider duck, a material prized in Victorian-era quilts for its unparalleled insulation value and high degree of compressibility.[34] High-quality down can expand up to nine hundred times its volume, in the process trapping significant quantities of air that confer it with unique insulating properties. A quick comparison highlights the massive weight changes undergone in sleeping bags over the past 125 years: made of furs arranged inside out so that the dense pattern of hairs trapped the heat emanating from the body, a typical nineteenth-century expedition sleeping bag weighed approximately 18 to 20 pounds. Rated to withstand a similar temperature range, the Nemo Canon -40 down sleeping bag does the job at 4.5 pounds, or roughly 25 percent of this weight.[35]

The use of loose insulation materials did pose unique design challenges. For one thing, kapok and especially eiderdown were expensive and could not be freely spared; unlike dried leaves or hay, they needed to become an integral and permanent part of the bag assembly. Further, the materials themselves required additional protection from the elements since they lost significant insulating value when exposed to

◐ **1976**

Margot Apple, *5 Types of Down Construction*, in Steve Futterman and Margot Apple, *Soft House*.

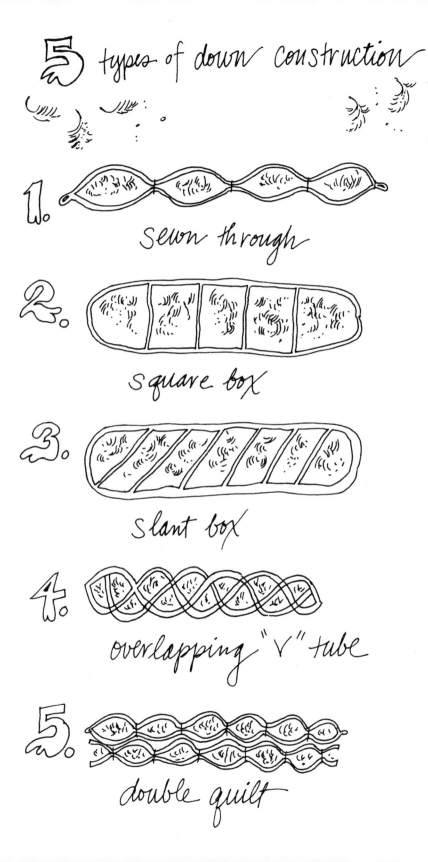

5 types of down construction

1. sewn through

2. square box

3. slant box

4. overlapping "v" tube

5. double quilt

water or humidity. Following the example of Russian dolls nested inside one another, the modern sleeping bag is in essence a multilayer system featuring not one but two separate bags: an innermost (warm) envelope housing the camper and contained inside a slightly larger outer (cold) shell between which is encased a layer of insulation. Discrete compartments created by stitching the two bags to one another, known as boxing or baffling, keep the loose material in place and prevent it from bunching up. This process allows for different parts of the body to be targeted with specific amounts of insulation. Areas typically requiring extra padding include the top surface of the bag, which remains in constant contact with outside air, as well as the knees, lower legs, and feet: these form the "bottom box," an area that Pierre Allain sought to protect with his pied d'éléphant.

Ever the perfectionist, Allain envisioned a complete bivouacking system—an assembly that provided waterproofing, cushioning, and thermal value all at once. Building on the example of the Russian dolls, Allain simply grew the *warm shell / insulation / cold shell* system outward by adding an inflatable pad; finally, he wrapped the whole package with a waterproof layer that could be used on its own as a knee-length rain smock (cagoule) or completed with a pied d'éléphant. One will note in the representation of Allain's system the diminutive size of the camper's head—the smallest doll nestled inside the innermost layer of this bulky package.

Allain's Sac-Bivouac is notable for its willingness to rethink the role of the mattress, an implement of gear that had historically constituted a separate feature from the sleeping bag. Nessmuk noted wryly that he "often had occasion to observe that stubs, roots and small stones, etc. have a perverse tendency to abrade the anatomy of people unused to the woods."[36] Like him, resourceful Adirondacks campers (or their guides) knew how to fashion their own rustic bedframes using loose branches or weaving a trellis

↑ c. 1930
An inflatable mattress is layered under an all-weather shell in Pierre Allain's Système Intégral. Photographer unknown.

➜ c. 1930
A cross section of Pierre Allain's Système Intégral, or Sac-Bivouac, reveals the triple layering of down components, inflatable mattress, and waterproof shell.

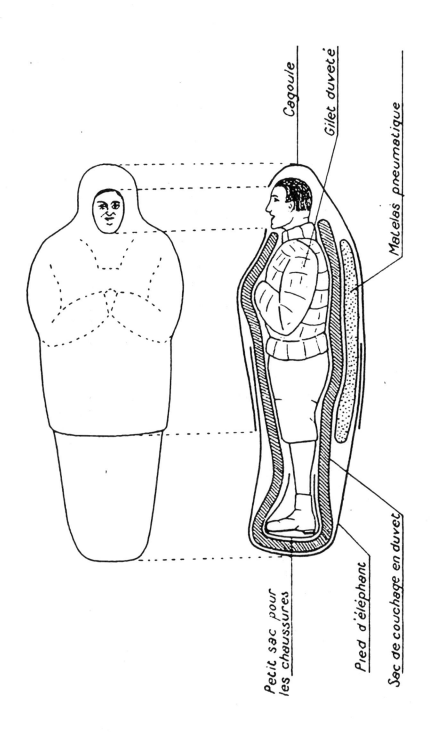

Cagoule

Gilet duveté

Matelas pneumatique

Petit sac pour les chaussures

Pied d'éléphant

Sac de couchage en duvet

126. — SAC-BIVOUAC.

with thin-gauge rope, in the process raising the body safely above the damp and cold ground. For his part, Galton observed that "eight pounds' weight of shavings make an excellent bed, and I find I can cut them with a common spokeshave, in 3 hours, out of a log of deal."[37] What about those campers with less time to spare (or no spokeshave)? Elon Jessup estimated that fifty sheets of newspaper also made for an inviting mattress, an ingenious system that predated modern preoccupations with recycling.[38] And because the automobile would increasingly and over time make the weight of camping gear a secondary concern, many twentieth-century motor camping enthusiasts set out on the road with old spring mattresses strapped to the roof of their vehicles—a reminder that many still remained unwilling to leave behind the comforts of home. This is not to say that mattresses were exempt from the state-of-the-art technology that was slowly converting heavy sleeping bags into lighter, more compact, and thermally efficient camping resources.

Among the first examples of the technological hybridity linking the car to the campsite occurred in the 1920s when spring beds cantilevered from the side of the vehicle and then hammock-like structures hung inside the vehicle itself (page 104). While historical evidence suggests they date back to the fifteenth century, it should come as no surprise that the first commercially produced air beds originated precisely at the same moment when sleeping bags became multilayer systems, for what is an inflatable mattress than yet another "bag," filled not with kapok or down but with air?[39] Indeed, an 1898 *Harper's Weekly* advertisement for the Mechanical Fabric Company's Perfection Mattress claimed that "air, not hair is the modern filling for mattresses and cushions."[40]

Building on technological advances of the period, the inflatable mattress solved several needs all at once. It was the Scottish chemist Charles Macintosh (1766–1843) who first patented a method for

Log Frame of Bed
Over lapping Boughs.

(Copyright Secured.)

" It is composed of but few parts which may be taken apart and all that is essential to camping in the forest,

(Copyright Secured.)

⬆ ⬆ **1913**
Log Frame of Bed, Ernest Thompson Seton, *The Book of Woodcraft*.

⬆ **1875**
Patent New Camp Lounge, Edwin R. Wallace, *Descriptive Guide to the Adirondacks and Handbook of Travel to Saratoga Springs; Schroon Lake; Lakes Luzerne, George, and Champlain; The Ausable Chasm; The Thousand Islands; Massena Springs; and Trenton Falls.*

➡ **c. 1512**
Woodcut from Flavius Vegetius Renatus, *De re militari*, depicting an inflatable mattress.

waterproofing fabric by dissolving rubber into coal-
tar naphtha in 1823. The application not only yielded
the modern raincoat but also found extensive use
in camping. The trail writer and physician Claude P.
Fordyce (1883–1953) noted of the waterproofed
ground cloth that it "is to a tent what a floor is to a
house. It keeps out dirt, vermin, dampness and wind
and in cold or wet weather, besides being an absolute
health necessity, it will add greatly to one's comfort."[41]
Portable cots like the Camp Lounge, a model published in Edwin Wallace's *Descriptive Guide to the
Adirondacks* (1875), also made use of wide strips of
waterproofed fabric, as did the outer shell of some
sleeping bags. However, the rubberized Macintosh
was also airtight and considered ideal for inflation.
Among the first to commercialize the invention was
the Pneumatic Mattress and Cushion Company of
Reading, Massachusetts, in 1890. Since then, PVC
rubber and modern synthetic materials have greatly
increased the efficiency of inflatable structures: there
would be no need to blow extra puffs of air into an
old, lumpy mattress as it slowly collapsed under the
weight of the camper during the night. But in an
unsurpassed stroke of ingenuity, modern air mattresses no longer require *any* mechanically assisted
inflation. First patented by Cascade Designs in 1975,
the self-inflatable foam pad introduced by Therm-a-
Rest (US Patents 3,872,525 and 4,149,919) employs
a unique, highly compressible foam inside an airtight
nylon sleeve that sucks in outside air as it slowly
expands.[42] All that is needed is for the camper to turn
open the inflation valve and watch the mattress take
shape while marveling at the savings in weight: a new
Thermarest NeoAir XLite Sleeping Pad weighs less
than one pound, while historical counterparts like
the nineteenth-century Perfection Mattress or the
portable army folding wood cot weighed ten to
fifteen pounds.

But even in an age defined by extraordinary
new synthetic materials, modern technology cannot

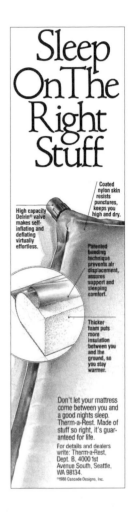

↑ 1989
"Sleep on the Right Stuff,"
Backpacker, March 1989.

➲ 1979
James M. Lea and Neil P.
Anderson, Method of Making
a Self-Inflating Air Mattress,
US Patent 4,149,919. In this
application, Lea and Anderson
sought to patent the mechanical
press required to bond the
open-cell foam of the Therm-
a-Rest mattress to its external
layers of impermeable, plastic-
coated fabric.

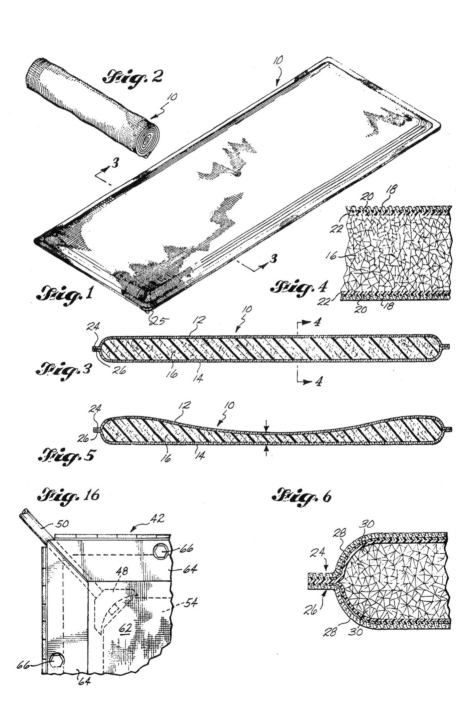

Fig. 2

Fig. 1

Fig. 4

Fig. 3

Fig. 5

Fig. 16

Fig. 6

always improve on nature: top-shelf three- and four-season sleeping bags are unique hybrid systems that combine the insulating capacity of down feathers with the unparalleled performance of waterproof, breathable, and fast-drying synthetic materials like nylon (1938) and Gore-Tex (1976) for constructing shells, zippers, elastic cords, and stitching.

The dramatic ramping up in military production during World War II, which helped secure the fortunes of the nylon manufacturer DuPont (tents, parachutes, parkas, sleeping bags) and the retailer Eddie Bauer (B-9 down jackets), recalls the 1876 contract that the Welsh entrepreneur Sir Pryce Pryce-Jones (of the previously mentioned Pryce Jones Company) engaged in with the Russian Army to produce sixty thousand examples of his popular Euklisia Rug. But when the Russians lost the war, Jones was left with a significant surplus, which he later dispersed around the world, an effort that no doubt contributed to the sleeping bag's early commercial successes. Harvey Manning noted in *Backpacking: One Step at a Time* (1972) that, during World War II, the US Army manufactured tens of thousands of its down sleeping bags, including the M-1942, for its troops.[43] After the war, commercial outfitters such as REI, Sierra Designs, Patagonia, Gerry, and Eastern Mountain Sports (EMS), all of which came of age in the 1960s, jumped into the fray to profit from Eddie Bauer's commercial spoils.

For DuPont, Bauer, and the United States military in particular, modern sleeping bag designs, with their unusual combination of natural and synthetic materials, created a wildly asymmetrical demand. In theory, nylon constitutes an endlessly renewable resource; however, this is not so for down, which has remained a popular resource not only in sleeping bags, but in jackets, winter suits, pillows, comforters, and even mattresses. So where do all the feathers come from that allow us to meet our endless appetite for newer, lighter, and warmer things? The renowned

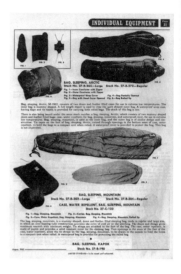

⊕ 1943

Sample page from the *Quartermaster Supply Catalog—Enlisted Men's Clothing and Equipment*. Featuring the heaviest grade of insulation, the M-1942 sleeping bag appears at the top of the page.

➔ 1942

Bob Law, photograph of a label tag inside an M-1942 arctic sleeping bag manufactured for the US Army by Irving & Co. Inc. of Portland, Oregon.

DON ASHMUS,

~99-1918, inclusi~

For use upon MATTRESSES

Oregon State Board of Health

№ 352313	ALL NEW MATERIAL	

Materials Used in Manufacture

State kind, grade and exact weight of each material

40% GRAY GOOSE DOWN

60% GRAY GOOSE BODY FEATHERS

Size	Net weight	Style No.	Order No.
Cover	Kind		Grade

Manufactured for **U. S. ARMY**

Manufactured by
IRVING & CO., INC.   Address   PORTLAND, ORE.

organization PETA (People for the Ethical Treatment of Animals) estimates that 80 percent of down feathers used in sleeping bags and other outdoor gear originates from farms in China. PETA has strongly denounced the use of the inhumane technique known as live-plucking, which involves removing feathers from the skin of waterfowl while they are still alive.

These efforts have led to a movement called Ethical Down and a search for alternate sources of insulation.[44] Despite their space-age names like ThermoBall®, Thinsulate®, PrimaLoft®, Omni-Heat®, and Climashield®, to name a few, many of the synthetics developed toward this end have consistently failed to attract the expert eye of many campers and gearheads.[45] Unlike down feathers, however, which lose their thermal value when wet, the most important advantage of synthetic downs is that they dry fast. The resulting bags, however, are not nearly as light and comfortable, but there is some hope. Companies such as Patagonia that found commercial success during the early 1970s are now on the leading edge of repair and recycle movements with the aim to extend the life of their gear beyond a few seasons. Among several notable examples is Patagonia's Worn Wear program, which offers high-end repair services as well as customer credit for trading in old clothing—an old jacket might be fully deconstructed, its fibers respun into new fabric, and its down feathers used to fill a completely new sleeping bag.[46] Today, the conscientious camper may no longer head to stores like REI or EMS but rather the local army supply store, where an M-1942, an ICW (intermediate cold weather), or an ECW (extreme cold weather) bag can still be purchased at a competitive price.[47] These efforts to connect past, present, and future would doubt have provided some measure of comfort to Albert Mummery and George Finch, who first introduced down into the outdoor gear market over a century ago, both unaware at the time that in our globalized economy, there can never be enough of a good thing.

⊖ 2020

Tim Davis, photograph of recycled down destined for Patagonia products. The company reports that used cushions, comforters, pillows, and other unsellable items in Europe are shipped to a down collector in France and cut open in front of a large vacuum that sucks in the contents. The down is then mixed, sorted, washed, heat sanitized, and shipped to Patagonia's factories to be sewn into new products.

TRASH

The vandals sacked Rome, but what 12,000,000 motor campers may do in this land of the free, unless good sportsmanship is the keynote of camping, will make the inroads of the Huns look like a fairy story for juvenile consumption by comparison.[1]
—FRANK E. BRIMMER

The solution to the trash problem seemed so simple: bears. To process the increasing mounds of food waste generated by tourists in Yellowstone National Park shortly after it was established in 1872, area managers quickly turned to new methods of onsite disposal. Hoping to kill two birds with one stone, they improvised an exclusive, bear-only "lunch counter," a wooden platform at which the famished park animals would lay waste to mounds of garbage. The popular daily event became a major tourist attraction on par with Yosemite National Park's Firefall in the late nineteenth century, and bleachers were soon constructed to accommodate the mobs of sightseers fascinated by this gruesome spectacle.[2]

◐◐ 1975
Dan Ing, photograph of the cleaning of Morning Glory Pool in Yellowstone National Park in Wyoming.

◑ 1933
Art Holmes, photograph of a garbage dump at Civilian Conservation Corps camp Lassen Volcanic National Park in California.

Touring the region around this period, the Wisconsinite Frank Carpenter no doubt experienced this dramatic display firsthand. Writing in *The Wonders of Geyser Land* (1878), he chose instead to recall another appalling activity—laundry day at Old Faithful. Fed up with hand-washing their clothing soiled by days of hard travel, park visitors had stumbled upon the idea of using the iconic geothermal feature as a washing machine:

> We hear the preparatory rumbling and the waters rise a few feet above the surface. Mr. Houston now gives the command to cast [our clothes] into the water. It goes down and remains so long that we begin to feel uneasy,…and the next instant, with a rush and a roar she "goes off" and the clothes, jacket, rags, &c., mixed in every conceivable shape, shoot up to a distance of a hundred feet or more and fall with a splash in the basins below. The water subsides, and we fish out the clothing which we find…nice and clean.[3]

Here was an Eden for the taking, its role not only to inspire but also to entertain and, perhaps, even assist with mundane chores. Carpenter concluded enthusiastically that "nature…keeps up her gratuitous exhibitions without intermission," even on Sundays.[4]

As discussed throughout this book, there are countless pleasures associated with both making and occupying the camp: the open air, the rustling leaves, the bright stars, the satisfying clicks, zips and whooshes of gear being assembled and dismantled, a cold drink after a long day on the trail, the rich and smoky smells of a meal cooking over the live campfire, and the like. And yet as the locus of intense consumption, the campsite is witness to an equally broad range of unwelcome side effects: food scraps; discarded cardboard, plastic, and metal containers; body waste washed away in streams; trees felled or exposed to nonnative insects and diseases; forest fires; compacted soils; and shrubs swiped by cars,

➲ **c. 1921–1935**
Lunch Counter—For Bears Only, Yellowstone National Park in Wyoming. Photographer unknown.

trucks, trailers, and RVs. For the modern enthusiast, learning to mitigate these impacts constitutes a critical challenge of contemporary camp craft. To this end, one of the most exemplary guidebooks of the pack-in, pack-out Leave No Trace movement that grew out of the 1980s is Kathleen Meyer's wonderfully didactic *How to Shit in the Woods: An Environmentally Sound Approach to a Lost Art* (1989), now in its fourth edition. But for Meyer's nineteenth-century counterparts, reading about bear lunch counters and improvised laundromats—or worse, witnessing these events in person—set a very dangerous precedent that appeared to minimize the inherent perils of camping to both humans *and* nature. In a disturbing cycle of events, these early Yellowstone park managers who invented the bear counter somehow believed that discarded refuse from hotels and campsites could be strangely alchemized. With the bears enlisted as consumers and unwitting performers, visitors walked away from the performance thinking they had charitably contributed to the animals' livelihood. In effect, the spectators had been treated to the deeply satisfying experience of seeing the remaining traces (and guilt) of their own consumption vanish into thin air. Unbeknownst to them, such practices would have far-reaching side effects that would not be well understood for decades. Even long after the National Park Service turned to waste incinerators and closed the food counters during the 1950s, or even after it began levying fines of up to $5,000 for littering geysers with coins, rags, bottles, sticks, and other refuse, the bears somehow did not receive the memo. They continued, undeterred, eagerly approaching moving vehicles and roaming through campgrounds, provisions stashes, and garbage dumps across the park, lured by the smells of food, which had to be secured in thick steel lockers or discarded in structurally reinforced trash cans.

◉ **c. 1946**
Tourists sitting in bleachers, watching grizzly bears eating on a stage, Yellowstone National Park in Wyoming. Photographer unknown.

Above Ground

We are living in the tin can era, and like the antediluvian
beasts, the can is leaving its imperishable records in every
geological strata on the earth today.[5]
—CORNELIA JAMES CANNON

The type of littering that gave rise to bear counters
was not limited to national parks. Describing the
cross-country Lincoln Highway a few years after it
first opened in 1913, the geographer and landscape
historian John A. Jakle described a trail "of trash and
swill…marked as effectively by discarded tin cans,
cheese rinds, whiskey bottles, and the other remains
of careless camping as by any other [road] signs."[6]
In fact, motor tourists of the period came to be
known by the single most visible item of trash they
ate from and later discarded, the tin can. More
broadly, the tin can also referred to the motor vehicles they drove (the affordable Ford Model T was
also affectionately known as the Tin Lizzie).

In fact, the origins of the expression *tin can tourist*
can be traced not as corollary, but rather as a retort
to the casually destructive ways of early motor campers. Founded in De Soto Park outside Tampa by James
M. Morrison in 1919, the Tin Can Tourists (TCT)
sought to promote ethical practices around camping
through a pair of biannual rallies held in Florida
during the winter and in Michigan over the summer.
In establishing this new association, Morrison was no
doubt channeling a broader and still-emerging consciousness in the field, with books such as Anthon L.
Westgard's *Official AAA Manual of Motor Car Camping*
(1920) and Frank E. Brimmer's *Autocamping* (1923).
Seeking to reverse the cultural stigma of this ubiquitous piece of trash, members of the TCT proudly and
defiantly affixed a single tin can to the radiator cap
of their vehicles as an emblem of membership.

In an era that predated the wide use of plastics
and recycling, metal and glass remained the most

❷ **1960**
Backcountry Cleanup, Smashing
Cans, Raes Lake, California.
Photographer unknown.

important forms of food packaging. As Cornelia James Cannon (1876–1969) had noted earlier, their durability (it takes fifty to one hundred years for metal to break down in a landfill and four thousand years for glass to do the same) made them particularly unenviable—this detritus would be around long after campers had left their site. But in an ironic twist, the dreaded can was simply reinvented into a larger version of itself, a new type of receptacle designed not for the purpose of containing packaged foods and other goods, but instead for holding refuse (which of course included plenty of discarded tins). Charles Parker Halligan, author of *Tourist Camps* (1925), described trash cans as compulsory in order "to maintain a neat, tidy, and sanitary condition about the campgrounds."[7] For the modern camper, it is easy to forget that, like the picnic table, what eventually became an integral element of campgrounds everywhere had hardly been in existence for a few decades at the turn of the century.

The trash can's origins are traced to Eugène Poubelle (1831–1907), a French lawyer who made the use of closed containers for the disposal of waste mandatory throughout the city of Paris in 1883. In what can only be perceived as equal parts affection and derision, the French eponymously nicknamed the device after its inventor: poubelle. Sadly (or not), the English language offers no such equivalent; the trash can was a can *for trash,* and not a piece *of trash.* Their sturdy and durable design offered many advantages: the large metal cans could withstand year-round outdoor use and the occasional encounter with a moving vehicle. Their fixed positions in campgrounds made daily, systematic garbage truck pickups a relatively simple task (and their contents could then be hauled to an incinerator or buried in a landfill). And the heavy lids, which were eventually "bear-proofed" in certain parks, helped suppress unfriendly odors.

The advent of modern synthetic materials like plastics and nylon in the first half of the twentieth

⊙ 1987
Jim Peaco, photograph of bearproof garbage can, Yellowstone National Park in Wyoming.

⊙ 1935
Campground Trash Can, Manzanita Lake Campground, Lassen Volcanic National Park in California. Photographer unknown.

century would yield further improvements in these rudimentary trash disposal systems. In 1951, the Canadian inventor Harry Wasylyk (1925–2013), together with Larry Hansen, a Union Carbide employee, created the garbage bag, a stretchy, waterproof polyethylene liner placed inside the can; once filled, the open end (top) was tied up and the bag extracted, its outer surface still clean to the touch. As such, the receptacle remained free from dried-up debris and residual odors day-to-day. In a wave of high-tech camping gear unleashed by these wondrous new materials, the garbage bag would scarcely merit attention except for one specific innovation, the kitchen-sized, single-deposit WAG (Waste Alleviation and Gelling) bag. Made of puncture-resistant, biodegradable plastic that contains small amounts of NASA-developed Poo Powder designed to reduce odors, each bag also includes some toilet paper and hand sanitizer to freshen up once the deed is completed.[8] Like the hiker exploring remote landscapes unserved by flush or chemical closets, the contemporary dog walker will recognize this familiar procedure, clipping their pet's poop bags to their leash in search of the next trash can.

Below Ground

The best line of defense for protecting our wild lands, our wild friends, and ourselves is to develop scrupulous habits of disposal—dig an environmentally sound hole and bury that shit![9]
—KATHLEEN MEYER

The essayist and cultural geographer J. B. Jackson (1909–1996) described the nineteenth century as the great "sanitary awakening," a period during which the connection between polluted water and deadly diseases like cholera was first scientifically established.[10] The problem did not simply lie in the sewage coursing

↑ 2020
Alex Schmidt, photograph of WAG bag kiosk at Jacob's Ladder trailhead, Long Peak Wilderness in Utah.

➜ 2022
The Original WAG BAG-GO Anywhere Toilet Kit is manufactured by the Montana-based company Cleanwaste.

GO anywhere toilet kit®

The original **WAG BAG**®

GO safe   **GO** clean   **GO** anywhere

Good for
multiple uses

Contains
NASA–developed
super-absorbent

Gels and deodorizes
32 oz. of liquid and
solid waste

Turns Liquid to **SOLID**

through urban waterways, it extended to human impacts in wild nature as well: writing of early camp-sites at the turn of the twentieth century, Horace Kephart articulated the concern in dramatic terms, noting: "I have seen one of Nature's gardens, an ideal health resort, changed in a few months…into an abomination and a pest-hole where typhoid and dysentery wrought deadly vengeance."[11]

Body waste is an important reference in the geography of the campsite: wind direction, the flow of a creek or stream, and the depth of the water table all constitute key vectors that influence the location of the encampment. Common sense dictates positioning the site away from offending odors and views but, far more importantly, out of reach of deadly bacteria. In this regard, the most important factor that guided the major expansion of campgrounds in Yosemite Valley during the twentieth century was not simply the dramatic views, but instead that the area would remain upstream—and thus free from—significant "intestinal discharges" flushed by the Yosemite Lodge and other touristic facilities down into the Merced River—a powerful reminder that links the intimacy of the lone campsite to the surrounding world, no matter how far one has traveled to escape its grasp.[12]

One of the great joys and challenges of camping is that the process of setting down roots is mitigated by the constant forward pull of mobility and explora-tion. By definition, the campsite constitutes a tran-sient setting, but this by no means suggests that it remains completely free of traces of past occupants. In an era that predated flush toilets and WAG bags, Kephart described best practices for disposing of human waste: below ground. In the 1930 edition of *Camping and Woodcraft*, he sketched out a simple latrine design, no more than a two-foot-deep ground trench dug at a short distance from the campsite, and where one and a half pounds of the originally excavated soil could be scooped back into the hole to deodorize the foul odors of each new stool and help

⊘ 1930
Latrine, Horace Kephart,
Camping and Woodcraft, 4th ed.

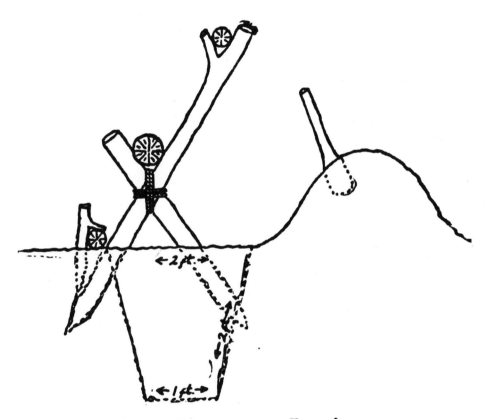

Fig. 113 — Latrine

accelerate the deterioration of deadly bacteria; for the relatively permanent camp deep into the woods, a rudimentary seat could be improvised from tied-up branches that spanned over the pit.

As camping grew in popularity and scale, and hundreds of incoming visitors set up camp at the very same spots vacated only a few hours before, the latrine concept had to be modified to meet the increasing demand—first with concrete-lined pits or "vault" toilets, then later with large septic tanks, flush toilets, and RV dumping stations. According to the laws of gravity, the waste maintained a downward trajectory, so to speak—but only to an extent: like the latrines, this new infrastructure remained below ground. Their contents, however, were not destined to forever remain in place. Instead, they could be pumped out with great regularity.

In the current era of off-grid camping, WAG bags, and urine-absorbent solidifiers, a new paradigm has emerged. For experienced campers, human waste, like discarded packaging and food scraps, becomes an integral part of the apparatus of camping gear, something to be packed out of the woods. Ironically, the same could also be said of the considerable autonomy afforded by modern RVs. Equipped with large freshwater tanks, gray water (i.e., sink, bath, shower) tanks, black water (i.e., sewage) tanks, gasoline tanks, generators, and massive batteries, the motor touring enthusiast can enjoy and maintain a "dry" (hook-up-free) camp for days, whether on the road or bivouacking in a Walmart parking lot.

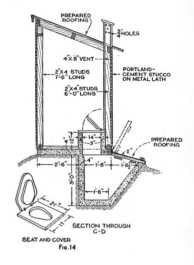

⬆ 1924

Design for a vault toilet, *Popular Mechanics Auto Tourist's Handbook No. 1.*

➡ 1925

Office Of Public Buildings & Public Parks of the National Capital, *Standard Septic Tank.*

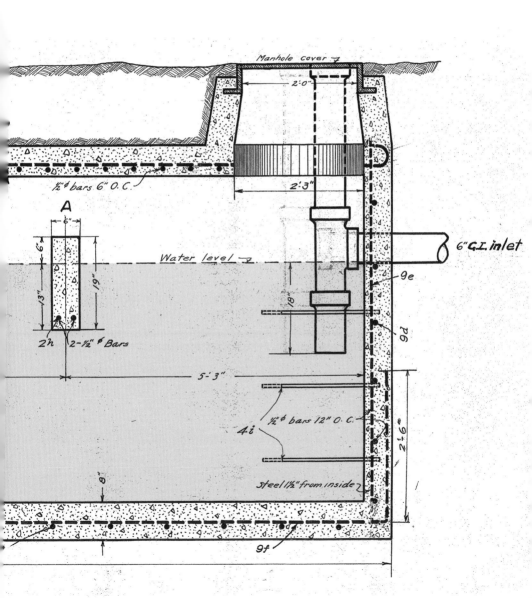

Manhole cover

2'0"

½"φ bars 6" O.C.

A

6"

6"

13"

19"

Water level

2h

2-½" φ Bars

2'3"

18"

6"G.I.inlet

9e

9d

5'-3"

½"φ bars 12" O.C.

4i

8"

Steel 1½" from inside

2'6"

9f

Conclusions

*American cities are like badger holes, ringed with trash…
and almost smothered with rubbish. Everything we use
comes in boxes, cartons, bins, the so-called packaging we
love so much. The mountains of things we throw away are
much greater than the things we use.*[13]
—JOHN STEINBECK

Amateurish campers place their trust in nature,
substituting the most recent gadgetry and prepackaged meals—often with their own massive carbon
footprints—for common sense and best practices.
For Steinbeck, it is at the campsite that "we can see
the wild and reckless exuberance of our production,
and waste seems to be the index."[14] As we seek to
escape the confines of modern life, our gear *and* our
trash follow close behind—the tent, the inflatable
mattresses, the sleeping bags, the lightweight cookware, the spent fuel cans, the crumpled maps, the
memories, and all the rest. Time to head back home!

⊘ **1970**
Madison Junction Campground
dumping station, Yellowstone
National Park in Wyoming.
Photographer unknown.

AFTERWORD

*We needed nothing else. With our stove, our screened
tents, our folding furniture, and our lamps, our air
mattresses, our ice box, we were able to enjoy a good
facsimile of our home comforts.*[1]
—FRANKLIN M. RECK AND WILLIAM (BILL) MOSS

The thing I remember most about my first camping
experience is the map.

Late in June 2000, I pulled off Route 44 just before
it crosses the White River, a few miles from Badlands
National Park in South Dakota. I was in the midst of
a month-long, ten-thousand-mile road trip that would
take me across the American West by way of New York,
Chicago, Salt Lake City, Las Vegas, and Austin. When
I'd told my friend Sheri about the trip and my plans to
visit 1960s and '70s art landmarks like Michael Heizer's
Double Negative (Overton, Nevada), Robert Smithson's
Spiral Jetty (Rozel Point, Utah), Nancy Holt's *Sun
Tunnels* (Lucin, Utah), and Donald Judd's Chinati
Foundation (Marfa, Texas), she suggested I borrow
her tent and sleeping bag. When I saw a big KOA
(Kampgrounds of America) sign looming in the

→ **2011**
The author at campsite #153,
Loop D, Madison Campground,
Yellowstone National Park,
June 22, 2011.

distance, I remembered the gear, which had remained out of sight in the trunk of my car for several weeks. Wouldn't it be nice to take a break from the cheap motels I had been patronizing during my trip?

The prospect of camping felt edgy, adventurous. I'd camped with the Boy Scouts during my childhood, but this would be my first solo experience. Was I prepared? Did I have enough gear to pull it off? A tent and a sleeping bag seemed like all I needed: shelter and warmth. Right? Maybe a few leftover snacks from the day's drive?

The main KOA building presented a hybrid mix of functions. It was part registration lobby, part gift shop, part convenience store. Once past the front door I was met by an attendant and I announced my plans to camp for the night, paid the $20 fee, and received a map of the campground. "We're here," the guy said, pointing with an open highlighter pen to the rectangular building inside of which we stood. "And your campsite," he added, highlighting the short route with his blue marker, then making a generous circle, "is here."

I had expected to be let loose on the grounds to claim a quiet, shady spot on my own, but instead a destination had been prescribed for me. Because the KOA was located along the White River, sites 118 to 122 would be best, the attendant offered. Did this mean there were at least 122 individual sites? I'm an architect by training and interested in the spatial planning of places—not only buildings but larger landscapes too. The map indicated there were RV sites and tent sites, bathrooms, a swimming pool, a miniature golf area, an off-leash dog area. It even showed streets with names. *This all felt and looked like a small village.* Since this was my first time at a KOA, I was admittedly a little surprised but also intrigued. Were all campgrounds like this?

Sites 118 to 122 were occupied by just a few families. My instinct was to look for a spot far away from the other tents, so I parked on a patch of dirt by a picnic

2000
KOA Badlands Kampground map, restaurant menu, and parking pass issued to the author on June 29, 2000. Rummaging through boxes of old materials on a recent Sunday afternoon, I was delighted to find that I had kept this important piece of evidence.

514083

HANG ON REAR-VIEW MIRROR • THIS SIDE OUT

SITE NO. **Tent**

CAR PASS

6/29

DEPARTURE DATE

JENKINS BUSINESS FORMS, MASCOUTAH, IL 62258

...e to Badlands/White River KOA

YOUR SITE # IS T
Please do not change your site unless approved by management

EMERGENCY NUMBERS:
Fire...433-5300 Local number
Police...1-605-837-2285

...ands National Park Visitor Center

WHITE RIVER

KAMPING KABINS
107 108 109 110 111 112 113
LASSO CIRCLE DRIVE

Owner's Home (Private)
MINIATURE GOLF

MAIN STREET

TENT VILLAGE
(Sheltered Deluxe Tent Sites)

Pet Walking Area
BALL FIELD

PLEASE NO FIREWORKS OR VEHICLE WASHING

Tenting Area

Shop Building (Private)

LOST DOG CREEK

KOA Kamping Kabins
FOR RENT, WITHOUT BEDDING

Catholic & Protestant
Church Services in Interior

SUNRISE BREAKFAST
7:00 - 9:30 A.M.
Includes pancakes, scrambled eggs, sausage, or bacon.

Adults	$4.25
Kids	$3.00
Coffee	$.60
Orange Juice	$.60
Milk	$.60

SUNDOWN SUPPER   6:00 - 9:00 P.M.
Your Choice of:

Sirloin Steak 8 oz	$10.25
Ribeye Steak 12 oz	$13.25
Buffalo Sirloin Steak 10 oz	$16.25
Buffalo Ribeye Steak 10 oz	$17.25
Chicken Breast 8 oz	$7.25
1/3 lb. Hamburger	$4.75
1/3 lb. Cheeseburger	$5.25
1/3 lb. Cheeseburger w/Bacon	$5.75
Buffalo Burger	$6.25
B-BQ Ribs Small Rack	$10.25
Whole Rack	$15.25

All dinners except burgers include corn on the cob, baked beans, potato salad and Texas toast.

B-BQ
Serving everyday Rain or Shine at the main building

ALA CARTE

Corn on the Cob	$.75
Potato Salad	$1.00
Baked Beans	$1.00
Coffee	$.60
Soft Drinks	$.75

Yellowstone Park KOA

table. My nearest neighbors were clearly far more prepared than I was—they had lawn chairs, a large tent, a stove, a cooler, with the open hatchback door of their minivan functioning as a kind of pantry. Reading the assembly instructions for my friend's tent, I tried to look casual, like I had done this before. And when my neighbors began cooking at their sites, with kids scrambling around to grab the first hot dog hot off the grill, it began to dawn on me just how little I'd thought this through and how unprepared I was. I'd spent the past few weeks staying in motels, relying on nearby fast food joints, gas stations, and highway family-friendly restaurants. Here, at my campsite, I didn't have food, cookware, utensils, or anything to start a campfire with. For a moment, I hoped they would notice me and invite me over for a bite (they didn't). I had noticed cold cuts, bread, and condiments at the KOA store, but my instincts wanted to do what was familiar so I drove out of the campground and headed a few miles down the highway to the nearby town of Interior, South Dakota, had a burger, and made it back to my campsite before dark. I walked around for a while, trying to peek into the RVs without appearing to, and even put in a load of laundry at the rear of the main KOA building, where I noticed campers surfing the internet using free telephone ports. I returned to my car and grabbed my laptop so I could send a few emails of my own, feeling as boastful as if I had been halfway around the world and had in fact a *real* story to tell. After a decent night's sleep on the hard ground, I rose early, awakened by the bright sun streaming into the tent. I packed up my stuff—it didn't take long—wolfed down a stack of pancakes at the very convenient KOA canteen, then set out to hike in the Badlands.

I did not return to my campsite, but it's a place I think about often.[2] It's been over two decades since that first solo camping experience, and since then I've visited many other campgrounds of various shapes and sizes. While some of these experiences have been

↑ **2001**

Sierra Designs, assembly instructions for Meteor Light CD tent. Though I have long since stopped reading them, this sheet has sat perfectly folded inside my storage sack ever since I purchased the tent over twenty years ago.

memorable, I can't say that I've come to really enjoy and love camping all that much. Sure, with each new arrival I did get faster and more confident setting up my tent. I did enjoy some magnificent scenery along the way, including walk-in site H09 at Schoodic Woods Campground in Acadia National Park (2015), site BB04 at Bridger Bay Campground at Antelope Island State Park in Utah (2002), and site 046, located in the upper loop of Spruces Campground in the Uinta-Wasatch-Cache National Forest (2002, 2003), among many others. Over this time, my partner, Lori, and I have enjoyed some truly great meals; however, a thought continued to persist. While in camp, I often felt like I was merely an actor in, or a spectator to, a series of tightly defined *scenes*: locating my site with the help of my campground map (yes, it turns out, there is always a map), setting up my camp, breaking it down the next morning, repeating it all the following night. Others around us might do more—build fires, cook food, hang out in lawn chairs. The scripts (theirs and ours) didn't change much from one campground to the next.

So where was all the mystery, the sense of adventure? At first, I wondered whether additional gear might enhance my experience. I purchased my own headlight, a pillow, a water bottle, and a camp towel. Would these make me a better camper, I wondered, or would they just make me *look like* a better version of one?

I know what you must be thinking: Why did you write a book about camping if you're not an avid camper, if you don't even truly enjoy it? I keep going back to that first night and the strangeness of walking into the main building of the KOA, of driving to my tent site, walking around the interior roads of the campground. Most importantly, I think, is the shock, the profound disconnect between the expectation of what I thought camping *might be like*—a mental image largely fueled by cultural narratives of wilderness and survival—and what the experience actually turned out to be. The form of camping I experienced

⊙ 2017
Walk-in campsite 9, Schoodic Woods Campground, Acadia National Park, Maine, July 15, 2017.

at KOA Badlands and many other facilities since has very little to do with the rituals, sights, and sounds that many associate with the practice, a cultural idea of camping fueled by movies of settlers on the Western range: sleeping under the open night sky under the warmth of a heavy blanket, the sound of a crackling flame, the smell of roasting meat, the pot of coffee precariously stationed on a burning log. While my own experience never came close, this strange disconnect continues to fascinate me—the prescriptive nature of the map, the numbered campsites, the highlighter, the gaze of my camping neighbors, the washing machines, the convenience store, the internet access. *Making Camp* represents the culmination of a long body of reflection on the topic. Over this period I have assumed shifting roles—sometimes as a regular camper, but, more often than not, also as an observer, "reliving" and carefully probing, comparing, and analyzing the surrounds with that initial experience at KOA in mind. In 2011, I was invited to conduct research and interview key executives at KOA at their headquarters in Billings, Montana. Later that summer, I began to commit some of these insights to paper through a series of short online histories (the campsite, and later the picnic table) that were well received, suggesting that I may, in fact, be onto something. These were followed in short order by an exhibition of maps, diagrams, and historical materials titled *925,000 Campsites: The Commodification of an American Experience* (2013-2017). With the help of my research assistant Liz Grades, I tried to estimate the number of campsites around the United States—a figure I still find staggering. This project was in turn followed by my first book, *Thirtyfour Campgrounds* (MIT Press, 2016), in which I set out to visit popular campgrounds around the country. I use the term *visit* loosely, since I did not actually set foot in any of these facilities. Instead, I decided to download from online reservation websites like recreation.gov and reserveamerica.com

⊙ 2016

Partial grid of individual campsites at Island Park Recreation Area Campground, a facility located at Pine Flat Lake in Sanger, California, and managed by the US Army Corps of Engineers. These images were downloaded at the online reservation website https://www.recreation.gov.

Island Park 054

Island Park 055

Island Park 056

Island Park 057

Island Park 060

Island Park 061

Island Park 062

Island Park 063

Island Park 066

Island Park 067

Island Park 068

Island Park 069

Island Park 072

Island Park 073

Island Park 074

Island Park 075

Island Park 078

Island Park 079

Island Park 080

Island Park 081

Island Park 084

Island Park 085

Island Park 086

Island Park 087

Island Park 090

Island Park 091

Island Park 092

Island Park 093

Island Park 096

Island Park 097

Island Park / Blue group site

Island Park / Buck group site

every single photograph of every single campsite for those campgrounds I had targeted. I felt that these 6,500 photographs, taken collectively, might begin to convey character and texture from the standpoint of the online shopper/camper. The systematic arrangement of these photographs in ascending numerical order by site number lays bare the administrative foundation of each campground as well as its coordinate system of driving loops and addresses.

During this period, I received a wonderful and unexpected invitation from my friend and colleague Emily Zaengle to design and maintain a small campground of my own during an artist residency in Cazenovia, New York, where for four summers I have staged *Camping at the Art Park*. In what may be the smallest campground in the state, the project features four individual campsites and a central social hub (campfire, Adirondack chairs, bathrooms) dispersed across 104 acres. With the art park already open 365 days a year from dawn to dusk, I proposed introducing camping as a new layer of activity to broaden the range of experiences for visitors and provide them with a unique opportunity to spend forty-eight uninterrupted hours within this beautiful, immersive Central New York landscape. As they tend to their campsites and socially interact with fellow participants and other visitors, the campers themselves also become part of the art inside the park, which is to say that they and their encampments are on display for visitors to see, as I had first been made aware of myself when I set down roots at the Badlands KOA.

And so a long loop spanning from South Dakota to New York provisionally closes. Through it all, our trusty Sierra Designs two-person Meteor Lite tent has endured to tell the tale. Assembling its three long poles and threading them through the nylon envelope have lost none of their appeal. Similarly, I hope this book is a resource that can be returned to over time, shedding new light on the intricacies, ironies, and rewards of the camping experience with each trip.

⬆ ⬆ **2019**
Camping at the Art Park facilities map, June 2019.

⬆ **2019**
Among the components of *Camping at the Art Park* are picnic tables, signage, chairs, a wheelbarrow, and even flashlights, all painted the same bright shade of blue so they can be easily identified. Photograph by the author.

⮊ **2017**
Camping at the Art Park. Campsite No. 2 is located near a sculpture titled *Center* by artist Margaret LaBounty. June 2017. Photograph by the author.

Acknowledgments

*One does not impose, but rather
expose the site.*
—ROBERT SMITHSON,
   "Toward the Development of an
   Air Terminal Site"

I owe a unique debt of gratitude to my
friend and former colleague Sheri
Schumacher. By lending me her camping
gear during the summer of 2000, it was
she who, unwittingly, sent me on the wild
twenty-two-year adventure that resulted
in this book. Though I didn't know it at
the time, the artifacts she lent me (tent,
sleeping bag) and those features I first
encountered at KOA Badlands (the map,
the campsite) would end up forming four
of the eight chapters in this book.

This is not to say that there weren't
water taps, picnic tables, and restrooms
at this particular facility; rather, it's only
that I hadn't yet truly grasped the entire
system of physical components described
in *Making Camp*. But even this is an
oversimplification: while shining a light
on those artists, adventurers, explorers,
experts, inventors, tinkerers, and patent-
holders who designed the crucial
innovations that undergird the modern
campground, it has been easy at times
to detach myself and my own camping
experiences from this broader historical
narrative. For if I was a solitary camper
parked at a lone site when I first pitched my
tent in June 2000, I've emerged from this
proverbial walk around the campground
surrounded by a growing community of
friends, scholars, and enthusiasts without whom this project could not have
progressed. I owe everything to my
wonderful wife and partner, Lori, who—
along with our dogs Stache and Iggy—
anchors the most intimate, crucial, and
life-sustaining ring in this extended
network, here at home, on the road, and
at the campsite (the time we spent together
at site BB04, Bridger Bay Campground,
Antelope Island State Park, Utah, in 2002 is
a deeply cherished memory of the first year
we spent together). Across a bright blue
picnic table lies another tent—my dear
friend René Fan's; for several years now, she
has joined us in Cazenovia, New York, for
Camping at the Art Park—a temporary
installation I created in 2018. I am deeply
grateful for her company and support.

Few campers can boast that they
designed their own campground, and I am
thankful to Emily Zaengle, executive
director at the Stone Quarry Hill Art Park,
for hosting *Camping at the Art Park* and for
giving me this unique opportunity to apply
insights gleaned from personal experience
and scholarly research. Being only a
middling camper myself, I have found that
the latter has offered perhaps the most
significant adventures and rewards. During
a period of the Covid-19 pandemic when
travel was very limited, remote access to
research materials worldwide provided an
invaluable means of moving this project
forward. I am particularly thankful to the
National Park Service, whose collections
are hosted at two principal websites, the
Digital Asset Management System (https://
npgallery.gov) and the Electronic Technical
Information Center, or ETIC (https://pubs.
nps.gov). When specific documents were
not available there, I was able to count on
rangers, archivists, and interpretive

specialists from across the Park Service to locate them, whether at Grand Canyon (Joelle Baird), Shenandoah (Kandace Muller and Claire Comer), Yellowstone (Anne Foster and Linda Veress), Yosemite (Virginia Sanchez and Paul Rogers), or Zion National Park (Jonathan Shafer), as well as in Denver (Samantha Noon and Lia Vella), Harpers Ferry (Nancy Russell and Jessica Scott), and Washington, DC (John Sprinkle). I'm also grateful to George Franchois, Director, US Department of the Interior Library; Lincoln Bramwell, Chief Historian, US Forest Service; and Eric Reinert, Curator, US Army Corps of Engineers, for their help. I'd also like to extend a very special thanks to LuAnn Beebe, Caitlin Holton, Bethany Dixon, Michelle Nair, Joy A. Thomas, Wendy Thompson, and Cammie June Wyckoff from my home library at Cornell University, whose vast holdings continue to inspire. Bethany and Joy's diligence in tracking down even the most obscure of titles from collections including the Sul Ross State University in Alpine, Texas, and the First Division Museum at Cantigny in Wheaton, Illinois, was nothing short of a miracle. Lastly, my friends Janny Chaiyavet and Stephen Sears have provided research support in locating critical, often non-circulating documents. Everything I know about Overland Park in Denver, I owe to Janny's patient research. And from the library at the University of Illinois at Urbana-Champaign, Stephen was able to personally handle and scan an original copy of E. P. Meinecke's *A Camp Ground Policy* (1932)—a foundational document for this book. How straight-up cool is that?

With the deepest respect to Meinecke, Kep, Nessmuk and their contemporaries, I'd like to recognize those fellow travelers whom I have been fortunate to engage, not simply through the pages of their books, but in live conversation as well: Margot Apple (*Soft House*), Bryan Burkhart (*Airstream: This History of the Land Yacht*; *Trailer Travel: A History of Mobile America*), Ethan Carr (*Wilderness by Design; Mission 66*), Jonathan Chew (*Dolly Copp and New Hampshire's Peabody Valley*), John Clayton (*Wonderlandscape*), Rachel Gross (*Buckskin to Gore-Tex: The Outdoor Industry in American History*), Charlie Hailey (*Campsite: Architectures of Duration and Place; Camps: A Guide to 21st-Century Space*), Peter Hiller (*The Life and Times of Jo Mora: Iconic Artist of the American West*), Katie Ives (*Imaginary Peaks: The Riesenstein Hoax and Other Mountain Dreams*), Jennifer K. Mann (*The Camping Trip*), Gilles Modica (*Alpinisme: La saga des inventions*), Marilyn Moss (*Bill Moss: Fabric Artist & Designer*), Mike Parsons (*Invisible on Everest: Innovation and the Gear Makers*), Susan Snyder (*Past Tents*), Abigail Van Slyck (*A Manufactured Wilderness: Summer Camps and the Shaping of American Youth*), Dan White (*Under the Stars: How America Fell in Love with Camping*), and Terry Young (*Heading Out: A History of American Camping*) patiently fielded my emails and shared generous insights over the course of this project—please check out their wonderful books! A special thanks to Paul Allain, son of the famed French alpinist Pierre Allain; Dale W. Cole, a member of the Washington State–based Cougar Mountaineers; Bob Goss, who maintains a wonderful website on the history of Yellowstone National Park; Jim Graff and Saskia Boogman at Kampgrounds of America; and Bob Law of the US Militaria Forum all generously contributed materials, insights, and encouragement.

I am also deeply grateful to Mark Warfel for his graphic support, expertise, and digital wizardry: from building a digital model of The North Face's Oval Intention tent in order to corroborate pole lengths to color-correcting the 260 images in this book to developing a script that gridded and randomized the sixteen icons that make up its endpapers, it is safe to say that there is not a single spread in *Making Camp* that Mark has not had a hand in.

As I first began to assemble the first strands in this body of research around 2010, Nancy Levinson, executive editor at the online journal *Places*, and Josh Wallaert, formerly a senior editor at *Places*, showed interest in and later published my summary histories on the campsite (2011), Kampgrounds of America (2012), and the picnic table (2018). It was especially after this last article that the outline for this book began to fall into place. H. James Lucas and Susan Branson reviewed early drafts of the work, and I am very grateful for their feedback and lifelong friendship. At Princeton Architectural Press, Jennifer Thompson, executive editor, and her team (Paul Wagner, Sara Stemen, and Laura Didyk) believed in the project from the very beginning and have helped make this a better book in every way. Special thanks to Cornell University and Furthermore: a program of the J. M. Kaplan fund, for their support.

Lastly, I dedicate this book to my friends, colleagues, and mentors Bruce, Jack, and Terry. It was Jack Williams who challenged me to take pleasure in writing and to find my voice. For his part, Terry Young, a leading authority in the field of camping, always showed a special knack for forwarding me the perfect article or image that captured the essence of the topic I was exploring at the time. (That hilarious scene with the tipped over picnic table? *That* was Terry's find!) And like me, the late Bruce Wade was an architect, who taught me to draw *everything* so that I could see, and therefore design, *everything*, and I'm sure he would be pleased to know that campgrounds could be such technical undertakings in their own right. During the last years of his life, he and his wife, Elaine, bought a Roadtrek 190 camper van and traveled the country, and I like to imagine that we may have visited some of the same campgrounds. He is dearly missed.

⊙ 1967
Wally Byam Airstream caravan, Birch Bay, Washington, July 1967. Photograph by Jack Carver. Byam (1896–1962) founded Airstream in 1931 and led his first caravan in 1951 on a journey through Mexico, Guatemala, El Salvador, Honduras, and Nicaragua. Today the tradition continues, with airstream owners invited to join the Wally Byam Caravan Club International (WBCCI) on rallies across North America.

Notes

Introduction

1 Ethan Carr, *Wilderness by Design: Landscape Architecture & the National Park Service* (Lincoln: University of Nebraska Press, 1999), 283.

2 "2017 American Camper Report," Outdoor Industry Association, accessed August 16, 2019, https://outdoorindustry.org/resource/2017-american-camper-report/.

3 Craig E. Colten and Lary M. Dilsaver, "The Hidden Landscape of Yosemite National Park," *Journal of Cultural Geography* 22, no. 2 (Spring/Summer 2005): 35.

4 Dan White, *Under the Stars: How America Fell in Love with Camping* (New York: Henry Holt, 2016), 273–95.

5 Horace Kephart, *Camping and Woodcraft* (New York: Macmillan, 1917), 77–82. Kephart's estimate for a two-person tent is twenty pounds, including poles and pins. In comparison, a similar modern nylon tent ranges from two to four pounds. "Best Backpacking Tents," Clever Hiker, accessed August 17, 2019, https://www.cleverhiker.com/best-tents-backpacking.

6 Colten and Dilsaver, "The Hidden Landscape of Yosemite National Park," 30.

7 White, *Under the Stars*, 23.

Water

1 Edward Abbey, *Desert Solitaire: A Season in the Wilderness* (New York: Simon and Schuster, 1968), 115–16.

2 Mary Roberts Rinehart, *Tenting To-Night: A Chronicle of Sport and Adventure in Glacier Park and the Cascade Mountains* (Boston and New York: Houghton Mifflin, 1918), 64.

3 William Henry Harrison Murray, *Adventures in the Wilderness; Or, Camp Life in the Adirondacks* (Boston: Fields, Osgood, 1869), 53.

4 Ralph Waldo Emerson, "The Adirondacs," in *May-Day and Other Pieces* (Boston: Ticknor and Fields, 1867), 60.

5 Cindy S. Aron, *Working at Play: A History of Vacations in the United States* (Oxford and New York: Oxford University Press, 1999), 224.

6 Elon Jessup, *Roughing It Smoothly: How to Avoid Vacation Pitfalls* (New York: G. P. Putnam's Sons, 1923), 222.

7 Marshall O. Leighton, "Report of the Acting Superintendent of Yosemite National Park—Appendix B: Sanitary Conditions and Water Supply," in *Reports of the Department of the Interior* (Washington, DC: Government Printing Office, 1908), 43–442.

8 Ibid., 437.

9 Susan Snyder, *Past Tents: The Way We Camped* (Berkeley, CA: Heyday Books, 2006), 39.

10 Frank A. Waugh, *A Plan for the Development of the Village of Grand Canyon, Ariz.* (Washington, DC : Government Printing Office, 1918), 5.

11 Warren James Belasco, *Americans on the Road: From Autocamp to Motel, 1910–1945* (Baltimore: Johns Hopkins University Press, 1979), 89.

12 Frank E. Brimmer, *Coleman Motor Campers Manual* (Wichita, KS: Coleman Lamp Co., 1926), 37.

13 Craig E. Colten and Lary M. Dilsaver, "The Devil in the Cathedral: Sewage and Nature in Yosemite National Park," in *Cities and Nature in the American West*, ed. Char Miller (Reno: University of Nevada Press, 2010), 162.

14 Murray, *Adventures in the Wilderness*, 126.

15 Linda Flint McLelland, *Building the National Parks* (Baltimore: John Hopkins University Press, 1998), 263; Carr, *Wilderness by Design*, 285.

16 Albert H. Good, ed., *Park Structures and Facilities* (Washington , DC: Department of the Interior, National Park Service, 1935), 86.

17 Ibid., 85.

18 United States Forest Service Region Five, *Public Camp Manual* (San Francisco: US Forest Service, 1935), 17.

19 E. P. Meinecke, "The Trailer Menace," *Journal of Forestry* 70, no. 5 (May 1972): 280. This paper was originally written in 1935.

20 Ibid.

21 Belasco, *Americans on the Road*, 52.

22 John Steinbeck, *Travels with Charley: In Search of America* (London: Heinemann, 1962), 41.

23 Richard Long, *Continuum Walk*. © 2022 Richard Long. All Rights Reserved, DACS, London / ARS, NY.

24 Ethan Carr, *Mission 66: Modernism and the National Park Dilemma* (Amherst: University of Massachusetts Press, 2007), 328.

25 "About Us," Refillnotlandfill, accessed December 12, 2021, https://refillnotlandfill.org/about-us/.

26 Bob Myaing, "The 13 Best Nalgene Water Bottles: Limited Edition, Rare & Iconic," Field Mag, accessed December 22, 2021, https://www.fieldmag.com/articles/cool-nalgene-water-bottles-limited-edition.

Campfire

1 Daniel Carter Beard, *The American Boys' Handybook of Camp-Lore and Woodcraft* (Philadelphia and London: J. B. Lippincott, 1920), 37.

2 David Wescott, *Camping in the Old Style* (Layton, UT: Gibbs Smith, 2009), 121.

3 Richard Wrangham, *Catching Fire: How Cooking Made Us Human* (New York: Basic Books, 2010), 1–14.

4 Frank H. Cheley, *Camping Out* (New York: University Society, 1933), 5.

5 Horace Kephart, *Camp Cookery*, (New York: Outing Publishing Company, 1910), 35.

6 The original materials for this chapter were assembled during the Camp Fire (2018), at that time the most destructive wildfire in California history that claimed the lives of eighty civilians and five firefighters (including two prison inmate firefighters) and ravaged over 150,000 acres.

7 Brimmer, *Coleman Motor Campers Manual*, 1.

8 Kephart, *Camp Cookery*, 28.

9 A. Hyatt Verrill, *The Book of Camping* (New York: Alfred A. Knopf, 1917), 66.

10 "shirk," "quitter," "side-stepper": Beard, *The American Boys' Handybook of Camp-Lore*, 37; "arrant [sic], thoughtless, selfish Cheechako": Ibid., 49; "tenderfeet" and "blooming idiot": G. O. Shields, *Camping and Camp Outfits: A Manual of Instruction for Young and Old Sportsmen* (Chicago and New York: Rand, McNally, 1890), 94.

11 Shields, *Camping and Camp Outfits*, 93.

12 Daniel Carter Beard, *The Field and Forest Handy Book* (New York: Charles Scribner's Sons, 1906), 230–231.

13 Brimmer, *Coleman Motor Campers Manual*, 5.

14 Frank H. Cheley and Philip D. Fagans, eds., *Camping Out and Woodcraft: A Complete Guide to Outdoor Life* (New York: Halcyon House, 1933), 38.

15 Beard, *Field and Forest Handy Book*, 229.

16 Verrill, *Book of Camping*, 71.

17 Kephart, *Camping and Woodcraft*, 238.

18 Ibid., 237.

19 Ibid.

20 Frank H. Cheley, *Camping Out*, 106.

21 T. G. Taylor and W. L. Hansen, *Public Campground Planning* (Logan: Utah Agricultural Experiment Station, 1934), 24.

22 Cheley, *Camping Out*, 125.

23 Reyner Banham, *The Architecture of the Well-Tempered Environment*, 2nd ed. (Chicago: University of Chicago Press, 1984), 20.

24 Marc-Antoine Laugier, *Essai sur l'architecture*, 2nd ed. (Paris: Chez P. T. Barrois, 1755), frontispiece illustration.

25 Banham, *Architecture of the Well-Tempered Environment*, 20; Charlie Hailey, *Campsite: Architectures of Duration and Place* (Baton Rouge: Louisiana State University Press, 2008), 96.

26 Banham, *Architecture of the Well-Tempered Environment*, 20.

27 Taylor and Hansen, *Public Campground Planning*, 24.

28 Wylie Permanent Camping Company, *Yellowstone National Park*, 1910 ed. (Livingston, MT: Wylie Permanent Camping Company, 1910), 12.

29 Good, *Park Structures and Facilities*, 80.

30 Ibid., 79.

31 Ibid., 80.

32 Ibid., 81.

33 Brimmer, *Coleman Motor Campers Manual*, 10–11.

34 Good, *Park Structures and Facilities*, 80.

35 Wescott, *Camping in the Old Style*, 121.

36 Beard, *Field and Forest Handy Book*, 229. Beard notes that the matches appeared "somewhere around 1827."

37 Unlike the Lucifers, safety matches could be lit only by striking the plate on the side of the matchbox.

38 Terence Young, *Heading Out: A History of American Camping* (Ithaca, NY: Cornell University Press, 2017), 107–9. The author insightfully notes of the grate implement that it "could support multiple pans and pots at once but a few inches above a wood fire, allowing the camper to cook the whole meal at the same time."

39 Philip G. Terrie, *Forever Wild: Environmental Aesthetics and the Adirondack Preserve* (Philadelphia: Temple University Press, 1985), 50.

40 Beard, *American Boys' Handybook of Camp-Lore*, 36.

41 Ernest Thompson Seton, *The Book of Woodcraft* (New York: Doubleday, Page), 193–94.

42 Cheley, *Camping Out*, 271.

43 Ibid., p.252.

44 Warren H. Miller, *Camping Out* (New York: George H. Doran Company, 1918), 265.

45 Young, *Heading Out*, 112.

46 Ibid.

47 Ibid.

48 Ibid., 113.

49 Ibid., 115.

50 Brimmer, *Coleman Motor Campers Manual*, 13.

51 This promotional copy for the Coleman Company is cited in Young, *Heading Out*, 115.

52 Combining a taste for the vintage and the high tech, Coleman now sells a contemporary version of its early portable lamp (with LED lighting) under the aegis of its 1900 Collection.

53 "GoSun Stove Introduces Fuel-free Solar Grill at CES 2016," GoSun Press & Media, accessed July 2, 2022, https://gosun.co/pages/new-press-and-media.

54 Warren H. Miller, *Camp Craft: Modern Practice and Equipment* (New York: Charles Scribner's Sons, 1915), 80.

55 Wescott, *Camping in the Old Style*, 122.

56 Belasco, *Americans on the Road*, 89.

57 Sarah Perez, "Domino's Will Now Deliver to 150,000 Parks, Pools and Other Non-Traditional Locations," Tech Crunch, April 16, 2018, https://techcrunch.com/2018/04/16/dominos-will-now-deliver-to-150000-parks-pools-and-other-non-traditional-locations/.

58 John Schwartz, "Climate Change Is Making It Harder for Campers to Beat the Heat," *New York Times*, updated July 22, 2021, https://www.nytimes.com/2021/07/05/climate/global-warming-summer-camp.html.

59 Hailey, *Campsite*, 62.

Campsite

1 Kephart, *Camping and Woodcraft*, 17.

2 John A. Jakle and Keith A. Sculle, *Motoring: The Highway Experience in America* (Athens: University of Georgia Press, 2008), 105.

3 A 2013 assessment conducted by my research assistant Liz Grades estimated the total number of campsites at 925,000 nationally, including 25,800 sites in national parks and 70,100 sites on lands managed by the US Forest Service.

4 "KOA Surpasses Record Year by Impressive 33 Percent in 2021," KOA Press Room, January 17, 2022, http://www.koapressroom.com/press/koa-surpasses-record-year-by-impressive-33-in-2021/.

5 White, *Under the Stars*, 23. The author notes the "standoff between domesticity and the wild."

6 Susan Sessions Rugh, *Are We There Yet? The Golden Age of American Family Vacations* (Lawrence: University Press of Kansas, 2008), 10.

7 Recreational Equipment Incorporated and Eastern Mountain Sports.

8 Frank E. Brimmer, *Autocamping* (Cincinnati: Stewart Kidd, 1923), 240.

9 Snyder, *Past Tents*, 49.

10 Brimmer, *Coleman Motor Campers Manual*, 36.

11 Victor H. Green, *The Negro Motorist Green Book: An International Travel Guide,* (New York: Victor H. Green, 1949), 71.

12 Candacy Taylor, *Overground Railroad: The Green Book and the Roots of Black Travel in America* (New York: Abrams, 2020).

13 Cheley, *Camping Out*, 46.

14 Hailey, *Campsite*, 7.

15 "The Great Spring Drive," *Municipal Facts* 1, no. 2 (April 1918): 7.

16 Belasco, *Americans on the Road*, 71; J. C. and John D. Long, *Motor Camping* (New York: Dodd, Mead & Company, 1923), 198.

17 "Tourist Increase at Overland," *Municipal Facts Monthly* 3, no. 10 (October 1920): 14.

18 The series is also known as *Ugly Americans* or *Ugly America*.

19 Kephart, *Camping and Woodcraft*, 20.

20 Abigail Van Slyck, *A Manufactured Wilderness: Summer Camps and the Shaping of American Youth, 1890–1960* (Minneapolis: University of Minnesota Press, 2006), 109.

21 McClelland, *Building the National Parks*, 277–78.

22 E. P. Meinecke, *A Camp Ground Policy* (United States Department of Agriculture, Division of Forest Pathology, 1932), 10.

23 Steinbeck, *Travels with Charley*, 87.

24 Kephart, *Camping and Woodcraft*, 20.

25 "Two Week's Vagabonds," *New York Times*, July 20, 1922. Cited in Belasco, *Americans on the Road*, 8.

26 Kephart, *Camping and Woodcraft*, 20.

27 Long and Long, *Motor Camping*, 168.

28 Brimmer, *Coleman Motor Campers Manual*, 39–40; Long and Long, *Motor Camping*, 197–98.

29 KOA operates several franchises in Canada and Mexico, too. Over the years, the company has in fact never publicized campground closings in its directory. From one year to the next, when facilities disappear, they are simply left out of the next edition of the company's directory, leaving no means of comparison over time. Even during the significant downturn from the late 1970s to the present, when the number of franchises shrank by over 40 percent, KOA continues to advertise with great fanfare every new campground, as if its growth could not be stopped.

30 Brimmer, *Coleman Motor Campers Manual*, 9; "Now Campers Can Enjoy Confirmed Reservations At Any KOA, Free of Cost to You!," *KOA Kampground Directory: 1969 Winter Edition* (Billings, MT: Kampgrounds of America, 1969).

31 Rugh, *Are We There Yet?*, 131.

32 "Free Nationwide Reservations Service," *KOA Kampground Directory: 1970 Winter Edition* (Billings, MT: Kampgrounds of America, 1970), 8.

33 "Cody," *Kampgrounds of America, Inc. Directory 1964* (Billings, MT: Kampgrounds of America, 1964).

34 "Cody," *KOA Handbook and Directory for Campers* (Billings, MT: Kampgrounds of America, 1972), D-39.

35 "Cody," *KOA Kampground Directory, 1983 Edition* (Billings, MT: Kampgrounds of America, 1983), D-86.

36 "Cody," *KOA 2013 Campground Directory* (Billings, MT: Kampgrounds of America, 2013), 221.

37 *2010 KOA Kampground Directory: 2010 Edition* (Billings, MT: Kampgrounds of America, 2010), 4.

38 In 2009, IAC sold ReserveAmerica to ACTIVE Network. In 2017, the company's Outdoors division, including ReserveAmerica, became the independent company Aspira, now owned by Alpine Investors.

39 Conversation with Terence Young, March 22, 2010.

40 Michael Levy, "In the Scramble for a Campsite, Everyone Deserves an Equal Chance," *New York Times*, posted June 21, 2022, https://www.nytimes.com/2022/06/21/opinion/camping-parks-access.html.

41 William L. Rice, Jaclyn R. Rushing, Jennifer Thomsen, Peter Whitney, "Exclusionary Effects of Campsite Allocation through Reservations in U.S. National Parks: Evidence from Mobile Device Location Data," *Journal of Park and Recreation Administration*, March 18, 2022, https://js.sagamorepub.com/jpra/article/view/11392.

42 There is a growing range of camping blogs, focused on a number of specialized topics like gear and cooking. Interesting examples include Megan and Michael van Vliet's *Fresh Off the Grid*, https://www.freshoffthegrid.com/about/; Allison Boyle's *She Dreams of Alpine*, https://www.shedreamsofalpine.com; Dave Collins and Annie Hopfensperger's *Clever Hiker*, https://clever.hiker.com; Ryan Cunningham's *Beyond the Tent*, https://www.beyondthetent.com/; and Clint Carlson's *50 Campfires*, https://50campfires.com/.

43 Donald Wood, *RV's & Campers: 1900–2000* (Hudson, WI: Iconigrafix, 2002), 150.

Map

1 Constant Nieuwenhuys, "New Urbanism," cited in Hailey, *Campsite*, 62.

2 Lewis Stornoway, *Yosemite: Where to Go and What to Do: A Plain Guide to the Yosemite Valley* (San Francisco: C. A. Murdock, 1888), 25.

3 Ibid., 8.

4 Ibid., 24.

5 Ibid.

6 Stanford Demars, *The Tourist in Yosemite, 1855–1985* (Salt Lake City: University of Utah Press, 1991), 65.

7 Ibid.

8 Wylie Permanent Camping Company, *Yellowstone National Park*, 1910 ed., 4–5. The brochure notes that the company had been operating the "Wylie Way in Wonderland" for twenty-seven years.

9 Ibid., 11.

10 Ibid.

11 Ibid.

12 Ibid.

13 Young, *Heading Out*, 77. KOA was imitating their peers in the food service or hospitality industry, a process that Young, borrowing from George Ritzer's 1993 book, referred to as the "McDonaldization" of services and "society's desire for greater efficiency, calculability, predictability, and control."

14 Wylie Camping Company, *Yellowstone Park*, 1910 ed., 11, 14.

15 This rough estimate is based on the 7,700 annual visitors over a three-month period of operation, June 15 to September 15. With arrivals daily, tours were on constant rotation across the camps, ensuring maximum occupation of its four-night camps. 7,700 visitors divided by 360 camp nights of operation = 21 campers per camp every night.

16 Demars, *Tourist in Yosemite*, 139.

17 Long and Long, *Motor Camping*. Some campgrounds offered free overnight stays.

18 Reau Campbell, *Campbell's Complete Guide and Descriptive Book of The Yellowstone Park* (Chicago: H. E. Klamer, 1909), 113; Frank Jay Haynes and Jack Ellis Haynes, *Haynes Official Guide: Yellowstone National Park*, 26th ed. (Saint-Paul: Pioneer Company, 1912), 59. The maps of the Upper Geyser contained in these two guidebooks are nearly identical from the standpoint of framing, linework, and labeling.

19 Charles Parker (C. P.) Halligan, *Tourist Camps—Rural Landscape Series No. 2* (East Lansing: Michigan State College Agricultural Experiment Station, 1925), 3.

20 Meinecke, *Camp Ground Policy*, 15.

21 Young, *Heading Out*, 166.

22 Good, *Park Structures and Facilities*; Albert H. Good, ed., *Park and Recreation Structures* (Washington, DC: United States Government Printing Office, 1938). The expanded 1938 edition featuring information on motor campgrounds including tent and trailer campsites, picnic tables, and firepits was reprinted by Princeton Architectural Press in 1999.

23 United States Forest Service Region Five, *Public Camp Manual*.

24 Loop C in this drawing would be completed later, but loop B was never implemented.

25 Jo Mora, Yosemite map, 1931, 1949.

26 Jonathan Chew, email message to author, December 17, 2018.

27 "Educator Describes 'Picture Esperanto,'" *New York Times*, January 10, 1933, 25.

28 The first commercial copier, the Xerox 914, was introduced on September 16, 1959. However, the patent on which the 914 is based was obtained by Chester Carlson in 1942.

29 Many KOA concessioners employ Southeast Publications of Deerfield Beach, FL, to develop colorful and slightly cartoonish campground maps.

30 Otto Neurath, "Isotype as a Helping Language," in *International Picture Language* (London: Kegan Paul, Trench, Trubner & Co., Ltd), 17–22.

31 Peter Hiller, *The Life and Times of Jo Mora, Iconic Artist of the American West* (Layton, UT: Gibbs Smith, 2021), 220–22. Hiller notes that the original 1931 version was published as a simple line drawing with no color. Color versions of Mora's map were later published in 1941 and 1949 by the Yosemite Park and Curry Company, with slight alterations.

32 Jo Mora, "Yosemite." The map was of limited use for campers, however: because he used a single white tent to represent each campground, there is no way of judging the size or capacity of these facilities.

33 "Join Now: Pick the perfect campsite every time," Campground Views, accessed December 21, 2022, https://www.campgroundviews.com/best-camping-tool-ever/.

34 General campground rules and norms generally stipulate a maximum number of tents (2) and occupants (6).

Picnic Table

1 Osbert Sitwell, *Sing High! Sing Low!* (London: Macmillan, 1944), 142.

2 The table was named after Rear Admiral Stephen W. Rochon, former Director of the Executive Residence and the first African American to act as White House Chief Usher.

3 "Home / Outdoors / Patio Furniture / Patio Tables / Picnic Tables," Home Depot, accessed June 20, 2022, https://www.homedepot.com. This search yields several items that may or may not be labeled as *picnic tables* in the most conventional sense.

4 Miller, *Camp Craft*, 236.

5 Walter Levy, *The Picnic: A History* (Lanham, MD: AltaMira, 2014), 45.

6 Mary Ellen W. Hern, "Picnicking in the Northern United States, 1840–1900," *Winterthur Portfolio* 24, no. 2/3 (Summer/Autumn 1989): 152.

7 Ibid., 147. Hern is citing from Susan Dunning Power, *Anna Maria's House-Keeping* (Boston: D. Lothrop, 1884), 331–32.

8 Deborah M. Gordon, *Ants at Work* (New York: Simon and Schuster, 1999), 46.

9 Levy, *The Picnic*, 19.

10 Hern, "Picnicking in the Northern United States, 1840–1900," 7.

11 Levy, *The Picnic*, 7.

12 Murray, *Adventures in the Wilderness*, 14–15. Note that the latter part of the quote was withheld because it is blatantly disrespectful of Indigenous Peoples of America.

13 Miller, *Camp Craft*, 237.

14 Verrill, *The Book of Camping*, 84.

15 Good, ed., *Park Structures and Facilities*, 60.

16 Charles H. Nielsen, Table, US Patent 769,354, filed September 28, 1903, and issued September 6, 1904.

17 There is no information in the patent regarding the materiality of the tabletop, the seats, or their respective weights.

18 Harold R. Basford. Folding Camp Table, US Patent 1,272,187, filed September 4, 1917, and issued July 9, 1918.

19 Young, *Heading Out*, 135.

20 E. P. Meinecke, "Camp Planning and Camp Reconstruction" report (US Forest Service, California Region, 1934), 11.

21 Good, ed., *Park Structures and Facilities*, 57.

22 This 1922 drawing was clearly widely reproduced, as it came up time and again in the archives of the National Park Service, in various states of clarity.

23 E. P. Meinecke, *Camp Ground Policy*, 12.

24 Good, ed., *Park Structures and Facilities*, 58.

25 Young, *Heading Out*, 166.

26 Levy, *The Picnic*, 48.

Tent

1 S. H. Walker, *The Way to Camp* (London: Pilot, 1947), 39.

2 George Washington Sears, *Woodcraft*, 14th ed. (New York: Forest and Stream, 1920), 34.

3 Charles W. Moss and Henry Stribley, Folding Portable Shelter, US Patent 2,953,145, filed July 19, 1955, and issued September 20, 1960. Moss later commercialized the invention under the name Pop Tent. In the 1960s space race, similar claims to instantaneity were made about the Pop-Tart, first introduced by the Kellogg Company in 1964.

4 Gail Sheehy, *Passages: Predictable Crises of Adult Life* (New York: E. P. Dutton, 1974), 322.

5 Stephanie Bunn, *Nomadic Felts* (London: British Museum Press, 2010), 119.

6 Godfrey Rhodes, *Tents and Tent-Life from the Earliest Ages to the Present Time: To Which is Added the Practice of Encamping an Army in Ancient and Modern Times* (London: Smith, Elder, 1859), 23.

7 Charles W. Moss, Flexible Hyperbolic Paraboloid Shelter, US Patent 3,060,949, filed January 30, 1957, and issued October 30, 1962.

8 Ibid., xi.

9 Daniel Carter Beard, *Shelters, Shacks and Shanties* (New York: Charles Scribner's Sons, 1916), 2; Rhodes, *Tents and Tent-Life*, 147.

10 "The Sportsman's Bookshelf Volume II—Camp and Camp Cookery," in Elmer Kreps, Warren H. Miller, William Holt-Jackson, et al., *A Camper's Guide to Tents: A Collection of Historical Camping Articles on Types of Tent and How to Construct Them*, (Redditch, UK: Read Books, 2011), 279.

11 Ferdinand Eberhardt, Combined Tent and Ground Floor Cloth, US Patent 1,057,628, filed December 21, 1912, and issued April 1, 1913.

12 Reinhaldt Lönnqvist, An Improved Tent, GB Patent 377,831, and issued September 7, 1931, and issued

August 4, 1932. Inexplicably, Lönnqvist's invention appears to only have been patented much later in his native country of Finland (1953) and in the United States (1957).

13 Francis Galton, *The Art of Travel Or, Shifts and Contrivances Available in Wild Countries*, 4th ed. (London: John Murray, 1867), 161; *Popular Mechanics Auto Tourist's Handbook No. 1* (Chicago: Popular Mechanics Press, 1924), 43. Similarly, an inspection of Bill Moss's 1955 *Pop Tent* reveals that the ends of each pole were pointed and could be poked into the ground for added stability.

14 Eugène Emmanuel Viollet-Le-Duc, *Histoire de l'habitation humaine depuis les temps préhistoriques jusqu'à nos jours* (Paris: Bilbiothèque d'éducation et de récreation, 1875), 38; E. M. Hatton, *The Tent Book* (Boston: Houghton Mifflin, 1979), 42.

15 Bryan Burkhart and David Hunt, *Airstream: The History of the Land Yacht* (San Francisco: Chronicle Books, 2000), 28.

16 William B. MacDonald Jr., Vehicle Trailer, US Patent 2,481,230, filed April 8, 1946, and issued September 6, 1949. The invention was commercialized as the Karriall Kamper.

17 Kephart, *Camp Cookery*, 12.

18 Henry Hopkins (H. H.) Sibley, Conical Tent, US Patent 14,740, issued April 22, 1856.

19 Hatton, *Tent Book*, 22.

20 Ibid.

21 Miller, *Camp Craft*, 37. Poles were initially not factored into the weight of the outfit since they were often sold separately.

22 Ibid., 35.

23 Kephart, *Camping and Woodcraft*, 97.

24 Ibid., 84.

25 Edward Whymper, *Scrambles Amongst the Alps in the Years 1860–'69* (Philadelphia: J. P. Lippincott & Co., 1872), 46–47.

26 A modest cheesemaker, Meynet faded into history after the Matterhorn climb.

27 Thomas Hiram (T. H.) Holding, *The Camper's Handbook* (London: Simpkin, Marshall, Hamilton, Kent, Ltd., 1908), 137. It is not clear whether the two poles were considered as part of this surprisingly lightweight design.

28 Ibid., 301.

29 Ibid., 280.

30 "Noepel's Steel Tent Poles," in *Abercrombie and Fitch Co.*, 1910 ed. (New York: Abercrombie & Fitch, 1910), 47.

31 James H. Blair, Rod For Cleaning Rifles and the Like, US Patent 933,285, filed November 21, 1908, and issued September 7, 1909.

32 Harry H. Harsted. Foldable Antenna, US Patent 2,379,577, filed January 25, 1943, and issued July 3, 1945.

33 *The Fall 1975 North Face Catalog* (Portland, OR: Northwest Publishing, 1975), 31. Note the presence of the word *tent* in Oval Intention. The shortest poles in the *OI* set are approximately 75 inches long and bent to an even higher, eye-popping height of 51 inches.

34 Susannah Handley, *Nylon: The Story of a Fashion Revolution* (Baltimore: Johns Hopkins University Press, 2000), 16.

35 This figure is based on visual observation and does not include the fly sheet.

36 R. Buckminster Fuller. Geodesic Tent, US Patent 2,914,074, filed March 1, 1957, and issued November 24, 1959.

37 Marylin Moss, *Bill Moss: Fabric Artist & Designer* (Rockport, ME: Chawezi, 2013), 25.

38 Mark Wilson, "Inflatable Geodesic Tent Makes Tent Poles Obsolete," *Fast Company*, accessed February 24, 2021, https://www.fastcompany.com/1670031/inflatable-geodesic-tent-makes-tent-poles-obsolete.

39 William S. Faulkner, Shelter-Tent Half and Poncho, US Patent 703,245, filed July 16, 1901, and issued June 24, 1902.

40 Isidor Mautner, Tent, US Patent 535,066, filed September 24, 1894, and issued March 5, 1895.

41 Frank H. Gotsche, Tent, US Patent 901,802, filed January 20, 1908, and issued October 20, 1908.

42 Banham, *Architecture of the Well-Tempered Environment*, 18.

43 Wallace Hume Carothers, Synthetic Fiber, US Patent 2,130,948, filed April 9, 1937, and issued September 20, 1938.

44 Handley, *Nylon*, 48.

45 Robert L. Blanchard, Explorer's Folding Tent, US Patent 2,543,684, filed February 20, 1948, and issued February 27, 1951.

46 "A Brief History of Tents," Fjällräven, accessed February 26, 2021, https://foxtrail.fjallraven.com/articles/history-of-tents/.

47 Francis Galton, *The Art of Travel, OR, Shifts and Contrivances Available in Wild Countries* (London: John Murray, 1855), 39; *Abercrombie and Fitch Co.*, 1910 ed., 46; Claude P. Fordyce, *Trail Craft: An Aid In Getting the Greatest Good Out of Vacation Trips* (Cincinnati: Stewart Kidd, 1922), 95–96. Galton was perhaps the first to recommend using gauze to guard against "musquitoes" (sic). Later, Abercrombie & Fitch Co. offered bobbinet, mosquito-proof tent fronts, as well as insect-proof cheesecloth liners. For his part, Fordyce reported that Stewart Edward White had proposed suspending a second tent entirely made of cheesecloth inside of the cloth tent.

48 Handley, *Nylon*, 7.

Sleeping Bag

1 Emerson Hough, *Out of Doors* (New York and London: Appleton and Company, 1915), 150.

2 Robert McClure, *The Discovery of the North-West Passage by HMS Investigator*, 2nd ed. (London: Longman, Brown, Green, Longmans & Roberts, 1857), 135; Sherard Osborn, *Stray Leaves From an Arctic Journal; Or, Eighteen Months in the Polar Regions, in Search of Sir John Franklin's Expedition, in the Years 1850–51* (New York: George P. Putnam, 1853), 117. Note that Osborn edited the McClure journals, so the term *sleeping bag* might have come from him.

3 "sleeping-sack": Elisha Kent Kane, *Arctic Explorations: The Second Grinnell Expedition* (Philadelphia: Childs & Peterson, 1856), 168, and Robert Louis Stevenson, *Travels with a Donkey in the Cévennes* (New York: Century Co., 1907), 118; "drugget bag": Galton, *Art of Travel*, 45; "blanket bag": Whymper, *Scrambles Amongst the Alps*, 20, and *Abercrombie & Fitch Co.*, 1916 ed. (New York: Abercrombie & Fitch, 1916), 15; "strong linen sack": Galton, *Art of Travel*, 3rd ed., 45; "knapsack bag": Galton, *Art of Travel*, 5ᵗʰ ed., 150; "peasant's sack": Ibid., 153; "traveling rug": *Pryce Jones, Royal Welsh Warehouse, North Wales. Newtown* (1888–89), 129; "sleeping valise": Harry Roberts, *The Tramp's Hand-book* (New York and London: John Lane, Bodley Head, 1903), 144; "sleeping-pocket": Edward Breck, *The Way of the Woods: A Manual for Sportsmen in Northeastern United States and Canada* (New York and London: G. P. Putnam's Sons, 1908), 57; "quilt bag": Miller, *Camp Craft*, 58.

4 John Steinbeck, "Camping is for the Birds," in *Popular Science* 90, no. 5 (May 1967): 204.

5 Frank A. Bates, "Comfort in Camp," in George S. Bryan, ed., *The Camper's Own Book: A Handy Volume for Devotees of Tent and Trail* (New York: Log Cabin Press, 1912), 22.

6 Kephart, *Camping and Woodcraft,* 125.

7 In choosing suitable bedding, Washington may have been tempted by the famed four-point wool blanket first introduced by the Hudson Bay Company in 1779, an item of such unimpeachable reputation that it was still advertised by outfitters like Abercrombie & Fitch Co. well into the twentieth century. However, it would have been his patriotic duty to refuse any such gift from the British-led trader.

8 Belasco, *Americans on the Road*, 129.

9 Sherard Osborn, *Stray Leaves from an Arctic Journal*, 117.

10 Bunn, *Nomadic Felts*, 90.

11 Ibid.

12 Jessup, *Roughing It Smoothly*, 73.

13 Raymond Gaché, "Le matériel de bivouac," *Alpinisme* 40, (1935): 163–66.

14 Fridtjof Nansen, *The First Crossing of Greenland* (London & New York: Longmans, Green, 1890), 43. Nansen had decided against a single six-man bag for the entire team in case they lost their only sled in a crevasse.

15 Claude P. Fordyce, *Touring Afoot* (New York: Macmillan, 1922), 107.

16 Apsley Cherry-Garrard, *The Worst Journey in the World: Antarctic 1910–1913* (New York: George H. Doran, 1922), 238.

17 Ibid., 293.

18 H. Hawthorne Manning, "Sleeping System Rather than Sleeping Bag?," *Summit* 5 no. 6 (July 1959): 28–29; Harvey Manning, *Backpacking: One Step at a Time*, 4th ed. (New York: Vintage Books, 1986), 268–69. Note that this is the same individual.

19 Murray, *Adventures in the Wilderness*, 23.

20 Dale W. Cole, email messages to author, November 26 and December 09, 2021. Cole, who, like Manning, was part of the Cougar Mountain group, confirms this fact.

21 Katie Ives, *Imaginary Peaks: The Riesenstein Hoax and Other Mountain Dreams* (Seattle: Mountaineer Books, 2021), 128.

22 The photograph is made even more poignant by the fact that Evans would die on the Beardmore Glacier less than a year later during their return journey from the South Pole, where Robert Falcon Scott and his men had arrived only to find the Norwegian flag planted there five weeks earlier by their competitor, Roald Amundsen.

23 Kephart, *Camping and Woodcraft,* 128.

24 Whitcomb L. Judson, Shoe Fastening, US Patent 504,037, filed November 7, 1891, and issued August 29, 1893; Robert Friedel, *Zipper: An Exploration in Novelty* (New York: W. W. Norton, 1994), 12–18.

25 Gideon Sundback, Separable Fastener, US Patent 1,219,881, filed August 27, 1914, and issued March 20, 1917.

26 *Motor Camper & Tourist* 2, no.2 (July 1925): 143.

27 *The Mountaineer* 20, no. 1 (December 1927): 79.

28 "NEMO Canon -40 Sleeping Bag, Long," Geartrade, accessed July 09, 2021, https://www.geartrade.com/item/719515/nemo-canon-40-sleeping-bag-long?gclid=CjwKCAjw55-HBhAHEiwARMCszhKUjl4PvcLMO-Mu2miQJtktxoDUh2sTG8u6BzSuCyjCSjJTKa1zvbhoC-QRgQAvD_BwE.

29 Galton, *Art of Travel*, 3rd ed., 41.

30 Francis Galton, *The Art of Travel; Or Shifts and Contrivances Available in Wild Countries*, 2nd ed. (London: John Murray, 1856), 38.

31 Kephart, *Camping and Woodcraft*, 124–25.

32 Galton, *Art of Travel*, 4th ed., 138.

33 Galton, *Art of Travel* 2nd ed., 38.

34 Mummery perished a few years later while attempting to climb Nanga Parbat, located in the Diamer District of Gilgit-Baltistan, Pakistan.

35 A turn-of-the-century Inughuit caribou skin sleeping bag from Cape York, Greenland (10.5 pounds), is 50 percent lighter than a Greely Expedition sleeping bag (18.5 pounds) from the same period.

36 Sears, *Woodcraft*, 14th ed., 24.

37 Galton, *Art of Travel*, 2nd ed., 36.

38 Jessup, *Roughing It Smoothly*, 68–69.

39 Flavius Vegetius Renatus, *De re militari* (Utrecht, NL: Nicolaus Ketelaer en Gherardus de Leempt, 1473).

40 "Perfection Mattress," *Harper's Weekly*, July 9, 1898, 680.

41 Fordyce, *Touring Afoot*, 111.

42 James M. Lea and Neil P. Anderson, Inflatable Foam Pad, US Patent 3,872,525, filed January 10, 1972, and issued March 25, 1975.

43 Manning, *Backpacking*, 4th ed., 242.

44 Susan Cosier, "Everything You Need to Know About Buying Ethically Sourced Down Products," National Aububon Society, December 18, 2020, https://www.audubon.org/news/everything-you-need-know-about-buying-ethically-sourced-down-products.

45 "Down Production: Birds Abused for Their Feathers," People for the Ethical Treatment of Animals, accessed June 29, 2021, https://www.peta.org/features/down-investigation/.

46 "Recycled Nylon," Patagonia, accessed July 12, 2021, https://www.patagonia.com/our-footprint/recycled-nylon.html. Today, 90 percent of the nylon used in Patagonia's gear contains recycled nylon.

47 "Genuine U.S. Military Issue ECW (Extreme Cold Weather) Sleeping Bag, Excellent Used Condition," B&M Military Surplus, accessed June 29, 2021, https://bandmmilitarysurplus.com/product/genuine-u-s-military-issue-ecw-extreme-cold-weather-sleeping-bag-excellent-used/.

Trash

1 Brimmer, *Coleman Motor Campers Manual*, 62.

2 Colten and Dilsaver, "The Devil in the Cathedral," 157; John Clayton, "Bears in Yellowstone," *Big Sky Journal*, Summer 2018, https://bigskyjournal.com/bears-in-yellowstone/.

3 Frank D. Carpenter, *The Wonders of Geyser Land* (Black Earth, WI: Burnett & Sons, 1878), 33. Note that the end of this quote was deliberately withheld because it is racist.

4 Ibid.

5 Cornelia James Cannon, "The Untidy Tourist," *Outing* 81, no. 3 (December 1922): 113.

6 John A. Jakle, *The Tourist: Travels in Twentieth-Century North America* (Lincoln: University of Nebraska Press, 1985), 158.

7 Halligan, *Tourist Camps*, 8.

8 Kathleen Meyer, *How to Shit in the Woods: An Environmentally Sound Approach to a Lost Art*, 4th ed. (Berkeley, CA: Ten Speed, 2020), 60–69; White, *Under the Stars*, 275.

9 Meyer, *How to Shit in the Woods*, 22.

10 John Brinckerhoff (J. B.) Jackson, *American Space: The Centennial Years*, 1865–1876 (New York: W. W. Norton, 1972), 219–29.

11 Kephart, *Camping and Woodcraft*, 222.

12 United States Forest Service Region Five, *Public Camp Manual*, 20.

13 Steinbeck, *Travels with Charley*, 25.

14 Ibid.

Afterword

1 Franklin M. Reck and William Moss, *Ford Treasury of Station Wagon Living* (New York: Simon and Schuster, 1957), 21.

2 Though I can't be sure, my partner, Lori, and I did visit KOA Badlands on another trip to the region in September 2004 and camped in the same area.

Further Reading

Author's note: In preparing this bibliography, I wanted to both acknowledge and expand on the range of titles referenced throughout this book. My goal was to assemble a broad historical cross section of materials that span the entire 150-year history of recreational camping in the United States, beginning with the Reverend William Henry Harrison Murray's *Adventures in the Wilderness* (1869) and ending with Phoebe Young's *Camping Grounds* (2021). Crucial to this timeline is a series of early volumes published during the early decades of the nineteenth century by authors such as Daniel Carter Beard, Frank E. Brimmer, Horace Kephart, Elon Jessup, George Washington Sears, Ernest Thompson Seton, and A. Hyatt Verrill. Many of these books are long out of circulation, but many of these titles are available in reprint form, as noted below. Those labeled * are available for free download from one of the following websites: Archive.org (https://archive.org); the National Park Service's Electronic Technical Information Center (https://pubs.nps.gov/); or the Forest History Society (https://foresthistory.org). Finally, a special designation ** is set aside for richly illustrated coffee-table books on the subject of camping.

Abercrombie & Fitch Co., 1916 ed. New York: Abercrombie & Fitch Co., 1916. https://archive.org.

Aron, Cindy S. *Working at Play: A History of Vacations in the United States.* Oxford and New York: Oxford University Press, 1999.

Barringer, Mark Daniel. *Selling Yellowstone: Capitalism and the Construction of Nature.* Lawrence: University Press of Kansas, 2002.

*Beard, Daniel Carter. *The American Boys' Handybook of Camp-Lore and Woodcraft.* Philadelphia and London: J. B. Lippincott, 1920. Reprint, Jaffrey, NH: Nonpareil Books, 2008. https://archive.org.

*———. *The Field and Forest Handy Book.* New York: Charles Scribner's Sons, 1906. Reprint, Jaffrey, NH: Nonpareil Books, 2000. https://archive.org.

Belasco, Warren James. *Americans on the Road: From Autocamp to Motel, 1910–1945.* Baltimore: Johns Hopkins University Press, 1979.

Blanke, David. *Hell on Wheels: The Promise and Peril of America's Car Culture, 1900–1940.* Lawrence: University Press of Kansas, 2007.

Breck, Edward. *The Way of the Woods: A Manual for Sportsmen in Northeastern United States and Canada.* New York and London: G. P. Putnam's Sons, 1908.

Brimmer, Frank E. *Coleman Motor Campers Manual.* Wichita, KS: Coleman Lamp Co., 1926.

*———. *Autocamping.* Cincinnati: Stewart Kidd Company Publishers, 1923. https://archive.org.

**Brunkowski, John, and Michael Closen. *Pictorial Guide to RVing.* Atglen, PA: Schiffer, 2010.

*Bryan, George S., ed. *The Camper's Own Book: A Handy Volume for Devotees of Tent and Trail.* New York: The Log Cabin Press, 1912. Reprint, Scholar Select, 2016. https://archive.org.

**Burkhart, Bryan, and David Hunt. *Airstream: The History of the Land Yacht.* San Francisco: Chronicle Books, 2000.

**Burkhart, Bryan, Phil Noyes, and Allison Arieff. *Trailer Travel: A Visual History of Mobile America.* Layton, UT: Gibbs Smith, 2002.

Carr, Ethan. *Mission 66: Modernism and the National Park Dilemma.* Amherst: University of Massachusetts Press, 2007.

———. *Wilderness by Design: Landscape Architecture & the National Park Service.* Lincoln: University of Nebraska Press, 1998.

Chamberlin, Silas. *On the Trail: A History of American Hiking.* New Haven: Yale University Press, 2016.

Cheley, Frank H. *Camping Out*. New York: The University Society, 1933. Reprint, Whitefish, MT: Kessinger, 2010.

Colten, Craig E., and Larry M. Dilsaver. "The Hidden Landscape of Yosemite National Park." *Journal of Cultural Geography* 22 (Spring/Summer 2005): 27–50.

Cunningham, Gerry, and Margaret Hansson. *Light Weight Camping Equipment and How to Make It*. New York: Charles Scribner's Sons, 1976.

De Abaitua, Matthew. *The Art of Camping; The History and Practice of Sleeping Under the Stars*. New York and London: Penguin Books, 2011.

Demars, Stanford E. *The Tourist in Yosemite, 1855–1985*. Salt Lake City: University of Utah Press, 1991.

Dilsaver, Lary. "Stemming the Flow: The Evolution of Controls on Visitor Numbers and Impact in National Parks." In *The American Environment: Interpretation of Past Geographies*, edited by Larry M. Dilsaver and Craig E. Colten, 235–256. Lanham, MD: Rowman & Littlefield, 1992.

**Duncan, Dayton, and Ken Burns. *The National Parks: America's Best Idea*. New York: Alfred A. Knopf, 2009.

*Fordyce, Claude P. *Touring Afoot*. New York: Macmillan, 1922. Reprint, Scholar Select, 2019. https://archive.org.

*Fordyce, Claude P. *Trail Craft: An Aid in Getting the Greatest Good Out of Vacation Trips*. Cincinnati: Stewart Kidd Company, 1922. Reprint, London: Forgotten Books, 2017. https://archive.org.

Franz, Kathleen. *Tinkering: Consumers Reinvent the Early Automobile*. Philadelphia: University of Pennsylvania Press, 2005.

Frisch, Emma. *Feast by Firelight: Simple Recipes for Camping, Cabins, and the Great Outdoors*. Berkeley, CA: Ten Speed Press, 2017.

**Futterman, Steve, and Margot Apple. *Soft House*. New York: Harper & Row, 1976.

*Galton, Francis. *The Art of Travel; Or, Shifts and Contrivances Available in Wild Countries*, 5th ed. London: John Murray, 1872. Reprint, Scotts Valley, CA: CreateSpace, 2016. https://archive.org.

**Gellner, Arrol, and Douglas Keister. *Ready to Roll: A Celebration of the Classic American Travel Trailer*. New York: Viking Studio, 2003.

Gilborn, Craig A. *Adirondacks Camps: Home Away from Home, 1850–1950*. Syracuse, NY: Syracuse University Press, 2000.

*, **Good, Albert H., ed. *Park and Recreation Structures*. Washington, DC: Department of the Interior, National Park Service, 1938. Reprint, New York: Princeton Architectural Press, 1999. https://archive.org.

*, **———. *Park Structures and Facilities*. Washington, DC: Department of the Interior, National Park Service, 1935. https://archive.org.

Green, Victor H. *The Negro Motorist Green-Book: An International Travel Guide*. New York: Victor H. Green, 1940. Reprint, Camarillo, CA: About Comics, 2016.

———. *The Negro Motorist Green Book Compendium*. Camarillo, CA: About Comics, 2019.

Grusin, Richard. *Culture, Technology, and the Creation of America's National Parks*. Cambridge, UK: Cambridge University Press, 2004.

Hailey, Charlie. *Camps: A Guide to 21st-Century Space*. Cambridge, MA: MIT Press, 2009.

———. *Campsite: Architectures of Duration and Place*. Baton Rouge: Louisiana State University Press, 2008.

Halligan, C. P. *Tourist Camps–Rural Landscape Series No. 2*. East Lansing: Michigan State College Agricultural Experiment Station, 1925.

Hart, John Fraser, Michelle J. Rhodes, and John T. Morgan. *The Unknown World of the Mobile Home*. Baltimore and London: Johns Hopkins University Press, 2002.

**Hatton, E. M. *The Tent Book*. Boston: Houghton Mifflin, 1979.

**Heister, Douglas. *Teardrops and Tiny Trailers*. Layton, UT: Gibbs Smith, 2008.

**Hillcourt, William. *The Golden Book of Camping*. New York: Golden Press, 1971.

**Hogue, Martin. *Thirtyfour Campgrounds*. Cambridge, MA: MIT Press, 2016.

*Holding, T. H. *The Campers' Handbook*. London: Simpkin, Marshall, Hamilton, Kent, Ltd., 1908. Reprint, Whitefish, MT: Kessinger, 2010. https://archive.org.

*Hough, Emerson. *Out of Doors*. New York and London: Appleton and Company, 1915. Reprint, Scholar Select, 2015. https://archive.org.

Jakle, John A. *The Tourist: Travels in Twentieth-Century North America*. Lincoln: University of Nebraska Press, 1985.

Jakle, John A., and Keith A. Sculle. *Motoring: The Highway Experience in America*. Athens: University of Georgia Press, 2008.

Jessup, Elon. *Roughing It Smoothly: How to Avoid Vacation Pitfalls*. New York: G. P. Putnam's Sons, 1923.

*———. *The Motor Camping Book*. New York: G. P. Putnam's Sons, 1921. Reprint, Eugene, OR: Doublebit, 2021. https://archive.org.

* Kephart, Horace. *Camping and Woodcraft*. New York: Macmillan, 1917. Reprint, Eugene, OR: Doublebit, 2021. https://archive.org.

*Kimball, Winfield A., and Maurice H. Decker. *Touring With Tent and Trailer*. New York: Whittlesey House, 1937. https://archive.org.

Kreps, Elmer, Warren H. Miller, William Holt-Jackson, et al. *A Camper's Guide to Tents: A Collection of Historical Articles on Types of Tents and How to Construct Them*. Redditch, UK: Read Books, 2011.

Levy, Walter. *The Picnic: A History*. Lanham, MD: AltaMira, 2014.

*Long, J. C., and John D. Long. *Motor Camping*. New York: Dodd, Mead, 1923. Reprint, Charleston, SC: Bibliolife, 2009. https://archive.org.

Löfgren, Orvar. *On Holiday: A History of Vacationing*. Berkeley: University of California Press, 1999.

Louter, David. *Windshield Wilderness: Cars, Roads, and Nature in Washington's National Parks*. Seattle: University of Washington Press, 2006.

McLelland, Linda Flint. *Building the National Parks*. Baltimore: John Hopkins University Press, 1998.

Magoc, Chris J. *Yellowstone: The Creation and Selling of an American Landscape, 1870–1903*. Albuquerque: University of New Mexico Press, 1999.

Mann, Jennifer K. *The Camping Trip*. Somerville, MA: Candlewick, 2020.

Manning, Harvey. *Backpacking: One Step at a Time*, 4th ed. New York: Vintage Books, 1986.

*Meinecke, E. P. *A Camp Ground Policy*. Washington, DC: United States Department of Agriculture, Division of Forest Pathology, 1932. https://foresthistory.org.

Meyer, Kathleen. *How to Shit in the Woods: An Environmentally Sound Approach to a Lost Art*, 4th ed. Berkeley, CA: Ten Speed, 2020.

*Miller, Warren H. *Camp Craft: Modern Practice and Equipment*. New York: Charles Scribner's Sons, 1915. Reprint, London: Forgotten Books, 2017. https://archive.org.

*———. *Camping Out*. New York: George H. Doran, 1918. Reprint, London: Forgotten Books, 2018.

Moss, Marilyn. *Bill Moss: Fabric Artist & Designer*. Camden, ME: Chawezi, 2013.

*Murray, William Henry Harrison (H. H.). *Adventures in the Wilderness; Or, Camp-Life in the Adirondacks*. Boston: Fields, Osgood, 1869. Reprint, London: Forgotten Books, 2012. https://archive.org.

*Nansen, Fridtjof. *The First Crossing of Greenland*. London and New York: Longmans, Green, 1890. Reprint, London: Gibson Square Books, 2022. https://archive.org.

*National Park Service. *Campground Study: A Report of the Committee to Study Camping Policy and Standards—Region Four*. San Francisco: National Park Service, 1959. https://pubs.nps.gov.

Parsons, Mike, and Mary B. Rose. *Invisible on Everest: Innovation and the Gear Makers*. Philadelphia: Northern Liberties Press, 2003.

Popular Mechanics Auto Tourist's Handbook No. 1. Chicago: Popular Mechanics Press, 1924.

Ratay, Richard. *Don't Make Me Pull Over! An Informal History of the Family Road Trip*. New York: Scribner, 2018.

Reck, Franklin M., and William Moss. *Ford Treasury of Station Wagon Living*. New York: Simon and Schuster, 1957.

Rhodes, Godfrey. *Tents and Tent-Life from the Earliest Ages to the Present Time: To Which is Added the Practice of Encamping an Army in Ancient and Modern Times*. London: Smith, Elder, 1859.

Riviere, Bill. *The Camper's Bible*, revised ed. New York: Doubleday, 1970.

Roberts, Harry. *The Tramp's Hand-book*. New York and London: John Lane, Bodley Head, 1903.

Rugh, Susan Sessions. *Are We There Yet? The Golden Age of American Family Vacations*. Lawrence: University Press of Kansas, 2008.

Rustrum, Calvin. *The New Way of the Wilderness*. New York: Macmillan, 1958.

Shaffer, Marguerite S. *See America First: Tourism and National Identity, 1880–1940*. Washington and London: Smithsonian Institution Press, 2001.

*Sears, George Washington. *Woodcraft*, 14th ed. New York: Forest and Stream Publishing Co., 1920. Reprint, Eugene, OR: Doublebit, 2019. https://archive.org.

Sellars, Richard West. *Preserving Nature in the National Parks: A History*. New Haven: Yale University Press, 1997.

*Seton, Ernest Thompson. *The Book of Woodcraft*. New York: Doubleday Page, 1912. https://archive.org.

**Snyder, Susan. *Past Tents: The Way We Camped*. Berkeley, CA: Heyday Books, 2006.

**Standards Manual*. *Parks*. Brooklyn, NY: Standards Manual, 2019.

*Steinbeck, John. *Travels with Charley: In Search of America*. London: Heinemann, 1962. Reprint, New York: Penguin Books, 1980. https://archive.org.

*Stevenson, Robert Louis. *Travels with a Donkey in the Cévennes*. New York: Century, 1907. Reprint, Mineola, NY: Dover Thrift Editions, 2019. https://archive.org.

Taylor, Candacy. *Overground Railroad: The Green Book and the Roots of Black Travel in America*. New York: Abrams, 2020.

Taylor, T. G., and W. L. Hansen. *Public Campground Planning*. Logan: Utah Agricultural Experiment Station, 1934.

*Terrie, Philip G. *Forever Wild: Environmental Aesthetics and the Adirondack Preserve*. Philadelphia: Temple University Press, 1985. https://archive.org.

United States Forest Service Region Five. *Public Camp Manual*. San Francisco: United States Forest Service, 1935.

**Van Slyck, Abigail. A. *A Manufactured Wilderness: Summer Camps and the Shaping of American Youth, 1890–1960*. Minneapolis: University of Minnesota Press, 2006.

*Verrill, A. Hyatt. *The Book of Camping*. New York: Alfred A. Knopf, 1917. Reprint, London: Forgotten Books, 2017. https://archive.org.

Walker, S. H. *The Way to Camp*. London: Pilot, 1947.

**Wescott, David. *Camping in the Old Style*. Layton, UT: Gibbs Smith, 2009.

**———. *Camping in the Old Style*, revised ed. Layton, UT: Gibbs Smith, 2015.

White, Dan. *Under the Stars: How America Fell in Love with Camping*. New York: Henry Holt, 2016.

White, Robert B. *Home on the Road: The Motor Home in America*. Washington, DC: Smithsonian Institution Scholarly Press, 2001.

*Whymper, Edward. *Scrambles Amongst the Alps in the Years 1860–'69*. Philadelphia: J. P. Lippincott, 1872. Reprint, Washington, DC: National Geographic Adventure Classics, 2002. https://archive.org.

Wilder, James Austin. *Jack-Knife Cookery*. New York; E. P. Dutton, 1929.

**Wood, Donald F. *RVs & Campers, 1900–2000: An Illustrated History*. Hudson, WI: Iconografix, 2002.

Young, Phoebe S. K. *Camping Grounds: Public Nature in American Life from the Civil War to the Occupy Movement*. New York: Oxford University Press, 2021.

Young, Terence. *Heading Out: A History of American Camping*. Ithaca, NY: Cornell University Press, 2017.

Index

Page numbers in *italics* refer to illustrations or their captions.

A

A16, 224
Abbey, Edward, 26
Abercrombie and Fitch Co., 214, *216*, 228
Acadia National Park, 84, *136–38*, 158, 160, *160–61*, 162, 307, *307*
Adventures in the Wilderness (Murray), 8, 188, 190, 254
air beds/mattresses, 274, 276
Airstream trailers, 94, 220, *314–15*
Ajungilak, 270
Albert Pike Recreation Area/ Campground, 100, *100–101*, 102
Albright, Horace, 106
Ali, Mahershala, *180–81*
Allain, Pierre, 250, *252–54*, 268, 272, *272–73*
Allen, Arthur Wigram, *186–87*
Alward-Anderson-Southard Company, *104*
American Gas Machine Company, 76
American Institute of Graphic Arts (AIGA), 168
Amistad National Recreation Area, 110
amphitheaters, *20–21*, *86–87*
Anderson, Neil P., *276–77*
Anderson, Ralph H., *66–67*
Anderson, Victor, *188–89*
Anderson, Wes, *176–78*
Antelope Island State Park, 307
Apple, Margot, *212*, *270–71*
automobiles. *see* motor vehicles
axes, 58
Ayres, Thomas, 28

B

Badlands National Park, 302
baffling, 272
Banham, Reyner, 62, 64, *64*, 236, *236–37*
bark drinking cup, *40*
Basford, Harold R., 194, 196, *196*
Bates, Frank A., 246

Beard, Daniel Carter, 26, 46, *52–53*, 54, 56, *56–57*, 58, 72, 74, *74*, *74–75*, *212–13*
bears, food waste and, 284, 288
beds
  air, 274
  mattresses and, 272, 274, 276
  portable, 246, 248, *248*, 276
  rustic, 266, 268, 272, 274
  see also blankets; sleeping bags
Belasco, Warren James, 10, 32, 36, 84
Bierstadt, Albert, 28, 48, *48*
Birch Bay, *314–15*
Bisphenol A (BPA) plastics, 40
Blair, James H., 228
blankets
  picnic, 182, 184
  wool, 256, 258, 260
body waste, 294, 296, 298
bonfires, 66
Bonham State Park, *200–201*
Book of Camping and Woodcraft, The (Kephart), 48, 50
Book of Camping, The (Verrill), *54–55*, 72, *190*
bow and drill, *54–55*, 74
boxing, 272
Boy Scouts of America, 26
Brandreth Preserve, *6–7*
Breck, Edward, 40
Bridges, Sheila, *182–183*
Brimmer, Frank E., 32, 50, 56, 70, 78, *78–79*, 80, 96, 98, 120, 284, 290
British Antarctic Expedition of 1910–1913, *240*, 252, 256, *256*
Bunn, Stephanie, 210, 212, 248
Byam, Wally, *314–15*

C

California Firewood Task Force, *60*
California Scenic Line collection, *144*
Camp Ground Policy, A (Meinecke), 156, *156–57*, 160, *202–3*
Campbell, Reau, 170, *170–71*
campfires
  building/starting, 52, 54, 56, 74, 76
  centrality of, 64, 66, 68, 70
  dangers of, 50

evolution of, 13
firepits, 66, 68, 70, *70–71*, 72
fuel for, 56, 58, 60
"gearing" of, 72, 74, 76
importance of, 46, 48, 84
starting, *54–55*, *74–75*
campgrounds
  amenities at, 120, 132
  commercial, 38
  as commodity, 118
  maps for, 110, 112, 128
  typical layout for, *26–27*
  unitization of, 108
Camping and Woodcraft (Kephart), 48, 224, 296, *296–97*
Campmor, *94–95*
campsites
  access and, 114
  amenities at, 94, 100, 102
  assignment of, 106, 108, 110
  as enclosure, *96–102*, *112–13*
  evolution of, 13–14
  importance of, 90
  laying claim to, 206, 208
  number of, 92
  numbering of, *6–7*, 162
  proximity of, 56
  as roofless cabin, 200
  rusticity of, 106
  typical layout for, *10–11*
Cannon, Cornelia James, 290, 292
Capitol Reef National Park, *174*
Carey, Reuben, *6–7*
Carothers, Wallace Hume, 238
Carpenter, Frank, 286
Carr, Ethan, 34, 38
cars. *see* motor vehicles
Carver, Jack, *314–15*
Cascade Designs, 276
Cedar Point, *178–79*, 186
cell phone reception, 130
Cheley, Frank H., 56, 58, 62, *62*, 72, 74, 102, *216–17*
Cherry-Garrard, Apsley, 252, 254
Civil Rights Act (1964), 98, 188
Civilian Conservation Corps (CCC), 18, 20, 34, 104, 158, 198, *284–85*
Clean Air Act (1970), 38
Cleanwaste, *294–95*
Clinton, Hillary, 178, 180, *180–81*
clothing, layers for, 236
Cole, Thomas, 180, *182–83*, 184

Image Credits

4–5: University of Southern California Libraries / California Historical Society. **7 top:** ADKX, Blue Mountain Lake, NY. **8 bottom:** *Motor Camper & Tourist* 1, no. 12 (May 1925): 708. **8:** Rondal Partridge Archives, Lopez Island, WA. **9:** Bancroft Library, University of California, Berkeley. **11:** National Park Service, *Campground Study: A Report of the Committee to Study Camping Policy and Standards—Region Four* (San Francisco: National Park Service, 1959), Plate no. 2. National Park Service, Electronic Technical Information Center (ETIC). **12 top:** *Motor Camper & Tourist* 1, no. 7 (December 1924): 412. **12 bottom:** The Coleman Company Inc. **13 top:** San Bernardino County Museum, Redlands, CA. **13 bottom:** National Park Service, NPGallery Digital Asset Management System. **14:** Special Collections & Archives, Merrill-Cazier Library, Utah State University. **15 top:** Pryce Jones, *Royal Welsh Warehouse, North Wales, Newtown* (1888–89), 85. Powys Archives and Information Management, Llandrindod Wells, UK. **15 bottom:** Robert Louis Stevenson, *Travels with a Donkey in the Cévennes* (New York: Century, 1907), frontispiece. **16, 17 top and bottom:** © Bruce Davidson/Magnum Photos. **19:** Albert H. Good, ed., *Park and Recreation Structures*, vol. 2, *Recreational and Cultural Facilities* (Washington, DC: Department of the Interior, National Park Service, 1938), 18. **21:** Good, ed., *Park and Recreation Structures*, vol. 2, 210. **23:** Albert H. Good, ed., *Park Structures and Facilities* (Washington, DC: Department of the Interior, National Park Service, 1935), 87. **24–25:** Library of Congress, Washington, DC. **27:** Good, ed., *Park and Recreation Structures*, vol. 3, *Overnight and Organized Camp Facilities*, 116. **29:** San Bernardino County Museum, Redlands, CA. **30:** Elon Jessup, *Roughing It Smoothly: How to Avoid Vacation Pitfalls* (New York: G. P. Putnam's Sons, 1923), 215. **31:** Rondal Partridge Archives, Lopez Island, WA. **32:** National Park Service, NPGallery Digital Asset Management System. **33:** National Park Service, Electronic Technical Information Center (ETIC). **35:** Good, ed., *Park Structures and Facilities*, 86. **37:** United States Forest Service Region Five, *Public Camp Manual* (San Francisco: United States Forest Service, 1935), 18. **39:** United States Forest Service Region Five, *Public Camp Manual*, 7. **40:** Edward Breck, *The Way of the Woods: A Manual for Sportsmen in Northeastern United States and Canada* (New York and London: G. P. Putnam's Sons, 1908), 82. **41:** *Science* 131, no. 3416 (June 1960): 1824. Courtesy of Nalgene Outdoor. **42:** Geyser Systems. **43:** *Science* 216, no. 4546 (May 1982): Suppl. k. Courtesy of Nalgene Outdoor. **44–45:** Metropolitan Museum of Art, New York, NY. **47:** ADKX, Blue Mountain Lake, NY. **49:** Timken Museum, San Diego, CA. **51:** Wadsworth Atheneum Museum of Art, Hartford, CT, the Ella Gallup Sumner and Mary Catlin Sumner Collection Fund, 1944.57. **53 top:** Daniel Carter Beard, *The American Boys' Handybook of Camp-Lore and Woodcraft* (Philadelphia and London: J. B. Lippincott, 1920), 36. **53 bottom:** Ernest Thompson Seton, *The Book of Woodcraft* (New York: Doubleday Page, 1912), 275. **55:** A. Hyatt Verrill, *The Book of Camping* (New York: Alfred A. Knopf, 1917), 75. **57:** Daniel Carter Beard, *The Field and Forest Handy Book* (New York: Charles Scribner's Sons, 1906), 231. **59:** Photograph by the author. **60:** California Firewood Task Force. **61:** New York State Department of Environmental

Conservation. **62:** Marc-Antoine Laugier, *Essai sur l'architecture*, 2nd ed. (Paris: Chez P. T. Barrois, 1755), frontispiece. **63:** Frank H. Cheley, *Camping Out* (New York: University Society, 1933), 254. **64:** Reyner Banham, *The Architecture of the Well-Tempered Environment*, 2nd ed. (Chicago: University of Chicago Press, 1984), 20. University of Chicago Press. **65:** Good, ed., *Park Structures and Facilities*, 173. **66:** Wikimedia Commons. **67:** National Park Service, Harpers Ferry Center for Media Services. **68:** *Parks & Recreation* 8, no. 5 (May–June 1925), 432. **69 top:** Good, ed., *Park and Recreation Structures*, vol. 2, 34. **69 bottom:** Good, ed., *Park and Recreation Structures*, vol. 2, 30. **70:** National Park Service, Electronic Technical Information Center (ETIC). **71:** Good, ed., *Park and Recreation Structures*, vol. 2, 36. **72 top:** Cheley, *Camping Out*, 143. **72 bottom:** Elon Jessup, *The Motor Camping Book* (New York: G. P. Putnam's Sons, 1921), 71. **73:** Jennifer K. Mann, *The Camping Trip* (Somerville, MA: Candlewick Press, 2020). **75:** Beard, *The Field and Forest Handy Book*, 230. **77:** © Bruce Davidson/Magnum Photos. **78:** *Motor Camper & Tourist* 1, no. 11 (April 1925): cover. **79:** Frank E. Brimmer, *Coleman Motor Campers Manual* (Wichita, KS: The Coleman Lamp Co., 1926), 51. **80:** *Motor Camper & Tourist* 1, no. 2 (July 1924): cover. **81:** The Coleman Company, Inc., *Catalog Outing Products, Parts Catalog 32B* (Wichita, KS: The Coleman Company, Inc., 1958), Burners 1. **83:** GoSun. **85:** Kampgrounds of America, Inc. **87:** National Park Service, NPGallery Digital Asset Management System. **88–89:** Arthur Fitzwilliams Tait, *Camping in the Woods—"A Good Time Coming"* (New York: Currier and Ives, 1863). ADKX, Blue Mountain Lake, NY. **91:** ADKX, Blue Mountain Lake, NY. **93:** © Bruce Davidson/Magnum Photos. **95:** Montage by the author using artwork from A. F. Tait, *Camping in the Woods*; *Campmor Spring 2011*, illustrations by Richard Heisse, © Campmor, Inc.; *Kampgrounds of America Kampground Directory, 1970–1971*, courtesy of Kampgrounds of America, Inc. **97:** Yosemite National Park Archives. **98:** Victor H. Green, *The Negro Motorist Green Book: An International Travel Guide* (New York: Victor H. Green & Co., 1949), cover. **99 top:** National Park Service, NPGallery Digital Asset Management System. **99 bottom:** National Park Service, NPGallery Digital Asset Management System; Green, *Negro Motorist Green Book*, 1949 ed., 71. **101:** © REUTERS / Alamy Stock Photo. **103:** Good, ed., *Park and Recreation Structures*, vol. 3, 9. **105:** Donald F. Wood, *RVs & Campers, 1900–2000: An Illustrated History* (Hudson, WI: Iconografix, 2002), 42. **105:** Jessup, *Motor Camping Book*, 79. **107:** National Park Service, NPGallery Digital Asset Management System. **109:** *Municipal Facts Bi-Monthly* 5, nos. 3–4 (March–April 1922), 6. **111:** Courtesy of Terence Young. **112, 113:** © Bruce Davidson/Magnum Photos. **115:** National Park Service, NPGallery Digital Asset Management System. **116:** © Bruce Davidson/Magnum Photos. **117:** Good, ed., *Park and Recreation Structures*, vol. 3, 14. **118:** Denver Public Library Digital Collections. **119:** J. C. and John D. Long, *Motor Camping* (New York: Dodd, Mead, 1923), 269. **121 top:** Denver Public Library Digital Collections. **121 bottom:** Kampgrounds of America, Inc. **122, 123:** KOA, *June, 1967 Directory* (Billings, MT: Kampgrounds of America, 1967), cover. **124, 125, 127 top**

and bottom: Kampgrounds of America, Inc. **129:** Created by the author. **131 top:** *KOA Kampground Directory, 1970–1971 Edition* (Billings, MT: Kampgrounds of America, 1970). **131 bottom:** *Directory, 2017 KOA Campgrounds* (Billings, MT: Kampgrounds of America, 2017), 16. **132:** © Bruce Davidson/Magnum Photos. **133:** Eric Whitehead (Flickr). **135:** jimbob_malone (flickr). **136–37:** National Park Service, Electronic Technical Information Center (ETIC). **139:** National Park Service, NPGallery Digital Asset Management System. **141:** © Campground Views, Inc. **143:** "Campground Maps," National Park Service, accessed January 31, 2010, https://www.nps.gov/romo/planyourvisit/maps.htm. **144:** Bancroft Library, University of California, Berkeley. **145:** Lewis Stornoway, *Yosemite: Where to Go and What to Do: A Plain Guide to the Yosemite Valley* (San Francisco: C. A. Murdock & Co., Printers, 1888), 8. **146:** Author's postcard collection. **147:** Wylie Permanent Camping Company, *Yellowstone National Park*, 1910 ed. (Livingston, MT: Wylie Permanent Camping Company, 1910), 1–2. **148:** "Browse All: Pictorial Map of Yellowstone National Park," David Rumsey Historical Map Collection, accessed December 4, 2021, https://www.davidrumsey.com/luna/servlet/view/all/what/Pictorial%2Bmap/where/Yellowstone%2BNational%2BPark?sort=Pub_List_No_InitialSort%2CPub_Date%2CPub_List_No%2CSeries_No&os=0&pgs=50&cic= RUMSEY%7E8%7E1. **151:** Jack Ellis Haynes, *Haynes New Guide: The Complete Handbook of Yellowstone National Park*, 1936 ed. (Saint Paul, MN: Haynes Picture Shops, 1936), 61. Courtesy of Bob Goss. **152:** *Popular Mechanics Auto Tourist's Handbook No. 1* (Chicago: Popular Mechanics Press, 1924), 74. **153:** Haynes, *Haynes New Guide*, 1936 ed., 76. Courtesy of Bob Goss. **155:** Charles Parker (C. P.) Halligan, *Tourist Camps: Rural Landscape Series No. 2* (East Lansing: Michigan State College Agricultural Experiment Station), 5. **156:** Ethan Carr, *Wilderness by Design: Landscape Architecture & the National Park Service* (Lincoln: University of Nebraska Press, 1999), 245. **157:** E. P. Meinecke, *A Camp Ground Policy* (United States Department of Agriculture, Division of Forest Pathology, 1932), 10. **159 top:** National Park Service, Electronic Technical Information Center (ETIC). **159 bottom:** Good, ed., *Park and Recreation Structures*, vol. 3, 15. **161:** National Park Service, Electronic Technical Information Center (ETIC). **163:** Jonathan Chew, "Dolly Copp," accessed October 10, 2018, http://www.dollycopp.com. **165:** "Mather Campground—South Rim," National Park Service, accessed April 23, 2019, https://www.nps.gov/grca/planyourvisit/mather-campground-south-rim.htm. **167:** "Campground Maps," National Park Service, accessed July 9, 2013, https://www.nps.gov/shen/planyourvisit/maps.htm. **169:** Long and Long, *Motor Camping*, 216. **170:** "Map Symbols & Patterns for NPS Maps," National Park Service, accessed January 8, 2022, https://www.nps.gov/carto/app/#!/maps/symbols. **171:** Reau Campbell, *Campbell's Complete Guide and Descriptive Book of The Yellowstone Park* (Chicago: H. E. Klamer, 1909), 113. **173:** Yosemite Conservancy. **174:** Campground Views. https://www.campgroundviews.com. **175:** "Big Meadows Campground, Shenandoah (VA)," Recreation.gov, accessed December 1, 2015, https://www.recreation.gov/camping/campgrounds/232459.

176–77: Focus Features/Alamy Stock Photos. **179:** Author's postcard collection. **181 top:** Barack Obama Presidential Library. **181 bottom:** Universal Pictures/Alamy Stock Photos. **183 top:** Sheila Bridges. **183 bottom:** Brooklyn Museum, Healy Purchase Fund. **185:** © Eames Office, LLC (www.eamesoffice.com). All rights reserved. **186 top:** "Albums of photographs of the Allen family, taken between 1890–1934 / Arthur Wigram Allen," Mitchell Library, State Library of New South Wales. **186 bottom:** *Motor Camper & Tourist* 1, no. 10 (March 1925): 637. **187:** Museum of Fine Arts, Boston. **188:** Shenandoah National Park. **189:** *Parks & Recreation* 11, no. 3 (January–February 1928), 166. Emphasis on the picnic grounds by the author. **190:** Verrill, *Book of Camping*, 81. **191:** ADKX, Blue Mountain Lake, NY. **193:** Frederick Van de Water, *The Family Flivvers to Frisco* (New York: D. Appleton, 1927), 65. **194:** Denver Public Library Digital Collections. **195:** Charles H. Nielsen, Table. US Patent 769,354, figs. 1–2. Google Patents. **196:** Harold R. Basford, Folding Camp Table. US Patent 1,272,187, figs. 1–5. Google Patents. **197:** Wikimedia Commons. **199:** National Park Service, Electronic Technical Information Center (ETIC). This drawing was lightly edited by the author. **201 top:** Good, ed., *Park and Recreation Structures*, vol. 2, 12. **201 bottom:** Good, ed., *Park and Recreation Structures*, vol. 2, 10. **202:** © Bruce Davidson/Magnum Photos. **203:** Meinecke, *A Camp Ground Policy*, 13. **204–5:** Bridgeman Images USA. **207:** George Washington Sears, *Woodcraft*, 14th ed. (New York: Forest and Stream Publishing Co., 1920), 35. **208:** S. H. Walker, *The Way to Camp* (London: Pilot Press, 1947), 47. **209:** The Moss Tents Family Archive and Moss Adventures. Inc. **211:** Bancroft Library, University of California Berkeley, Robert B. Honeyman, Jr. Collection of Early Californian and Western American Pictorial Material. **212:** Steve Futterman and Margot Apple, *Soft House* (New York: Harper & Row, 1976), 44. **213:** Beard, *American Boys' Handybook*, 205, 209. **214:** Druce Raven, *Let's Go Camping*, in Elmer H. Kreps, Warren H. Miller, William Holt-Jackson, et al., *A Camper's Guide to Tents: A Collection of Historical Articles on Types of Tents and How to Construct Them* (Redditch, UK: Read Books, 2011), 152. **215 top:** Godfrey Rhodes, *Tents and Time-Life from the Earliest Ages to the Present Time: To Which is Added the Practice of Encamping an Army in Ancient and Modern Times* (London: Smith, Elder and Co., 1858), 82–83. **215 bottom:** Charles W. (Bill) Moss, Flexible Hyperbolic Paraboloid Shelter. US Patent 3,060,949, filed January 30, 1957, and issued October 30, 1962, fig. 2. Google Patents. **216:** *Abercrombie and Fitch Co.* catalog, 1910 ed. (New York: Abercrombie & Fitch Co., 1910), 37. **217 top:** Cheley, *Camping Out*, 64. **217 bottom:** Ferdinand Eberhardt, Combined Tent and Ground Floor Cloth. US Patent 1,057,628, filed December 21, 1912, and issued April 1, 1913, fig. 3. Google Patents. **218:** *Sopu* (Helsinki: Kirjapaino Aa osakeyhtiö, 1957), 7, 11, 12. **219:** Reinhaldt Lönnqvist. An Improved Tent. GB Patent 377,831, filed September 7, 1931, and issued August 4, 1932, figs. 1–3. Espacenet. **220:** Wood, *RVs & Campers: 1900–2000*, 76. **221:** William B. MacDonald Jr., Vehicle Trailer. US Patent 2,481,230, filed April 8, 1946, and issued September 6, 1949, figs. 3–4. Google Patents. **223:** Elon Jessup, *Motor Camping Book*, 134.

224: Horace Kephart, *Camping and Woodcraft*, 18th ed. (New York: Macmillan, 1957), 84. **225:** © The Metropolitan Museum of Art. Art Resource, NY. **226 top:** Whymper, *Scrambles Amongst the Alps in the Years 1860–'69* (Philadelphia: J. P. Lippincott & Co., 1872), 125. **226 middle:** *Practical Camp Equipment* (Denver: Stoll Manufacturing Company, 1926), 6. **226 bottom:** *Sierra Designs 69/70* (Berkeley, CA: Sierra Designs, 1969), cover. **227:** Edward Whymper, *Scrambles Amongst the Alps*, 47. **228:** Thomas Hiram (T. H.) Holding, *The Camper's Handbook* (London: Simpkin, Marshall, Hamilton, Kent & Co., Ltd., 1908), 5. **229 top:** Holding, *Camper's Handbook*, 304. **229 middle:** Holding, *Camper's Handbook*, 280. **229 bottom:** Harry H. Harsted, Foldable Antenna, US Patent 2,379,577, filed January 25, 1943, and issued July 3, 1945, figs. 1–5. Google Patents. **231 and 232:** The North Face. **233 top:** Holding, *Camper's Handbook*, 290. **233 bottom:** R. Buckminster Fuller, Geodesic Tent, US Patent 2,914,074, filed March 1, 1957, and issued November 24, 1959, figs. 5–6. Google Patents. **234:** Isidor Mautner, Tent, US Patent 535,066, filed September 24, 1894, and issued March 5, 1895, figs. 1–2. Google Patents. **235:** William S. Faulkner, Shelter-Tent Half and Poncho, US Patent 703,245, filed July 16, 1901, and issued June 24, 1902, figs. 1–3. Google Patents. **237:** Banham, *Architecture of the Well-Tempered Environment*, 18. University of Chicago Press. **238:** *The DuPont Magazine* 37, no. 2 (April–May 1943), 6. **239:** Franklin M. Reck and William Moss, *Ford Treasury of Station Wagon Living* (New York: Simon and Schuster, 1957), endpapers. **240 top:** Gilles Modica et Jacky Godoffe, *Fontainebleau—100 ans d'escalade* (Les Houches, FR: Les Editions to Mont Blanc, 2017), 109. **240 bottom:** Scott Polar Research Institute, University of Cambridge: ©Fjällräven. **242–43:** Photograph by Paul Mutino. Barnum Museum, Bridgeport, CT. **245:** Whymper, *Scrambles Amongst the Alps*, 37. **246:** Roger Frison-Roche and Sylvain Jouty, *A History of Mountain Climbing* (Paris and New York: Flammarion, 1996), 310. **247 top:** Holding, *Camper's Handbook*, 169. **247 bottom:** Harry Roberts, *The Tramp's Hand-book* (New York and London: John Lane, Bodley Head, 1903), 144. **248 top and bottom:** Photographs by Rudy Ruzicska. The Henry Ford, Dearborn, MI. **249:** Museum of the Rockies, Bozeman, MT. **251:** Seyit Konyali. **252:** Raymond Gaché, "Le matériel de bivouac," *Alpinisme* 10, no. 40 (1935), 164. **253:** Courtesy of Paul Allain. **255 top:** Fridtjof Nansen, *The First Crossing of Greenland* (London and New York: Longmans, Green, and Co., 1890), 42. **255 bottom:** James G. Phillips & Gordon K. Scott, Sleeping Bag With Snorkel Hood and Draft Curtain, US Patent 4,787,105, filed February 10, 1987, and issued November 29, 1988, figs. 1, 2, 5, 6. Google Patents. **256:** Scott Polar Research Institute, University of Cambridge. **257:** Smithsonian Institution, National Museum of the American Indian, Washington, DC. **259:** S. H. Walker, *The Way to Camp*, 39. **260 top:** Gustav Jaeger, *Health-Culture* (Montreal: John Lovell & Son, Limited, 1907), 101. **261 bottom:** Jessup, *Roughing It Smoothly*, 116. **263:** Gideon Sundback, Separable Fastener, US Patent 1,219,881, filed August 27, 1914, and issued March 20, 1917, figs. 1–8. Google Patents. **264 top and bottom:** NEMO. **265:** *The Mountaineer* 20, no. 1

(December 1927), 79. **266:** Courtesy of Dan White. **267:** Francis Galton, *The Art of Travel; Or, Shifts and Contrivances Available in Wild Countries*, 3rd ed. (London: John Murray, 1860), 48. **269 top:** *Summit* 6, no. 6 (June 1960), 11. **269 bottom:** *Motor Camper & Tourist* 1, no. 12 (May 1925): 761. **271:** Futterman and Apple, *Soft House*, 61. **272:** Modica et Godoffe, *Fontainebleau—100 ans d'escalade*, 106. **273:** "Pierre Allain (1904–2000)," Outdoor Gear Coach, accessed September 1, 2021. http://www.outdoorgearcoach.co.uk/innovation-history/pierre-allain-innovator-extraordinaire/#.U7Q6AvldXHk. **274 top:** Seton, *Book of Woodcraft*, 269. **274 bottom:** Edwin R. Wallace, *Descriptive Guide to the Adirondacks and Handbook of Travel to Saratoga Springs; Schroon Lake; Lakes Luzerne, George, and Champlain; The Ausable Chasm; The Thousand Islands; Massena Springs; and Trenton Falls* (New York: American News Company, 1875), 253. **275:** Flavius Vegetius Renatus, *De re militari* (Erfurt, DE: Knappe, c. 1512), 34. **276:** *Backpacker* 17, no. 2 (March 1989), 89. **277:** James M. Lea and Neil P. Anderson, Method of Making a Self-Inflating Air Mattress, US Patent 4,149,919, filed May 25, 1977, and issued April 17, 1979, figs. 1–6, 16. Google Patents. **278:** *Quartermaster Supply Catalog, Section I—Enlisted Men's Clothing and Equipment* (Quartermaster General—ASF, 1943), 31. **279:** Courtesy of Bob Law. **281:** Tim Davis / Patagonia. **282–83:** Yellowstone National Park Heritage & Research Center. **285, 287:** National Park Service, NPGallery Digital Asset Management System. **288:** Yellowstone National Park Heritage & Research Center. **291:** National Park Service, NPGallery Digital Asset Management System. **292:** Yellowstone National Park Heritage & Research Center. **293:** National Park Service, NPGallery Digital Asset Management System. **294:** Save Our Canyons. **295:** Cleanwaste. **297:** Horace Kephart, *Camping and Woodcraft*, 4th ed. (New York: Macmillan Company, 1930), 223. **298:** *Popular Mechanics Auto Tourist's Handbook No. 1*, 73. **299:** National Park Service, Electronic Technical Information Center (ETIC). **301:** Yellowstone National Park Heritage & Research Center. **303:** Lori Brown. **305:** KOA Badlands / Kampgrounds of America, Inc. **306:** Sierra Designs. **307:** Photograph by the author. **309:** Martin Hogue, *Thirtyfour Campgrounds* (Cambridge, MA: MIT Press, 2016), 246. **310 top:** Drawing by the author. **310 bottom:** Photograph by the author. **311:** Photograph by the author. **315 and back cover:** Photograph by Jack Carver. Whatcom Museum, Bellingham, Washington.

Published by
Princeton Architectural Press
A division of Chronicle Books LLC
70 West 36th Street
New York, New York 10018
papress.com

Editor: Jennifer Thompson
Design concept: Martin Hogue
Cover design: Paul Wagner

Library of Congress Cataloging-in-Publication Data
Names: Hogue, Martin, author.
Title: Making camp : a visual history of camping's most essential items &
    activities / Martin Hogue.
Description: New York, N.Y. : Princeton Architectural Press, [2023] |
Includes bibliographical references and index. | Summary: "An illustrated
    history of the evolution of camping from the late nineteenth century
    through present day through its most significant components: the
    campsite, the campfire, the picnic table, the map, the tent, the sleeping
    bag, water delivery, and trash collection"—Provided by publisher.
Identifiers: LCCN 2022036114 | ISBN 9781797222523 (hardcover) |
    ISBN 9781797224169 (ebook)
Subjects: LCSH: Camping—History. | Camping--Equipment and
    supplies—History.
Classification: LCC GV191.7 .H65 2023 | DDC 796.5409—dc23/
    eng/20220825
LC record available at https://lccn.loc.gov/2022036114

Special thanks to Cornell University and Furthermore: a program
of the J.M. Kaplan fund, for their support.

 Cornell University

Furthermore:
a program of the J.M. Kaplan Fund